PRAISE FOR SOMETHING FIERCE

"The stories that fill this book feel like the stories of several lives, not the adventurous, exhilarating and harrowing adolescence and early adulthood of one extraordinary person."

NATIONAL POST

"Aguirre has written a fascinating, warts-and-all portrait of herself, her family, and South America. The book is a brave document, written by someone who is clearly no stranger to bravery."

QUILL & QUIRE

"A coming-of-age story that blends birthday parties and puppy love with indoctrination in the tradecraft of subversion: how to arrange the delivery of secret documents, how to lose a police tail, how to lead a double life."

TORONTO STAR

"A brutally honest and wryly funny story, told through the eyes of a girl young enough to yearn for cork-soled platforms... but old enough to know the people arriving at her parents' safe house in La Paz, Bolivia, are limping and exhausted because they've been tortured."

GEORGIA STRAIGHT

"An insightful journey into the formation of a revolutionary soul."

GLOBE AND MAIL

"This extraordinary memoir is long overdue. I recommend it to everyone who loves life and needs to know what some give up so life is possible."

MARGARET RANDALL, author of *To Change the World*

SOMETHING FIERCE

SOMETHING

MEMOIRS OF A

REVOLUTIONARY DAUGHTER

FIERCE

CARMEN AGUIRRE

Douglas & McIntyre

D&M PUBLISHERS INC.

Vancouver/Toronto/Berkeley

12 13 14 15 16   5 4 3 2

Douglas & McIntyre
An imprint of D&M Publishers Inc.
2323 Quebec Street, Suite 201
Vancouver BC Canada V5T 4S7
www.douglas-mcintyre.com

Cataloguing data available from Library and Archives Canada
ISBN 978-1-55365-462-9 (cloth)
ISBN 978-1-77100-036-9 (pbk.)
ISBN 978-1-55365-791-0 (ebook)

Editing by Barbara Pulling
Cover and text design by Peter Cocking
Cover and interior photographs courtesy of Carmen Aguirre
Printed and bound in Canada by Friesens
Text printed on acid-free paper
Distributed in the U.S. by Publishers Group West

We gratefully acknowledge the financial support of the
Canada Council for the Arts, the British Columbia Arts Council,
the Province of British Columbia through the Book Publishing
Tax Credit and the Government of Canada through the
Canada Book Fund for our publishing activities.

For my son, Santiago, love of my life,
the greatest teacher of all

In memory of Bob Everton, 1949–2004

VALOR

Te dije:
"Se necesita mucho valor
para tanta muerte inútil."
Pensaste que me refería a América Latina.
No, hablaba
de morir en la cama,
en la gran ciudad,
a los ochenta o a los noventa años.

CRISTINA PERI ROSSI, *Estado de Exilio*

COURAGE

I said to you:
"One needs a lot of courage
for so much useless death."
You thought I was referring to Latin America.
No, I was talking
about dying in bed,
in a great city,
at eighty or ninety years old.

CRISTINA PERI ROSSI, *State of Exile*

PART ONE

THE
RETURN
PLAN

I

As MY MOTHER bit into her Big Mac, her glasses caught the reflection of a purple neon light somewhere behind me. Barry White's "Love's Theme," my favourite song, blasted from the loudspeaker. Mami looked hilarious in her new aqua eyeshadow. Her plucked eyebrows gave her a surprised expression. Then there was her frosted pink lipstick, which was smeared across her chin now, and the unfamiliar scent of Charlie. I'd helped her choose that perfume. The picture on the box showed one of Charlie's Angels doing the splits in mid-air, wearing a white pantsuit and platform shoes. In dressing for our trip that morning, my mother had followed her lead, though not the splits part, because she was four foot ten and round. Now here we were in a food court at Los Angeles International Airport, which my mother referred to as "L-A-X." She and I and my sister, Ale, had walked for ages through the terminal, looking for our gate, and the whole time she'd rubbed the palms of her hands into the small of her back, muttering, "Firing squad to the woman hater who invented heels."

It was June 1979, and the day before, in Vancouver, Mami had been a hippie. She'd been a hippie for as long as I'd been her daughter, in fact, which was eleven years now. That's why Ale and I had giggled when we saw her this morning, and why we'd been shocked a few weeks earlier when Mami announced we were going to a mall. She'd tried on most of the inventory at Suzie Creamcheese before settling on the white polyester pantsuit and some matching platforms at Aggies. She was usually dressed in frayed jeans with patches on the ass and a pair of old clogs. But this was a special occasion, requiring a new wardrobe to go with it, my mother had explained. We'd found her in the kitchen that morning blowing on her toenails, which were wet with red polish, humming Victor Jara's famous song "The Right To Live in Peace." Our passports were laid out like a fan on the table. The three of us hadn't looked back as we left our basement suite. Canada had taken us in after the coup in Chile five years earlier, but my mother had made it clear from day one that the refugee thing in the imperialist North was not for us. So our suitcases had been packed again, and our posters of Ho Chi Minh, Salvador Allende and Tupac Amaru taken down and given away. Rulo drove us to the airport in my mother's orange vw Bug, and Mami had several attacks of the giggles along the way, because he'd only just learned to drive. "Clutch, Rulo, clutch, you idiot!" she yelled. I'd never seen Rulo so excited, and I knew it was because he'd get to keep the car from that day on.

This part of the imperialist North, LAX, was very different from anything I'd seen so far. In Vancouver, we and the few dozen other Chilean families had been the only Latinos. That city, where you could buy tropical fruit in the dead of winter, was full of white people who kept their bodies and faces perfectly still when they talked. At LAX we were surrounded by the sound of Mexican Spanish, and there were black people everywhere. I could see palm trees and turquoise sky just beyond the glass walls of the airport. The lady who'd sold me a cheeseburger with no patty (I'd been a strict vegetarian since I was eight) had touched my cheek and spoken to me in Spanish. She'd recognized herself in me, and somehow I understood that. For the first time in five years, I thought maybe I belonged somewhere. But it couldn't possibly be here, because the North was the forbidden place of belonging.

A Colombian family at the table next to us argued and laughed and broke into spontaneous cumbia. When I went up to the counter for a second banana milkshake, one of the Colombian ladies asked me if I was going to Bogotá, like her. I shook my head. I couldn't explain where I was going or where I was coming from. There were too many winding roads leading each way. But she had recognized herself in me, too, and I swallowed down some tears hard and fast.

Back at our table, Mami was finishing her hamburger, her eyes far away. I'd never seen her eat a Big Mac before. McDonald's was the ultimate symbol of imperialism, so we had always boycotted it. Ale showed off a new helium balloon featuring a portrait of Ronald McDonald. It had been given to her by Ronald himself, who'd passed through moments ago. Two years before, when she was eight, Ale had run away from home. My parents and the other adults had never learned about my sister's bold attempt at a new life; they'd been too busy printing *Victoria Final* (Final Victory), the monthly newsletter they put out from our dining room table. It was my cousins Gonzalo and Macarena and I who followed Ale down the street and brought her back. She'd been clutching her Easy-Bake Oven, given to us by a church group that helped refugees. I sucked the airport milkshake past the knot in my throat.

Our stepfather, Bob, had left Vancouver a few months earlier, and now we were flying to join him in Costa Rica, revolutionary Central America. Goodbye to my elementary school city, to the land of late-night janitor work, hand-me-down Barbie dolls and Salvation Army clothes. Goodbye to my father, who was staying behind.

My mother and father had gotten a divorce, joining so many other Chileans whose marriages had not withstood exile. One afternoon when Ale and I got home from school, my parents were waiting for us at opposite ends of the living room. Mami's glasses were all steamed up, and Papi was staring out the window, his chin quivering. My mother explained that she was moving out, that she couldn't be with my father anymore but she'd always be our best friend. She was going to live with some other women in a communal apartment, and we could visit her there and go to the park. After a long hug, she drove away in the orange vw, its trunk held down by a coat hanger, and just like that, our family was broken forever. The next time we saw Mami, she was on stage, singing with Rulo, my uncle Boris and the other Chileans with whom she'd formed the folk group Revolución. When we met up with her after the show, a terrible shyness hit me. I'd never had to meet my mother anywhere before, the way you meet a stranger.

Our house got filthy, and my father and Ale and I ate hot dogs for weeks. But the plants always looked nice, because Papi watered and trimmed them. Whenever we walked through the botanical garden at the university, where he worked part time as a gardener, he would point out his favourite ferns. Then he'd ask us how to spell cloud and ocean and highway, because he was revalidating his physics degree and studying English at the same time. He was a car washer at a Toyota dealership and had a paper route and janitor gigs, but his favourite job was at the botanical garden. Papi was a great admirer of nature. That's what he always said. A couple of months after the separation, he'd found solace in the arms of another Chilean exile who had split with her husband. We called her Aunt Tita.

Ale was licking ketchup off her fingers. My mother looked around, lit up a Matinée, then cleared her throat.

"Girls, we're not going to Costa Rica," she said.

Ale and I stared at her, one of us mid-swallow, the other mid-lick.

"We were never headed to Costa Rica, actually. That was a facade."

"What's a facade?" Ale asked. Ronald McDonald spied on us from the balloon bobbing above her head.

"A facade is when you make up a story because it's dangerous to tell the truth," Mami said. "It's a story you make up when you're involved in something bigger than yourself and you don't want to risk your life or the lives of others."

My mind raced back to the afternoon in Seattle when my mother had addressed a crowd wearing a long-haired wig and cat's-eye glasses. The organizers had introduced her as María. She'd explained to us

4

later that it was safer that way; she'd been talking about the struggle in Chile, and not all of the photographers in the crowd had been with the newspapers. We'd stayed at a communal hippie house there, and a couple of the men had shaved off their beards and cut their long hair before we left for the rally. The men were in solidarity with us, my mother said. They were activists against the war in Vietnam, and they understood the danger of the situation.

Ale said, "You mean a facade is when you tell a big fat lie."

My mother looked weary. Her eyes moved around, as if she was searching for the right words. She shifted in her seat, crossing her legs as she sucked on her cigarette. Finally, she said, "It's not quite like that."

"Well, where are we going then?" I asked.

She reached for our hands.

"I wish I could tell you, my precious girls, but I can't. Right now, we'll be taking a plane to Lima, Peru. Nobody else has this information about us. It has to do with being in the resistance, and I know you'll understand because you are both so strong and so smart and so mature."

I hadn't realized we were in the resistance. I'd just thought we were in solidarity with the resistance. But I felt too embarrassed to say that.

The plane to Lima wasn't leaving for two more hours, my mother told us. She leaned in close, her face super-serious. I knew better than to look away or to practise the hustle in my mind, as I sometimes did when I was worried. The resistance was underground, my mother said in a low voice. That meant it was top secret. We couldn't tell anybody, under any circumstances. There was a story we had to memorize, and she was going to go over it with us many times, so that when somebody asked us about ourselves, we'd know exactly what to say.

"When someone asks where you were born, for example, you say Vancouver. If somebody asks you who Bob is, you say he's your father. In the blood sense. I know I can trust you girls to do this. That's why I brought you along. There are many other women going back to join the resistance, and they've left their kids behind or sent them to Cuba to be raised by volunteer families. But children belong with their mothers. I know that if we're careful, everything will be okay. And we'll all be together, the way we're meant to be."

Bob and my mother had moved in together after the divorce. He was a longshoreman, and he often brought us goodies from the port. He suffered from a terrible temper, but he kept a drawer full of Kit Kats in the kitchen and always offered us one after a fit of rage. We'd heard Bob's story many times. When he was nineteen, he'd hitchhiked all over the world, and because of what he saw he became a revolutionary. After Salvador Allende was elected in Chile, Bob hitchhiked there to offer his support. Lots of foreigners had done that. Allende was the first Marxist president in the world to take power through an election. He believed it was possible to make revolutionary changes without a revolution. Bob spent a year in Santiago, helping to build houses in the New Havana shantytown. Then the coup happened, with General Augusto Pinochet, whom Allende had recently appointed commander-in-chief of the armed forces, at the helm. When the military raided New Havana, Bob was arrested and put in the national stadium, which wasn't for soccer games anymore but had become a concentration camp. Bob had a line about that. "It was during my time there that I became a revolutionary with a capital R," he would say. He got this look in his eye sometimes, and his Adam's apple started quivering. My mother explained that it had to do with what had happened to Bob in the stadium during those two weeks, and what he saw happen to other people.

Three Canadians were being held in Chile right after the coup, and the Canadian embassy got them out. Out of jail, out of the country and onto the dictatorship's blacklist. When Bob got back to Canada, he formed a solidarity committee and organized a cross-country caravan. They set up camp on Parliament Hill until the prime minister, Pierre Trudeau, agreed to offer asylum to Chilean refugees. We'd been one of the first families to arrive, and Bob had helped us from the start. He became my gringo uncle after a while, then my stepfather. And now he was supposed to be my father, which was kind of funny. I guessed people would believe Ale and me, because Bob was Black Irish. That's how he explained his black hair and beard. Black Irish, raised on the wrong side of the tracks. My heart burst for him, for the fact he had almost died for Chile.

My mother continued with the new official story.

We were to tell people she was Peruvian, she said. The Chilean blood that ran through our veins could be no more. Our family was moving south because Bob was starting an import-export company. We'd shopped at the mall for the first time ever to put together a middle-class look. It all made sense now: my mother's Charlie's Angels attire, Ale and I in our brand-new shoes, all the rage with their white platforms and blue suede tops, the Pepsi logo stitched on the side. We had to look normal. Mainstream. We had to stand out for the right reasons from now on, not the wrong ones.

Lots of our friends in Vancouver had come straight from the detention centres in Chile. They'd arrived with crooked spines, missing an eye or their balls or nipples or fingernails. Like Rulo. He'd been held in the Dawson Island concentration camp, near Antarctica, and he was skinny as a skeleton when we picked him up at the airport. He was carrying a charango, a little guitar made from an armadillo shell. Rulo was seventeen when he landed in Vancouver, and Bob had taken him in. Rulo had tried to teach me how to play his tiny charango, but it was too hard to get my fingers into the right position. So I'd taught him the hustle instead. He really liked that.

I tuned back in to my mother as she squeezed our hands.

"To be in the resistance is a matter of life and death. To say the wrong thing to the wrong person is a matter of life and death. And it's impossible to know who the wrong person is. You must assume that *everybody* is the wrong person. In the resistance, we agree to give our lives to the people, for a better society. I'm asking a lot of you, but you must remember that the sacrifices you'll have to make are nothing compared with the majority of children in this world. So many of them die of curable diseases and work twelve-hour shifts in factories, without ever learning to read and write. We are fighting for a society in which all children have the right to a childhood. I'm so proud of you girls for being a part of that."

I was glad my mother had chosen to take us along, because I wanted to fight for the children, for the people of the world. I thought about the sacrifices Rulo had made. He told us he'd handed his bones over to be broken methodically by the military, and he'd do it all again if he had to. He'd shown me his scars and let me touch them. Our sacrifice, my mother said, was a bit different. It would involve us acting as if we were rich, pretending to be something we were not. I swallowed past the stupid knot in my throat. It felt as if a huge vitamin pill had gotten stuck in there.

"That's all I can say for now," my mother was explaining. "So please don't ask me any questions. When one is in the resistance, one simply does what one is told to do. And for the time being, you will not be able to send letters or postcards to anybody." Her cigarette made a sizzling sound as she stamped it out in the ashtray. She kept her gaze down, avoiding our eyes. I thought of the stationery from Chinatown in my carry-on bag. My father had given it to me, with explicit orders to write often. I remembered him that morning, seeing us off at the airport, his shoulders heaving. "My girls, my girls, my girls," he'd murmured in our ears, his hands clutching the backs of our heads.

Ale asked my mother if she could get some more french fries. As she dug in, I watched the long shadows created by the setting sun. Were the planes I could hear all around me coming or going, I wondered? What if I were to pick up my travel bag right now and walk to the Canadian Pacific counter and get on a plane back to Vancouver? What if I were to join the Colombian family at the next table and become one of them? What if I were to walk through the glass doors that led to the vast city of L.A. and get on a bus and just stay in the part of town that it took me to? When I looked over at my mother, she was hugging her canvas carry-on bag to her chest and gazing off somewhere unreachable. A fresh Matinée burned between her fingers.

8

When the time came, we lined up at the Braniff counter with the other passengers, Peruvians and Ecuadorians. Our plane was due to stop in Quito before reaching Lima, and a lady in a beehive and pearls asked me if that's where I was from. No, I said. I was from Santiago. The lady smiled. "Santiago is one of the jewels of South America," she said. Wow. I hadn't known that. But then my mother elbowed me, and I remembered I was from Vancouver now, a place so distant it was already as if it had never existed. We were no longer exiles. We were a resistance family headed who knows where.

There was a kerfuffle at the counter up ahead, and a lady who looked like Julie from *The Love Boat* explained over the loudspeaker that since our plane was having technical difficulties, the airline was going to put us up at a hotel near the airport until morning. Ale and I gave each other a high-five. The only hotel we'd ever stayed in was the hotel for refugees the Canadian government had paid for when we first got to Vancouver.

In the bus lineup, a woman who had gel nails decorated with the U.S. flag shyly approached my mother. "I'm from Ecuador," she said in a rush, clenching her white clutch purse. "I'm twenty-five years old, and I came to L.A. to visit my uncle and auntie. He's the baseball sportscaster on Radio La Raza. Do you know him? Anyway, my nerves have gotten the better of me because my plane is delayed. I noticed that you are a señora with two girls. Would you mind taking care of me as well?"

My mother nodded. I'd never spoken to one of these ladies before, with their feathered hair and heavy perfume. Ladies Mami had always referred to as a "bunch of fucking idiots." And now we'd get to share a room with one.

The hotel was actually a motel. Just like Malibu Barbie's house, I thought, except this motel was for economy-class Latinos whose flights had been delayed. The paint was peeling, and the Astroturf was stained. Ale and I smeared our faces with cream from the mini-containers in the bathroom and modelled the shower caps. There were so many channels on TV it made us dizzy.

It was four in the morning by the time we got into our beige double bed. My mother was supposed to share her bed with the lady, who was called Jackie. But Jackie was stationed at the plastic-wood vanity, rollers in her hair, putting different creams on her face and then wiping them off. From where I was lying, I could see her tweezing her eyebrows and then a trail of hair that led from her belly button to her vagina. My mother always called the private parts of the body by their proper names. If you said "down there," she would look you straight in the eye and say, "*Vagina.* Repeat after me: *va-gi-na.* Good." I wondered if Mami was asleep or just pretending.

Our plane took off without a hitch a few hours later. As we flew toward the equator, the passengers cheered and clapped and talked about their final destination: home. The last time Ale and my mother and I had been on a plane we'd flown north, in the middle of the night, as people wept into their hankies. Someone had spread a Chilean flag and a banner of Allende in the aisle. When the pilot announced over the loudspeaker, "We have crossed the border into Peru. We are out of Chile," the passengers, grown men and strong women, had cried even more loudly. Someone started singing the Chilean national anthem, and everyone joined in. My parents had put their arms around us and said, "You will never forget this. You. Will. Never. Forget." Their faces were distorted from all the crying. And now here we were, five years later, heading somewhere else. Somewhere south again.

2

LIMA KNEED ME in the gut. This city of cathedrals was full of people who looked like me, dressed in their best and smelling of
cologne. Crowds jammed the cobblestone streets, and vendors sold
shakes from stationary bicycles with blenders attached, whistling
boleros as they pedalled. Flies landed on the papayas as fast as the
vendors could peel them, but they threw the fruit into the blenders
anyway, topping it with milk that had been sitting in the sun for hours.

All around us there were people hawking jackets and gold chains
and little trinkets, explaining that they needed money for the bus ticket
to their grandma's funeral, and that's why they were selling this unique
cuckoo clock that had been in the family for forty years. Indian peasant
ladies sold seeds arranged in little mounds. Beggar children missing arms and legs were pushed around on homemade skateboards by
bigger children whose feet were black with dirt. The boys who passed
by winked their eyes and made kissing sounds, murmuring "Mamita" in your ear. Everywhere you looked, even on the cathedral steps,
there were couples making out. Church bells rang and nuns asked for
donations. Music blasted from every store, and groups of yelling men
pressed up against shop windows to watch a soccer game on TV. Buses
never stopped honking their horns. The honking and the yelling and

the traffic noise made you think you were going to go deaf, but then you got used to it. The air stank of sewers and diesel. You got used to that, too. I stuck close to my mother, taking it all in with a quivering chest.

We had checked into a hotel for rich people in the centre of the city. We spent our days walking through the crowds, my mother in her white pantsuit, Ale and I in our new Adidas sweatshirts and Pepsi shoes. At night we stayed inside, because downtown Lima was the most dangerous place in the world when it was dark, my mother said, especially if you were a girl pretending to be rich. Night was when the uniformed men we saw during the day, driving around in their green trucks and monitoring everything with their machine guns, disappeared into the shantytowns.

It was still just the three of us. Mami hadn't said a word about how long we'd be there or where Bob was. She lit one cigarette after another up in our room, watching the news on TV non-stop, while Ale begged me to play Monopoly or Parcheesi, both of which she'd made sure to pack in her suitcase. I'd hit her on the arm when my mother wasn't looking, because I was trying to read my book, *Are You There God? It's Me, Margaret.* Also, I had a lot to chew on. Now I realized what I'd been missing in Vancouver all those years: human heat. Heat coming from strangers, shoulder rubbing against shoulder, full eye contact with every person you passed. Here it was as if everyone on the street was a house with its windows wide open. By the end of the day, you'd encountered a thousand souls and looked into their hearts. Memories were flooding me now that we were south of the equator again. Before the coup, my grandmother Carmen, the person I loved most in the world, had lived in a big wooden house overlooking the ocean in Valparaíso, with my grandfather Armando, my uncle Boris—the greatest storyteller of all time—my aunt Magdalena and my cousins Gonzalo and Macarena. My uncle had been the first Chilean refugee to arrive in Vancouver after an epic solo journey that took him from Valparaíso to Santiago to Seattle and then across the border into Canada. My aunt and cousins had joined him there a few months later. But before all that happened, Mami, Papi, Ale and I would get into our yellow

Citroën every summer and drive all the way from Valdivia, where my parents taught at the university, to Valparaíso, the biggest port in Chile, to spend the summer in that wooden house on top of the hill. One morning, my grandmother had woken me up at the crack of dawn and quietly got me dressed, so no one else would hear. We'd walked to the train station together, and she'd taken me on an outing to Santiago, where she'd bought me churros at Santa Lucía Hill and cotton candy and glazed peanuts and anything else my heart desired. We'd come back late at night, and I'd slept on her lap on the train. It had been the happiest day of my life thus far.

On our third day in Lima, we were out walking when suddenly the crowds pressed into us full force. Mami, knocked off balance in her platforms, screamed out our names as we slammed against a wall. There was smoke everywhere, something like acid in my eyes, a cougar in my throat clawing it raw. Explosions, breaking glass, sirens so loud your ears popped and a stampede of feet.

"Whatever happens, don't let go of my hand!" my mother yelled at us.

Liquid poured from our eyes and noses. Ale was whimpering, and I knew I was going to puke any minute. But then a lady dressed like a secretary in patent-leather spike heels grabbed us and shouted: "All the women come with me!" The secretary was pressing an embroidered hanky to her mouth, smearing her red lipstick. She was about twenty, and obviously an expert on how to get out of sticky situations. We ran behind her through a set of bronze doors. She locked them just as some peasant Indian women were trying to get in, and the whole group of us ran up the spiral stairs with their gold railings to the top floor. When we stopped, I swallowed the puke that was sitting in my mouth, and it burned my insides all the way down. The tear gas wasn't so bad up here, the secretary was explaining. She looked Indian, though she acted and dressed as if there was no Indian in her at all. She was pretending to be something else, just like us.

From the windows we could see hundreds of teenagers, boys and girls both, fighting with the paramilitary, the militarized police force commonly deployed against protesters. Bandanas over their faces, the

youths were hurling little balls with nails sticking out of them, tossing flaming Molotov cocktails made from Coke bottles and firing
stones from slingshots. When the paramilitaries got their hands on
a teenager, they'd beat the kid down with their batons and then drag
him or her to a waiting military truck. They kept shooting tear gas,
and their machine guns were at the ready. A water cannon drove by
slowly, spraying acid water with so much force that it threw people
to the ground. Some trapped bystanders had covered their faces with
their hands, pressing the fronts of their bodies against the buildings.
I could see them retching, and their legs wobbled like noodles. Street
vendors had had their tables overturned and their trinkets smashed.
The women scurried away with their babies on their backs. The men
ran with their broken blender bicycles held up to protect their faces. A
short man in a beat-up suit jacket dashed around opening up his jacket
to display a collection of hankies. Some of them were big and striped,
for men, and some were delicate and white, for ladies. People would
give him a coin, snatch a hanky and then clamp it over their mouths
and noses. Within a few minutes he was out of stock.

"There's a protest in Lima every day," the secretary informed us
with a sigh. "Today it's these kids, who've marched for hours from
the shantytowns. They're mad because the hike in bus fare is meant
to stop them from going to school. It's the third hike in fares this year.
They'll go to the presidential square and light a few buses on fire." A
gold tooth flashed in her mouth as she spoke.

The women around us were talking excitedly about the high cost
of living, inflation, corruption and the escalating price of milk. It was
impossible to come downtown anymore, they complained. If it wasn't
the peasants protesting, it was the teachers, and if it wasn't the teachers, it was the students or the domestic workers or the miners or the
doctors or the priests. My mother listened closely, but she kept her
mouth shut and her face still as she clung to Ale and me. Ale stood
with her back to the window, but I was transfixed by the scene below.
The teenagers didn't look scared. They just kept getting up from the

ground when they fell, adjusting their bandanas and firing off another stone with their slingshots. The secretary popped a piece of gum into her mouth and blew a bubble half the size of her face. My mouth watered as the tear gas started to clear from my sinuses.

The fighting moved down the street, block by block, and after a while the secretary announced in her expert tone of voice that the path was clear. As we emerged into the aftermath, my mother took our hands again. I felt a tug on my jeans and looked down into the black eyes of a small boy.

"Do you have a Sublime, señorita?" he asked. His eyes had hooks that wouldn't let me go.

I'd been eating a Sublime chocolate bar, my new favourite snack, when the protest hit us. He must have seen me and been waiting outside the building the whole time. I knew my mother would disapprove of me buying the little boy a chocolate bar, because that would be charity, and we didn't believe in charity. Charity was vertical, keeping the relationship between the haves and have-nots intact. We believed in revolution. Back in Vancouver, when I'd come home from school once and said, "Please help UNICEF," my uncle Boris had declared he'd rather take a shit in the little box of coins I was holding up. "Hold that box still, Carmencita. Don't move it till I'm done taking a shit in it." He'd started unbuckling his belt, and my mother had fallen to the floor laughing. I laughed too. The image of my uncle, who was five foot five and weighed over three hundred pounds, trying to balance his big behind over the teeny box was just too much. A classless society was what we were fighting for, so I leaned down and kissed the boy all over his round face instead. We kept walking, and his little fingers clutched my jeans the entire way. When we reached the hotel, the guard at the door scared him away with the open palm of his hand: "Shoo, boy, shoo!" Before he dashed out of sight, the boy mouthed the words "No Sublime?" He shrugged his shoulders.

Upstairs, my mother collapsed onto the bed and pulled Ale down beside her. Ale was still whimpering a little, but before long both of them were asleep. I closed the bathroom door quietly and then crumpled onto the toilet, sobbing and sobbing. It was lifetimes since we'd left Vancouver. My father had explained to us that time and space didn't really exist; they were human constructs for trying to make sense of things that didn't make sense at all. Thinking of Papi, I wanted to go back to the exile land. To the solidarity dances, to the school where my friend Dewi and I climbed trees, to putting on plays with my cousins and spying on the late-night meetings where tactics and strategies were discussed. I wouldn't be able to wear my Ché Guevara red star here, or tell the story of the murder of Allende, because we were in the resistance. Instead, Ale and I would probably have to learn to fight like those teenagers in the street. My aim was really bad. I knew I'd aim a stone at those paramilitaries and miss, and then I'd be tortured with electric shocks and sent to the firing squad like my father's best friend, Jaime, who'd been taken from his house in Iquique during lunch for all to see.

When I came out, my mother and Ale were still fast asleep. Mami was usually a light sleeper, but today she was out like a log. I pried her denim handbag from her grip, reached for a coin and went downstairs into the street. Tear gas still hung in the air, and it took me a while to find a kiosk that hadn't been destroyed. But I did, and when I did I bought a Sublime, in its wax-paper wrapping with the swirly blue letters across the front. On my way back to the hotel, the teeny boy found me. His fists latched onto my shaking pants. They were shaking because I was scared to be walking alone in the centre of the city. I didn't have the balls those teenagers had. I never would. Why couldn't the revolution just hurry up and win? Couldn't it see that the teeny boy was hungry and just wanted to play in a sandbox somewhere?

ON OUR FIFTH DAY in Lima, just as Margaret in my book was getting her period, someone knocked on our hotel room door. It was nighttime, and my mother was taking a bath. I opened the door, cautiously, to see a tall man wearing a beige corduroy suit and brown suede shoes.

He had pale skin and very short black hair and a dimple in his chin. He was carrying a brown suitcase and a briefcase with combination locks. The man smiled and then spoke to me in perfect English.

"Hello, Carmencita."

I stared at him. I was holding the Judy Blume book close to my chest, making sure not to lose my page.

"It's Bob," the man said.

I looked at him again. Bob with the long black hair and beard to match. Bob with the lumberjack shirt and kaffiyeh scarf from Palestine. Bob coming home from the port with bags full of groceries, making spaghetti and meatballs while he whistled along to a Pete Seeger album. Bob with his outbursts. Bob, who'd stay up till the wee hours working on the banner to be held up outside the grocery store, urging people to boycott the Chilean grapes sold inside. The great love I'd always felt for him flooded through me.

Bob chuckled. "So? Are you going to let me in?"

The next thing I knew, Mami was behind me, wrapped in the hotel robe. She pushed me aside and pulled Bob in and started climbing all over him. Ale was doing jumping jacks and Mami was crying and Bob was holding her and saying, "It's okay. I'm okay. We're all okay." I understood now that my mother had been scared since we'd gotten to Lima. I couldn't stop smiling, and I practised saying "This is my father" in my mind until this new Bob rubbed his hands together and said: "Let's go get some fish and papa a la huancaína. I'm starving."

Every afternoon for the next seven days, Ale and I stayed alone in the hotel room, playing Parcheesi. We had strict orders to keep the noise down and not to open the door to anyone. Mami and Bob would leave all decked out in their new looks and come back just in time for dinner.

Late at night, when they thought Ale and I were asleep, I'd spy them sitting cross-legged on their bed, talking in hushed tones while they studied photographs of papers and maps. It looked as though someone had covered a wall with papers and then taken a snapshot of every sheet. They would read the papers using a magnifying glass and then go into the bathroom and close the door. I'd hear the click of a lighter, then the toilet flushing over and over again.

I wasn't worried during the times they were gone, except about one direction they'd left me with—only me, not my sister. "If twenty-four hours pass and we don't come back, call this number and say you're with the Tall One and Raquel. Then hang up. Within an hour someone will knock on the door. Answer it, and then you and Ale go with that person."

The paper they'd handed me looked blank, but that's where the lighter Bob had given me came in. If circumstances required, I was to go into the bathroom, close the door, and hold the flame underneath the paper, making sure not to burn it. After a moment, a number would appear in brown letters. My instructions were to memorize the number, burn the paper and flush the ashes down the toilet before making the call. All of this should be done only at the twenty-four-hour mark. Not before. In the meantime, I was to keep the paper in a secret place. Above all, I must not mention this to anyone.

I folded the piece of paper in two, wrapped it in a small piece of cloth, and sewed it into the inside of my travel bag. I felt lonely after I'd done that. Up to that point, Ale and I had both been in on everything. Now I had secrets from her, too. But the twenty-four-hour thing never happened, and the only person who kept knocking on the door was the chambermaid, begging for money for her children who had chronic diarrhea. I never answered, because what if she was an informer for the secret police? Ale and I would get really quiet until she gave up.

On the eighth day, Mami announced that we were leaving. She brushed out her hair, releasing it from its tidy bun, and both she and Bob pulled on jeans and sneakers. Ale and I stuffed the bare essentials in our new orange backpacks. Everything else would be packed into our Samsonites and sent away. We walked from the hotel to a massive bus station swirling with people, where we got onto a bus with the name HUANCAYO written on the front. Bob and I sat together, with

Mami and Ale behind. I pressed my nose to the window to watch Lima disappearing. Vendors ran up to our bus at every traffic light. The people on the bus were poor, and we seemed to be the only non-Peruvians. My mother chatted with an older woman with callused hands.

"Oh, yes, I'm from Tacna," she told the woman. "And my husband and daughters are Canadian. They've always wanted to see Peru, so here we are."

As we reached the outskirts of the city, I thought again about my father. Papi was probably out in the garden right now. He'd be imagining us frolicking in the waves in Costa Rica, green parrots flying around our heads. I swallowed hard, and Bob rubbed my back.

"I love you, Carmencita. I love you."

I nodded and looked out the window. My eyes met the steady gaze of a girl my age, a baby on her back, a barefoot toddler holding her hand. She stood on the island of the great boulevard, holding up a bag of oranges as we passed.

3

I'D NEVER BEEN on a bus like the one to Huancayo, packed to the rafters with families, chickens, piglets and giant sacks of fruit. Babies cooed and screamed throughout the ride, and the driver played a soccer game full blast on the radio. What should have been a six-hour journey ended up taking twelve, because of the bus breaking down every so often. A few of the wooden bridges along the way were missing sections, too, which meant we all had to disembark and walk across the planks put down to cover the holes. Then the driver, with the help of the male passengers, had to figure out how to get the vehicle across, going inch by inch to avoid the places that would snap and send the bus hurtling into the abyss. When we weren't hopping on and off, I was holding my breath as our bus hugged the side of one cliff after another, a green valley always waiting at the bottom to catch us if we fell.

We stayed for a few days in a rundown colonial hotel in Huancayo inhabited by European and North American hippies. There was only one bathroom and one shower for everyone, so the lineups in the morning were long. Each room had a pail for emergencies, though. Mami and Bob disappeared every day until dinnertime. This time, our only instructions were to stay in the hotel room. Nothing was said about making a phone call at the twenty-four-hour mark. I couldn't decide if that meant things were less dangerous here or more so.

On the all-night bus to Ayacucho, I watched the stars of the southern hemisphere from my window. We were in the Andes now, the mountains my parents and their friends referred to constantly, and it felt right to be there. At one point we passed a burning village in the distance. The flames licked the sky. Everyone around me was asleep, and I wondered if the bus driver would stop and get us to help, but he didn't. Our vessel continued on through this landscape of beauty and horror.

There were rallies in the streets of Ayacucho, and Mami and Bob whispered about a civil war. It was the first time I'd heard them use the term. Something was different here in Peru, and it had to do with those words. I knew from earlier conversations that the general in power, Francisco Morales Bermúdez, was dangerous to us because he participated in Operation Condor, which had been set up by Pinochet and the surrounding dictatorships to catch revolutionaries operating anywhere in South America. Operation Condor was an illegal, top secret affair, officially denied by the governments in question, but foreigners in Peru were disappearing all the time. There was a new movement rising in the country, based right here in Ayacucho, and its members believed that peasants, not the working class, should lead the war against the powers that be and take over the cities.

Late at night, when Ale and I were supposed to be sleeping, Bob took photographs of papers that he'd taped to the wall. In Lima, he and Mami had read photos of documents. Now they were the ones producing the photos. Whenever a roll of film was done, Bob would hide it deep in his backpack. On our last morning in Ayacucho, very early, Bob wrapped the rolls of film in plastic, put them in a small cardboard box and taped the box shut. He grabbed his wallet and passport and slipped out of the room. When he came back, he announced that we were going to have fun that day. We bought chirimoya ice cream and ate it sitting in the square. Then we all had diarrhea. That was the thing about Peru. If you didn't have diarrhea, you were either puking or doubled over in pain, because your gut was seizing. My mother said it was good for us to build up our immune systems.

At dawn the following day we boarded a bus for Cusco, which Bob explained had been the capital of the Inca empire. For the next twenty-four hours we wound our way along narrow Andes roads so high up that sometimes we looked down on the clouds. We passed tiny villages and flocks of llamas tended by four-year-old shepherds wearing sandals made from tires. Every so often the bus would stop for a villager who needed to travel only a little ways, and he or she rode for free, chitchatting in Quechua with the driver. Quechua was the native tongue of the Andes, and ever since Huancayo, it was pretty much all we'd heard.

Every so often the driver would stop and yell out: "Time to go to the bathroom!" Everyone would scurry off the bus. Ale and I knew better by now than to look for the toilet; everyone just went over a little hill and squatted. The ladies and children went over one little hill, and the men went over another. In Peru, if you wanted to look up the definition of a word, you'd need two dictionaries: the Poor Peru dictionary and the Rich Peru dictionary. If you looked up the word *bathroom* in the Poor Peru dictionary, the definition would be: "Just over the hill there." If you looked it up in the Rich Peru dictionary, the definition would read: "Marble room with gold taps and its own servant to keep it sparkling." I'd been in a Rich Peru bathroom in Lima, when we'd gone to a fancy restaurant on our last night there.

Cusco was bustling with activity. My mother had bought us a kids' book about the history of Peru, and as we walked around town, I could see that the city was constructed on the foundations of Inca buildings destroyed by the invaders. When we got to the main square, I thought about Tupac Amaru, the native leader who had been murdered by the Spaniards here. They'd tied each of his limbs to a horse, and then each horse had galloped away in a different direction. Tupac Amaru had held on so tight, my uncle Boris told us, that the horses had had to use all their might.

We spent the day buying oranges, grapefruits, apples, chocolate—for energy, Bob said—and lots of quinoa, the local grain. We were going on a hike, and I was pretty sure I was starting to get the picture. Chile was lined by the Andes from north to south, and the only way to get there was by crossing those mountains, the highest in the Americas. We couldn't get into Chile by plane or bus or train or car, with Mami and Bob on the blacklist, so I figured we were headed there on foot. That night we redid our packs, making room for a few litres of water in canteens and a new pot to cook the quinoa in. At four the next morning, Bob woke us up, and we ran to the station and jumped on the train to the trailhead just as it was leaving.

The Inca trail was actually about twenty thousand miles long, Bob explained, but we took the stretch that led right to Machu Picchu. Bob was happier than I'd ever seen him as we set off up the towering mountain, whistling with his pack, stopping to admire the unbelievable beauty around us while he took a sip from his canteen. We were covered in dirt and sweat within minutes. In places the trail was only a sliver, and one wrong move would send you rolling down into the river hundreds of feet below. Ale spent most of the day crying, with Mami calling encouragement from behind. We pitched our tent that night under millions and millions of stars. It made my mother very emotional. "These are our mountains, Carmencita, these are our stars," she kept saying. As we hugged by the fire, I felt proud that I belonged to the Andes too. The Urubamba River shone like silver at the bottom of the world.

We climbed and climbed for the next three days. Once I got lost, surging too far ahead of the others, but Bob rescued me with the help of two Quechua men. I wrapped my legs around his waist and he carried me, backpack and all, up the trail to where my mother and Ale waited. The night before we reached Machu Picchu, we camped in an abandoned Inca city made of stone, bonfires burning around us. Bob told us that the city had been deserted hundreds of years before, during the time of the Conquest. The courtyards and houses and stairways were now open to the stars, which were the size of light bulbs in the ebony sky. A group of Austrians joined us for a chat while a family of twenty Indians set a table with starched white tablecloths and gleaming silver forks.

I'd been the first to spot the group that afternoon. Rounding a corner of the trail, I'd seen a little army carrying tables, chairs, mattresses and trunks on their backs, winding their way along the side of the mountain. Even the youngest, a girl about four, was carrying a pillow. Her shoes had no laces, which made her ankles twist. Like the others, she chewed vigorously on a ball of coca leaves. The oldest woman, who looked about a hundred, transported an enormous pot on her back, secured with ropes. She grunted as she climbed. One of the Indian men walked with a giggling Austrian woman in his arms, sweat pouring down his back in a perfect stream. The rest of the Austrians were pointing at the scenery, putting their palms to their hearts before clicking away with their cameras.

The Austrians feasted at the table while the Indian family squatted around a bonfire, sucking on corncobs and drinking chicha morada and chicha amarilla, liquor made from purple and yellow corn. We'd pitched our tent close to theirs, and when Mami said it was time to get water from the stream at the bottom of the abandoned city, Bob stayed behind, sharing cigarettes and jokes with the Indian family.

There was a full moon lighting our passage, and my knees were wobbly from excitement as we clambered down the steep stone stairs: one of the boys from the Indian family had been peering at me across the fires. His skin was like copper, and he wore an alpaca sweater with little llamas frolicking on it. He carried himself as if he might break into a cumbia at any moment. His eyes were so black you could see the fire reflected in them, two little bonfires blazing away. Halfway down the steps made by his ancestors, I looked back, and sure enough, there he was, standing at the top, hands in his pockets. When his eyes met mine, I smiled and leaned into one of my hips, just as Olivia Newton-John had done after John Travolta collapsed at the sight of her in *Grease*.

But I'd leaned too far, because now I was rolling down the stairs. My head made knocking sounds against the stone. I tried to stop myself, but it was no use. I remembered what my father had told me about gravity: sometimes you just had to give in and let it pull you down. Hikers came running toward the steps from all over the abandoned city, yelling in a variety of languages. I landed like a flopping fish, then leapt to my feet, brushed off my knees and resumed my Sandy stance. I looked for the boy, but he was no longer at the top. I never saw him again. He left with the other men in his family the next day before dawn, carrying the furniture in order to get a head start.

THE TRACKS WE were following led to Quillabamba, a jungle town on the edge of the river. The Urubamba River was brown like chocolate here, and banana trees lined its shores. We'd started out on the train, but when it broke down and nobody came to fix it, we climbed out the window and started to walk. Hours passed as we trudged along with our backpacks. Bob kept the wild dogs at bay with sticks. We still made it to town faster than the train, which arrived so late at night that we'd already eaten, bathed and gone to bed. But one of the passengers from the train started running through the streets, yelling that the Sandinistas had just won the revolution in Nicaragua, so we got up again and went out to a local bar. We ordered Inca Kolas and beer and then sat without uttering a word so Mami and Bob could hear what people were saying. The Sandinista National Liberation Front had been fighting for almost twenty years. They'd named themselves after Augusto César Sandino, leader of the resistance against the U.S. occupation in the 1930s, and they'd finally overthrown the U.S.-backed dictatorship of Anastasio Somoza. Against all odds, another socialist revolution had won in Latin America—the second, after Cuba, in the twentieth century. Mami and Bob could hardly contain their joy. When we did a secret toast, their eyes were filled with tears. "To the Sandinistas," my mother whispered. "To bread and dignity for everyone." I beamed with pride to be part of it. Ale yawned over and over again.

We boarded a train back to Cusco the next afternoon. I figured all these different stops had been to throw the secret police off the scent. There had been no meetings or hushed conversations in the middle of the night since Ayacucho, so the road we were following must have been mapped out then. The smell of rotting onions, chickens and sweat was so familiar by now that I liked it. It was the smell of Peru. Poor Peru.

The four of us were crammed onto one wooden seat, our knees knocking into the pile of people facing us. By the time night rolled around, our bones were sore. Mami massaged my neck and shoulders, and Bob put his arm around Ale, pressing her close. The train rocked from side to side, lulling everybody to sleep. Except me, and the couple across from me. The man's knees pressed into mine as the woman rode him like a bike. Her blouse had come undone. I stayed as still as I could, because I knew if people were humping in the dark across from you, you shouldn't cramp their style. That was my cousin Gonzalo's favourite expression. He would be doing his Elvis impersonation in our East Vancouver living room, and I'd go up and try to poke him. He'd push me away, put his hands on his hips and say, "Carmencita, you're cramping my style." Then he'd go back to being Elvis, singing "All Shook Up," and I was allowed to watch only as long as I stayed on the couch. Thinking of him now brought tears to my eyes. I wondered if I'd ever see him again, with his Fonzie gestures and car collections.

We spent the day in Cusco, then boarded a night bus that said COPACABANA, BOLIVIA, on the front. Another detour to confuse the secret police, I figured. We made the usual pit stops at the villages along the way, and after one of them, Bob got into an argument with another passenger, a loud big-city guy. The dispute revolved around who was to blame for Bob getting hit in the chin when the seat in front of his flew back. Bob had been holding ten kilos of onions in his lap at the time and clutching a baby to his chest, as a favour for one of the standing women. Her feet were swollen to the size of cantaloupes. The argument got so fierce that when the big-city guy accused Bob of being a pretentious hippie come to help lazy Indians with their shit-stinking babies, Bob flew into one of his rages and yelled that he and the big-city guy should go outside and duke it out at the next stop. To my amazement, my mother jumped in and shouted that we'd take their whole family on. She was going to punch out the big-city guy's wife, who had dyed red hair and blotches on her face from skin bleach, and she wanted me to deal with their fifteen-year-old daughter.

"Roll up your sleeves and get ready to fight these racist, social-climbing sons of bitches, Carmencita," she commanded.

I was seized by terror. Ale sat stunned at my side. We'd never seen Mami or Bob fight anybody. Fist fighting was as foreign as a game of cricket. The daughter was bigger than me, and I'd probably get creamed. One look at the wife's pointy nails and you knew that a scratch from that hand could tear your face apart. Bob was tough, but the husband was big, and I could see it getting really bloody before one of them went down. Plus, if we were arrested, our cover would be blown and the dictator of Peru would send us marching right into Pinochet's grip. I didn't know what had come over my mother, who usually talked Bob down from his rages, but now we were doomed. My heart pounded ferociously in my chest.

It was hours until the next stop, and I spent the time practising to see if I could make a tight fist. But once we got there, Ale, Bob and Mami were fast asleep, and the fight had been forgotten. I peered out the window as the big-city guy loaded his family's suitcases onto the back of a very old Indian man. This was referred to as muling it, I'd learned. Mules were Indian men who waited outside the markets and stations to offer their services. They had pieces of rope dangling from their bodies, and their bare feet looked like old shoes. If you accepted his offer, the mule bent over, and his back became the counter on which you piled your belongings. He would grunt as the load grew, his eyes focussed on the ground. After a while, all you could see was two brown legs with the feet shifting around, trying to find the right balance. When you were done loading, you kicked the mule in the shins.

Two hands would appear from beneath the boxes, bundles, suitcases and pieces of furniture. They'd throw rope around the pile, making a web, and then the mule's fingers tied the ropes tight around his chest. You kicked the mule in the calves, so that he knew it was time to go, and he carried your belongings home.

Mules didn't live long. They looked ninety, but the oldest they lived to be was about thirty-five. Usually they died from being mules, but sometimes they died at the hands of the military or the secret police, who liked to use mules for torture practice and then throw their bodies into unmarked common graves. I'd learned about the lives of mules when we were in Ayacucho, because a mule had been telling his story to a school kid with a typewriter in the main square. Bob and I were sitting on the next bench. The mule spoke in Quechua, but the kid translated out loud into Spanish as he typed. At the end of the story, the mule said in Spanish, "My name is Señor Condori Mamani, and this is my story." He'd wanted his story to be written down, and the kid had promised to take it to the library for him. The kid tucked the mule's story into the pocket of his starched white smock and then turned to the next person in line.

That night, from the bus window, I watched as the big-city guy kicked and spat on the old mule who stood in perfect stillness, his dignity intact. I was sorry that Peru wouldn't be our last stop. I wanted us to join the resistance here so we could help the angry teenagers in the streets and the little boy outside the hotel and the chambermaid whose children were dying of diarrhea and the Indian family who had carried the tables and chairs for the Austrians and this old mule take the streets and squares and mountains and make Peru their own. I'd be ready to participate in whatever way they wanted me to.

A TIGHT CIRCLE of men pushed in on us, hands shifting in their pockets. Night had fallen at the Copacabana bus station. We'd made it safely across the border, and Mami and Ale and I were holding down the fort while Bob searched for accommodations. Surrounding us now was a group of Bolivia's best pickpockets. My mother stabbed the air in front of her face with a rusty butcher knife she'd pulled out of her bag.

"One step closer and you're dead, sons of bitches," she snarled.

Ale and I clung to her like the koala bears from Australia we'd seen pictures of. We must have looked ridiculous, because we were both taller than she was.

"Don't worry, my precious little girls. I've got everything under control. Watch and learn, kids, how to deal with motherfuckers."

Mami took a step forward, dragging us with her. The tip of her knife touched the chin of one of the pickpockets. The circle broke, and the men scattered. I wondered if they had gone to get reinforcements to really do us in.

As we waited for Bob, I replayed the border scene for the millionth time.

We'd changed buses in Puno, a small city on Lake Titicaca. "Documents. We're at the border with Bolivia," the driver had announced soon afterward. When I caught Mami and Bob glancing at each other, a shard of terror pierced my gut. Now I got it: They were carrying something. They were carrying something dangerous in their packs. Bob's Adam's apple moved up and down, and my mother's nostrils flared. I remembered Uncle Jaime, my father's best friend in Chile. They said before he was shot by the firing squad, his tongue and testicles were burned black. As we moved toward the front of the bus, I saw men in dark glasses with guns and German shepherds waiting at the door. An invisible axe struck me in the chest. But when the men with guns had asked my mother what she had in her pack, she'd looked them in the eye, shrugged her shoulders and said, "Clothes. Dirty underwear." Some U.S. dollars had changed hands, and then we'd been ordered back on the bus. The four of us hadn't been taken to the shack where the people refused entry were sent. They were all Indian, all poor, all Peruvian. There were two young guys with fear clamped in their jaws, a woman with a baby on her back, a girl who'd kept her chin up. The

German shepherds had bounded around them barking, stirring up dust that landed in their shining black hair. I was afraid for them, and I swallowed and swallowed what felt like broken glass cutting its way down my esophagus. Bob rubbed my back.

That afternoon, a boat with our bus on board had crossed Lake Titicaca, the highest lake of its size in the world, delivering us into Bolivia. The boat was more like a raft, really, and the driver put bricks all around the tires to keep the bus from rolling off. Everybody cheered when we were firmly back on land.

I'd been confused when Copacabana first came into view. From watching Barry Manilow sing his hit song on TV, I'd thought Copacabana was a place where you fell head over heels in love while doing the kick ball change in platform shoes. But I'd gotten it wrong. Copacabana was the home of a brown Virgin with pink neon lights flashing off and on all around her. She commanded the top of a steep hill, and people crawled up to her on their knees like little ants, murmuring prayers in Spanish, Aymara and Quechua. We'd arrived on August 6, Independence Day. Bolivia had freed itself from Spanish control in 1810, and every year thousands of people came to this sacred place to celebrate. Everywhere we looked there were temples and shrines and candles burning. Our Lady of Copacabana was the country's patron saint. She kept the roads safe, and seemingly every car, cart, bus, truck, taxi and bicycle in the land was here to be blessed. Everybody prayed for protection from accidents that would kill them or turn them into vegetables or leave them deformed.

As we walked through town, it became evident that every thief in Bolivia was here as well, using razor blades to rip people's pockets and purses open. The thieves robbed everybody: gringos, skinned-kneed believers, nuns, students, whole families. They didn't care. People chased them through the streets and markets, but they were fast, and they helped each other out. Also, if you made too big a scene, they might slide a palm across your face, razor still in place, and leave you with a scar you'd have forever.

Under the circumstances, my mother decided it would be best to keep her butcher knife visible. She held it up against her chest as we manoeuvred around the processions and offerings that littered the sidewalks. Since she was a kill-two-birds-with-one-stone kind of person, she took the opportunity to remind Ale and me that organized religion had been invented by the rich and powerful to keep the poor down. "See?" she said, gesturing to the prostrate pilgrims. "Who's on their knees right now? The Indians, the most exploited of all." She gripped her knife with ferocity. "Once upon a time, Bolivia was the richest country in the world. The city of Potosí was crowned by a shining silver mountain. But the Spaniards arrived and enslaved these people—though they resisted, they put up a damn good fight—and made them mine that mountain until every last ounce of silver was gone, across the Atlantic to Europe, along with all the gold taken from the Incas and every last resource in the South. Genocide was committed in the name of the Church and progress. That's why we are atheists."

We passed a red-haired priest who was sprinkling a procession of taxis with holy water as he recited prayers in gringo Spanish. The priest was Irish, probably, Bob said. Buses had their own separate procession, as did trucks. Shiny Mercedes-Benzes driven by men in Ray-Bans lined up as well. The streets were packed, with everybody wolfing down chuño, charcoal-black potatoes, and meat patties called salteñas. Boys and men winked and puckered their lips, murmuring "Mamita" and "Delicious" and other, ruder comments. I noticed that there were mules in Bolivia, too, waiting in perfect stillness with their ropes. The ones with bleeding knees must have climbed the hill to ask for protection from the Virgin.

We left Copacabana on a newly blessed bus with its own little shrine to the Virgin at the front. The highlands stretched for thousands of miles around us, interrupted by the sharpest mountains I'd ever seen. Our fellow passengers crossed themselves every two seconds. I kept my face still so my mother wouldn't know what I was doing in my head: asking the Virgin to keep the roads clear and open for my family's journey. Whatever the journey was. Wherever our destination might be.

We drove for hours, until the land broke like a Greek plate and there was a drop in the road. I looked out to see nothing but sky. The universe. Then I looked down, and there below us was a city in a bowl. A bowl like the deepest crater on the moon, with a little house stuck to every last square inch of it. The bus drove over the edge of the bowl and down. Independence Day and the Virgin were being honoured here as well, because hundreds of people were dancing in hand-woven clothes with matching hats. Ladies with ten skirts in every possible colour twirled in unison, bright threads woven through their braids. We continued our spiral into the belly button of the South. Little kids chased after a homemade ball, wild dogs fought over a bone, armies of men carried big bundles on their backs, and finally our bus reached the bottom, honking its way along cobblestone streets with gold-encrusted cathedrals growing out of them. The air stank of shit and rotting garbage. The sounds of Aymara, Quechua and Spanish filled my ears.

A couple of guys in moth-eaten sweaters threw our packs down from the roof of the bus. We stood on a sidewalk in Plaza Murillo, which looked to be the main square, amid the bustle of newspaper boys, shoeshiners, pinstriped businessmen, Indian women on errands, secretaries, beggars and office workers in baby-blue smocks. There were Indian women selling tiny dried-up llama fetuses and kiosks displaying beautiful cards made of carved bronze and wood and silver. If we'd been allowed to write to our father, I would have bought one to send him.

"This is La Paz. The highest capital city in the world," my mother said.

I looked up to see if that meant the sky was closer.

"This is where we'll live."

A group of girls about my age were passing us on the sidewalk. They carried leather school bags and had their hair in immaculate braids. They laughed as they walked hip to hip, arms around each other's shoulders and waists. I looked at Ale. She looked at me. It had always been the two of us, and here we were, still together. I moved closer to her, and she leaned into my side. Bob flagged down an empty taxi as the bells of the cathedral announced evening mass. I was surrounded by people who must know all about life, I thought. There was no way you could live in a crater, closer to the sky than anyone else, in the heart of South America, in the continent's poorest country, and not know about life.

4

THE KETTLE BOILED its way to exhaustion as Jimmy Cliff sang "You Can Get It if You Really Want" for the tenth time in a row. It was one of Bob's favourite songs, and he played it day and night. Even though we put iodine in the water, we still had to boil it for thirty minutes before we could drink it. There was diarrhea and vomiting to be wary of, but also typhoid and cholera.

The four of us were seated around the table, which was set with bread and jam, waiting for our tea so we could celebrate the chairs. We'd carried them home from the San Francisco open market, almost killing ourselves on cobblestones. The hills in La Paz were so steep you couldn't help breaking into a run as you headed down. People had screamed when they saw us coming and jumped out of the way. A couple of mules had followed us, elbowing each other and laughing, perplexed as to why we hadn't just piled the chairs onto their backs.

Our new home in Miraflores, a lower-middle-class neighbourhood with the national stadium at its centre, was at the end of an alley off one of the great boulevards that criss-crossed this part of town. We'd found the house through Tammy's connections. Tammy was from Wyoming, but she'd lived here since the sixties, which was when Bob first met her. They'd both been hitchhiking through these parts and ended up volunteering at a hospital in the highlands. Tammy's hairy legs indicated to me that she was On the Left. But when I announced how excited I was to live in the country where Ché Guevara had died a mere twelve years earlier, a fact I remembered from one of my uncle Boris's stories, Bob pulled me aside and said sharply: "Don't do that. Tammy's not a revolutionary. She's a pacifist. She has no idea what we're really doing here." The loneliness I'd been feeling off and on since we'd begun our underground life dropped like a stone into my gut and stayed there.

Our house consisted of two rooms separated by a little staircase. We slept on the floor of the upstairs room in our sleeping bags. Both rooms were spacious, though, and there was a bathroom off the upstairs room and a kitchen off the downstairs one. We shared our courtyard with the landlords: Señora Siles, a matriarch in pearl earrings and a housecoat; her daughter Liliana, a woman in her thirties with a Dorothy Hamill haircut and wobbly high heels; her younger son, Juan, a playboy who rode a motorcycle and had papered the walls of his room with pictures of butt-naked women; and Liliana's eight-year-old son, Pedro. They were part of a clan that stretched back to the time of the Conquest, a prominent family of politicians ranging from the far right to the left, and they liked to tell us as often as possible that they were of full-blooded Spanish descent.

Bob and my mother filled us in on the details. Señora Siles's father, Hernando Siles, had been president of Bolivia from 1926 until 1930. Her brother, Hernán Siles Zuazo, had taken part in the 1952 revolution that led to the nationalization of Bolivia's most important mines and to major agrarian reform. Siles Zuazo became vice-president after the revolution had triumphed, and then president. During the Second World War South America had flourished, Mami explained, because the United States was otherwise occupied. But by the mid-fifties, the U.S. had turned its full attention back to the South, and during Siles Zuazo's term as president, Bolivia was pressured to adopt economic programs that were to the benefit of the United States and the local bourgeoisie. In 1971, General Hugo Banzer, who had trained at the U.S. Army's infamous School of the Americas, was installed by Richard Nixon after a military coup overthrew the left-leaning president, Juan José Torres. Banzer had Torres killed, and during his rule, thousands of Bolivians were imprisoned and tortured. Many disappeared, and hundreds were murdered. The International Monetary Fund (IMF) and the World Bank poured millions in credit into Bolivia as the country's natural resources were handed over to multinational corporations. Half a year before we arrived, Banzer had called elections to calm the volatile political climate. Through massive fraud, a general of his own choosing was elected, even though Siles Zuazo, the leader of a coalition of left-wing parties, had actually won. Now a conservative politician named Walter Guevara was serving as interim president. Bolivia was a powder keg, my mother said, and nobody knew what was going to happen next.

The Siles family's three maids, two young teenagers and an older woman, slept on bundles of hay brought into the landlords' kitchen late at night. They washed themselves in the morning in the cement laundry sink in the courtyard, using pails to shampoo their hair in the five o'clock highland cold, when a veil of frost covered the city. I loved to watch them braid their hair and weave coloured wool into it. The maids talked in Aymara. They liked to laugh long and loudly, but I could also hear them cry late at night. They scrubbed the landlords' clothes in the cement sink in ice-cold water until their hands bled. Often Señora Siles would monitor them: "More bleach on that one, you Indian. Or don't you know the meaning of white?" The clothes were hung to dry, and when they were taken down in the late afternoon, every last piece was ironed. The maids swept, washed and waxed the floors in the landlords' vast house, on all fours. They cooked four meals a day from scratch, kept an eye on Pedro, made the beds, scrubbed the three bathrooms clean, tended to the garden and did the shopping at a nearby market, where they were allowed to go for only half an hour at a time. The walls of the courtyard were topped with broken bottles encased in the cement. The jagged edges pointed straight up to keep thieves out and the maids in. If they were late getting back, Señora Siles would pull their braids and spit in their faces. Her shrieks of "Stupid, lazy Indian!" overtook house, garden and alley. Ale and I watched it all from our kitchen window, where we were peeling potatoes and boiling the corn. On a day when the punishment was particularly harsh, Ale exclaimed, "I will never be poor. If you're poor, that's how people treat you."

"But that's why we're here," I said. "To participate in the struggle to change all this."

"No. I don't care about the struggle. I will never be poor."

The maids got two hours off on Sundays, between three and five in the afternoon. In preparation, they shined their braids, added coloured pompoms to the ends and put tiny gold hoops in their ears. Each pulled out a velvet skirt and pinned an embroidered shawl over her shoulders. A bowler hat and a pair of flats with starched bows completed the look. They were beaming by the time they boarded the bus to Plaza Murillo, and didn't seem to mind that Ale and I were tagging along, although of course we'd go our own way once we got there. Dozens of buses were headed to the centre of the city, crammed with maids and the men who would woo them as they walked in big circles around each other in the plaza. Shoeshine boys grabbed the buses' back bumpers, their wares on their backs and their feet on homemade skateboards. Vendors in white pleated smocks held cotton candy like little pink clouds above their heads. University students with ancient typewriters strapped to their backs made the pilgrimage along the cobblestones, card table under one arm, block of paper under the other. They hoped to make a few bucks by taking dictation from the maids, who maybe had to send a letter to an important someone. The men who received the letters would pay some other student to have them read.

Organizers from the domestic workers' union were also out in full force, speaking urgently to maids of all ages about a planned general strike. Most maids were new to the city, and many of them didn't get paid. They simply worked as slaves in exchange for room and board. If a maid was impregnated by one of the males of the house, she'd get fired and thrown into the street, and then what? Ale and I heard all this from a woman shouting through a bullhorn. We didn't get too close to the action, though. Bob had warned us that no matter how much solidarity we felt for the maids, we had to come across as neutral Canadians who just felt sorry for them; otherwise our cover might be blown.

ONE SUNDAY EVENING in late August Ale and I pulled out the two white smocks we had bought at the San Francisco market and two leather school bags. Five notebooks each, a jar of black ink and a calligraphy pen. Tomorrow was the first day of school.

The public school, only three blocks from our house, was one of the best in the city, but the naked eye wouldn't have told you that. It was a falling-down building with rubble strewn around it. No glass in the windows, cracks in the walls. There were three shifts for students. Morning was for boys, afternoon was mixed, and night was for adults who'd never made it past their primary studies. Our shift would begin at 1:00 PM and go until 6:00.

We set off the next day. Hair braided so tight it hurt, socks pulled up to the knee, nails, ears and teeth clean. Mami and Bob waved goodbye from the corner. My mother wiped tears from her eyes; seeing us back in school in South America made her sentimental. As we entered the school's central courtyard, Ale and I were met with lines and lines of students, raven hair shining in the midday sun, girls in starched white smocks and boys in navy-blue sweaters and grey pants. A tattered flag was raised during the national anthem, and the school principal, a middle-aged man in a suit, faced the assembly from a wooden riser, singing at the top of his lungs. A metre-long stick held in his right hand moved to the beat. Dozens of women teachers, also in white smocks, stood in neat lines next to him. Each carried a book in her left hand and a stick in her right. Young men in leather jackets walked through the lines of students, wooden stick held in the right hand, tip of the stick caressed by the left. A few times the anthem was punctuated by the whack of a stick against a child's thigh, but everyone sang all the same, chests puffed and proud.

Next the principal pulled Ale and me up onto the wooden riser, where we looked down on the hundreds of brown faces.

"These two new students are from Canada. You will treat them with respect. If you don't, I'll hit you."

He punctuated the air with his stick for effect.

"Where's Canada?" The principal pointed to a male student with his stick.

"With your permission I will answer the question, sir," responded the boy.

"You have my permission to continue."

"Thank you, sir. Canada is the second-largest country in the world, sir, after the Union of Soviet Socialist Republics. It is situated just north of the United States, and it is part of our great continent of America. The population is Anglo-Saxon, and their religion is Protestant. There is one province, Quebec, where the population is French and their religion is Catholic. It is a First World capitalist country with a liberal democracy, and it has access to both the Pacific and the Atlantic, as well as the Arctic Ocean. Shall I go on, sir?"

The principal shook his head. He sent Ale to join one line of girls and me to another. One of the leather jackets placed me at the very back of my line, because I was the tallest in my grade seven class.

As a series of whistles sounded, I was swarmed by my new classmates. They took turns hugging and kissing me, bombarding me with questions. A stick cut through the air with a snap and landed, hard, on one of the boys' butts. He flinched, and the rest of us ran. The whole group took the marble stairs two at a time, telling jokes and passing each other love notes and bits of toffee. Inside the classroom, each person stood next to an ancient wooden desk, following a seating plan based on gender: boy, girl, boy, girl, boy, girl. My desk, beside a paneless window, looked out onto one side of the bowl that was La Paz. Every bit of the desk's wooden surface was engraved with hearts, dates, initials, political slogans and fragments from the poetry of the beloved Peruvian César Vallejo: "I shall die in Paris, in a rainstorm. On a day I already remember."

A crest hung above the blackboard: "1879–1979, the one hundredth anniversary of the Great War of the Pacific: OH, PACIFIC, HOW I CRAVE YOUR RETURN TO BOLIVIA, OH, PACIFIC, YOU WHO THE CHILEANS STOLE FROM US WITH THEIR CRIMINAL HANDS. THE PACIFIC IS BOLIVIAN." The war, fought for five years over who would control the mineral-rich Atacama Desert, had been started by the British as part of their divide-and-conquer tactics in South America. Bolivia had lost, and hence become landlocked. One more good reason to avoid saying I was Chilean. A leather jacket entered the room to take roll call. Much to my surprise, I was not the only Aguirre. The other was a boy with light brown hair who looked at me with a luminous smile and winked. Suddenly the students chanted loudly: "Good morning, teacher! How are you!" A bespectacled man carrying a briefcase walked to the head of the class, the indispensable stick under his left arm. We watched him snap his briefcase open and pull out a stick of chalk and a rag. "I'm fine, ladies and gentlemen. Señorita Flores, the board, please."

Our teacher roamed the aisles with his stick, checking everyone's ears and nails, before addressing us again. "Welcome to art class, ladies and gentlemen. Homework on your desks." The students around me opened their drawing tablets. The teacher walked again from desk to desk, holding up a few sketches for everyone to admire: charcoal portraits of a boy sitting on his shoeshine box, a girl leaning against a washbasin, a young vendor holding out a box of Chiclets. These students with their perfect posture and greased-back hair clearly knew and loved their people to the core, and this strict teacher understood how to pass on the skills that allowed them to capture their world and its inhabitants. As he moved among us, he held forth on dark and light, contours, depth and perspective. The students nodded furiously and took notes on his every word.

I sat with my hands crossed in front of me, lost for a moment in memories of macramé hour at my old school. A drumming on my desk brought me back to reality. It was the menacing stick, which led to a hand, which led to an arm, which led to a crisp white shirt and a wide black tie. Then there was an Adam's apple and a mouth and a pair of goldfish-bowl glasses.

"Homework."

My mouth refused to open. A girl in front of me turned around to say I was new, but the teacher glared at her, and she fell silent.

"Stand up."

I did so.

"Hands."

Students were gesturing to me to offer my palms. I willed my hands to stay in place as the stick cracked through the air, coming down hard. Two tears shot like projectiles from my eyes as I took my seat.

From the front of the class, the teacher lectured on art and revolution, accompanying his words with lively quick sketches on the blackboard. The artist must be ruthless in his pursuit of the truth, he said, and when he found the truth, he must utter it with love and beauty, whatever the danger involved. "An artist who does not risk his art and himself is to be pitied." My hands were smarting from being hit. But I liked him, because he talked to us like adults. There was nothing in his voice or demeanour to indicate that we were intellectually incapable of grasping these concepts. When the class was over, I stood with the other students and recited: "Thank you, teacher, for the lesson of today!" We bowed as he left the room.

At recess, the whole class ran to the courtyard together, everybody holding hands. People passed coins to a girl they called La Grandma. When she got back from the kiosk, the candy she'd bought was split evenly, and then everyone played together.

At eleven, it turned out, I was the youngest in my class. Most of the other grade seven students were between thirteen and fifteen, and almost all of them worked, the girls as maids and the boys as shoeshine boys. Not all masters were like our landlords, I learned. Some girls spoke highly of the families they worked for, and all were grateful they were given the freedom to go to school. The shoeshine boys lived with their own families and helped provide for them. When times got tough, school sometimes had to be dropped for the year.

Señorita Flores took me under her wing, telling me her secrets as if we'd known each other forever. She was fifteen, a maid, possibly pregnant and thinking of getting married to her twenty-year-old boyfriend. He would save her from a life of servitude, because he was an elevator operator at a downtown office building. Since she was wise in the ways of romance, I showed her the note somebody had passed me during art class. "Señorita Aguirre: I have been admiring you from afar for precisely fifteen minutes. And I have come to the conclusion that I am profoundly in love with you. This is my declaration of love. Do you accept? Your fantastic admirer, Eugenio Aguirre. P.S. How convenient that we already have the same last name, don't you think?" I must wait at least twenty-four hours before I gave my answer, my mentor advised, and even then only at his request. In the meantime, I should restrict myself to brief eye contact and half smiles.

We had four more classes that afternoon: literature, mathematics, French, and embroidery for girls and carpentry for boys. When the day was over, it seemed as if everybody had a sweetheart they'd been dying to make out with, and they were doing that now, no holds barred. Hundreds of night students rushed in through the rubble, pulling combs through their hair. Every teacher worked a morning, afternoon and night shift, my classmates explained, but few had the privilege of teaching all day at the same school. Some of them taught at the university as well. Like the students, they were required to provide their own tools: books, chalk, paper and pens.

The shoeshine boys from my class, including Eugenio Aguirre, chased after a bus, their homemade skateboards under their arms. Some of the maids were discussing the tasks waiting for them at home: one had to wax all the floors that evening, one had to help prepare a five-course meal, another had to wash a week's worth of laundry. Since they had the day's homework, too, they decided they'd go from home to home and do the housework as a group. The other girls in my class offered to walk me home. On the way we bumped into Ale, who was balancing six hot dogs given to her by her classmates and chatting animatedly with a large group of boys and girls. When I came alongside her, we talked about the hitting. Together, we decided never to mention it to my mother and Bob. They might take us out of that school, and we would rather die than leave now. We really would.

That night, I pulled out my Chinatown stationery. The letter-writing ban was off now, and this was the first time I'd written my father a letter. "My dearest Papi: I cannot tell you how much I miss you. Revolutionary Central America was not meant to be, so here I am writing you from the highest capital city in the world, La Paz. Today was the first day of school, where I went to grade seven. My classmates are working children who don't seem like children at all . . ."

5

THERE WERE TWO people sitting in our new chairs one day when Ale and I got home from school, a man and a woman about Mami and Bob's age. The man was blond and blue-eyed. The woman wore John Lennon spectacles.

"This is Lucas. And this is Trinidad. They're going to stay with us for a while," said my mother. "They'll be like your uncle and auntie. Just don't tell them anything about yourselves. And if anyone asks, say they're distant cousins of mine visiting from Mexico."

The newcomers didn't bat an eyelash. An open bottle of wine stood on the table, and all of the adults were smoking like crazy. I could tell Mami and Bob were happy to have company. We cooked a Chilean cazuela together for dinner, a stew made with potatoes, squash, rice and meat. Darkness fell, we pulled the curtains shut, and it was just like the old days in Vancouver. The adults drank more wine, the ashtrays overflowed, and our shortwave radio, usually tuned in to news stations from all over Bolivia and the rest of the world, was playing Andean music instead. Hours passed as we swapped stories and jokes. My mother and Trinidad kept grabbing each other's shoulders for support as they laughed. My mother had always had lots of girlfriends, and I could see how much she'd been missing them. Bob and Lucas spoke in hushed tones about the mounting crisis in Bolivia. Walter Guevara, the interim president, was faced with a critical economic situation, thanks to the Banzer dictatorship, which had robbed the country of millions. The military were nervous about the planned elections, because they did not want to respond to questions about the bloodshed during the Banzer years. Poverty was out of control, and people were clamouring for change. Bolivia was growing tenser by the day.

Trinidad had mashed up her food during supper, and every so often she got out of her chair and lay down on her back. She'd lie there laughing at one of my mother's jokes, and everyone continued as if it was the most normal thing in the world to have Trinidad on the floor like that. Lucas had wavy fingernails from torture, and there were two bullet-hole scars on his right forearm. At least that's what they looked like to me. Trinidad and Lucas reminded me of my uncles and aunties back in Vancouver. The ones who'd been fresh off the boat, direct from the concentration camps, with their scars and broken bodies. We all did janitor work together, in a group. The broken ones would have to take breaks from using the big vacuum cleaners and mops to lie on their backs on the floor. There was always someone who was crying uncontrollably, and someone else would explain it like this to us kids: "The Great Sadness has overtaken Aunt Lidia today. That's all."

For the first time since we'd arrived in Bolivia, my heart ached for my people in Vancouver. I got up from the table and went outside to the courtyard. When I came back in, the adults were singing banned songs in whispers: the music of Violeta Parra and the exiled Chilean groups Quilapayún and Inti-Illimani. Those two groups had been touring Europe when the coup had happened. If they'd been in Chile, they probably would have suffered the same fate as the great singer Victor Jara, who had been tortured and murdered in Chile Stadium days after the coup. In Vancouver, the Chilean solidarity commit-tee held monthly peñas at the Ukrainian Hall, benefits with singing, dancing, empanadas and wine. Hundreds of people—Chileans, gringos from the labour movement and the Communist Party, hippies, U.S. draft dodgers and exiles from everywhere from Palestine to Uganda—jammed into the place. Speeches would be made and documentaries shown and cumbia danced. The kids ran around, falling asleep under the tables while the adults cleaned deep into the night. The money raised was sent directly to Chile, because an active resistance demanded an active solidarity, as my mother always said over the microphone, her left fist in the air. Snow sometimes covered the ground as we drove through Chinatown and back home, where there was always a place on our couch for a new refugee.

Lucas and Trinidad stayed with us for months. Lucas would sometimes leave for a week or so, but he always returned. Soon after their arrival, Bob landed a marketing job at Bolivia's first computer company. My mother started teaching English at the American English Centre. They both set off early every morning, leaving Ale and me to do our homework. Once that was finished, the two of us went to the market, haggled for food and cooked lunch. We ate together; working hours in Bolivia provided for a long lunch, the most important meal of the day. After that, Ale and I would go to school.

In the mornings, before breakfast, Lucas greased his hair back, dabbed on English Leather cologne and ironed his white shirt. He owned only two shirts, and he rotated them, washing one every night in the bathroom and hanging it to dry. At breakfast, he and Trinidad listened to the shortwave radio and commented on the news. Lucas, who was as cool and collected as an oyster lying on the bottom of the sea, would shake his head and murmur while Trinidad yelled out obscenities at the right-wing general being interviewed or praised the miners who were denouncing their horrific working conditions and demanding a change in government. Some of the miners in the highlands had started their own radio stations, and everybody listened to these to get local news and reports on Bolivia's political situation. Sometimes Trinidad would pull Ale or me onto her lap and caress our arms and hair. She found all kinds of things funny, and it was easy to make her laugh. She liked to have things clean, so she spent a lot of time scrubbing our floors. She was a voracious reader who could read a book in a night, and often did, since she was an insomniac. She liked black coffee for breakfast and had a tendency to stare off into space for long periods of time, cigarette held near her face, hand shaking just a touch.

At night I'd sit quietly at the top of the stairs and listen to the adults talk. Trinidad and Lucas were on the blacklist in Chile, I'd figured out. They had both been in the leadership of the resistance when the coup happened. Lucas had been sent to the notorious Colony of Dignity, a concentration camp run by an ex-Nazi who was one of Pinochet's right-hand men. The camp received political prisoners of German descent with special glee, torturing them for being traitors to the Aryan cause. Nobody got out of the Colony of Dignity, Bob said, shaking his head in admiration, but somehow Lucas had. Trinidad had been sent from Villa Grimaldi, an underground detention centre near Santiago, to Chacabuco, a concentration camp in the Atacama Desert. Both of them had sought asylum in Mexico, since Mexico City had become the new resistance headquarters.

Those who joined the resistance believed in a revolution that would topple the existing capitalist structure in Chile, kick out the multinational corporations and create a socialist, democratically run state. They believed in armed struggle because the status quo was defended tooth and nail by the military, armed with the latest gadgets funded by foreign backers. When those weren't enough to keep people down, the United States sent in its own military to oversee and even carry out the dirty work. The resistance had recruited members from all sectors of Chilean society: students, peasants, priests, workers, miners, artists, anarchists and native leaders. Internationalists who had come to Chile from all over the world to support Allende joined the resistance as well. Allende had believed that socialism could be achieved peacefully, through the existing structures, but on the day of the coup, he himself,

48

along with other members of his government, had taken up arms. The resistance was virtually destroyed by Pinochet, its members murdered, disappeared or exiled. But now people believed it was ready to build itself up again from within Chile. This year, 1979, had been deemed the Year of the Return, I heard the adults saying. An international call had been made for remaining members, along with new recruits from around the globe, to go to Lima. Now I understood what we had been doing there. The Return Plan was very dangerous, I understood. All three countries bordering Chile—Peru, Bolivia and Argentina—were under right-wing dictatorships, and Operation Condor was in full swing. Captured resistance members were either disappeared by the local secret police or illegally transported across borders and handed over to Pinochet.

My nighttime life was separate from my daytime one, though each informed the other. I'd accepted Eugenio Aguirre's declaration of love at school, which meant we walked together in the courtyards at recess. He sent me love notes, but he never touched me. That was a relief. Señorita Flores, whose first name was Valentina, had become my best friend, and the rest of my classmates were so close they felt like cousins.

One day after school a girl invited me to her house for dinner. We climbed for what seemed like hours up the steep cobblestone streets. The higher we went, the darker the streets got, until we reached a point where it was pitch black. The dirt road was full of holes, and there were no stone steps anymore to lead the way. Life surrounded us in the dark: packs of barking dogs, children playing, men laughing. Everywhere there was the sound of mortars crushing chili peppers—the sound of La Paz at mealtimes. Finally we reached a muddy courtyard surrounded by dozens of little structures made of bricks, cardboard, wood and cement. Faint light issued from most of the houses, and women and children had gathered at a tap at the centre of the courtyard, pails in hand. My mother had drilled into our heads that there was no reason to fear the poor; on the contrary, the rich were the ones

49

not to be trusted. In Canada, people had sometimes crossed the street when they saw us coming, just because we were poor and brown. But I was still afraid now.

My friend led me inside one of the little structures, where kerosene lanterns lit a tiny living room. The dirt floor, packed solid, was covered with a little rug. The couch and armchair, their arms carved with intricate designs, would go for a fortune in Canada, I thought. The dining room set crammed into the small space shone as if the wood got polished every day. The obligatory shrine to the Virgin stood in one corner, and a portrait of Ché Guevara gazed down at us from the wall.

My classmate's mother offered me coca-leaf tea and a cheese pastry. She was young and beautiful, and an educated person, I could tell. She worked as a secretary, she said. As we were talking, I heard someone cough behind a curtain, and my friend's mother pulled it open to reveal the bedroom: three single beds right next to each other, only inches from the back of the couch. My friend's grandparents were in one of the beds, sitting straight as rods and smiling wide at me. The grandfather had a head full of white poofy hair and was in starched baby-blue pajamas. The grandmother wore a pink flowery housecoat, and her hair, black with hints of grey, had been pulled back into a braid, then rolled into a bun. A small gold cage encircling a white pearl hung from each of her ears.

My friend's mother served us peanut soup for dinner at the antique table. Her father and brother were home from work by now, and the grandparents joined the dinner conversation from their place on the bed. It was late when I left, and my friend's brother offered to walk me home. He was fourteen, I learned. He worked at the bus station handling luggage and went to school on the morning shift. His dream was to become an airplane pilot. On the way down we bumped into my French teacher, who was climbing the hill with his bag of books and chalk. The next day, from our desks in the classroom, my friend pointed out the part of the hill where she lived. It wasn't even halfway up the mountain. That made sense, actually, because the higher you lived, the poorer you were. Only the Indian working class lived at the top. And those were the people who had somewhere to live. The starving class lived on the streets, by the thousands.

WE'D BEEN IN BOLIVIA for almost four months by now, and I had turned twelve in the interim. On the morning of November 1, after my mother and Bob had left for work, I set off for the boulevard as usual to buy fresh bread. It was the beginning of the rainy season. Black clouds were forming, signalling the kind of storm that could send houses rolling down the hills. Oddly, the regular hum of the city was absent when I reached the street. Suddenly, there was a deafening roar, and military jets flashed across the sky in formation. We'd been living in Valdivia at the time of the coup in Chile, but I'd seen the footage of warplanes over Santiago many times since. The jets crossed the sky again, the roar of their engines echoing against the sides of the bowl of La Paz.

I stood frozen, my spine tingling. Before I could decide what to do, a man in plain clothes and sunglasses threw a stone at me from a few feet away. I ducked, and he pointed a semi-automatic pistol at my face.

"Get off the street, señorita! Run! Fast! Before I shoot!" He was erratic in his movements, obviously very nervous.

My eyes darted from side to side. All the stores were closed, and the curtains in every house were drawn tight. There wasn't a soul in sight except soldiers and plainclothes men in dark glasses. I smelled burning rubber, heard the distant sound of sirens, and it hit me all at once: this was a coup. I started running back down the alley, then hesitated. The man in plain clothes was at the mouth of the alley now, his gun pointed at the ground. If I kept going, he'd see where I lived, where Trinidad and Lucas were staying. My mind jumped to Mami and Bob.

An explosion threw me to the ground. This was it, I thought wildly. I would die in the heart of South America, killed by a man shooting children in the streets. My heart pounded in my ears. I didn't want to die, though, not yet. I hadn't had the chance to devote my life to a greater cause, for a better world, as my mother and Bob and my aunts and uncles in Vancouver were doing.

A clap of thunder cracked the sky in two. Buckets of water drenched me, giving me the strength to bounce to my feet and run. I decided I'd let my legs take me home, then figure out where the bullet had hit me once I got inside the courtyard. Knees skinned and bleeding, I made it to the gate, looked back one last time—and there the man was, gun still pointed down. He hadn't shot me. The ferocious clap of thunder had struck me down.

Hail was bouncing off the tiles like marbles. Señora Siles was looking up at the sky from her window, her face tight with fear. She drew the curtains when she saw me, and I heard her scream: "Pedro! Get under the bed and stay there!" When I made it into the house, Trinidad grabbed me. She took me onto her lap while Lucas tried to get a station on the shortwave. All he could find was military marches. Ale drank a glass of milk, seemingly unaware that anything was wrong. I decided to keep the story of the secret policeman with the gun to myself.

By noon, Lucas and Trinidad were pacing the floor, worrying about what had happened to my mother and Bob. I couldn't let myself think about that. The military marches continued to play on the radio, and jets flew back and forth across the sky. In the early afternoon, Mami finally arrived by herself. She hugged us for a long time. Had Bob come home yet? Had we seen him? At that moment, Bob walked through the door.

Mami had been trapped downtown, she told us. "It was the usual throng of workers on the buses this morning. But when we got to the centre of the city, everything changed. Jets started flying, and the military took the streets. It was incredible how quickly it happened. Young men from the poor neighbourhoods came down from the hills and started resisting, fighting with stones and Molotov cocktails." She drew in a shaky breath. "I was so worried about Bob, and you girls, and Lucas and Trinidad, of course. Those young people who are fighting are so brave it breaks my heart." I stood close behind her, caressing her shoulder as she spoke.

Bob had walked toward home for hours, he said. He'd been scared that, as a foreigner, he'd be arrested immediately, as he had been in Chile. "All the buses were packed, speeding by, with people hanging off even from the roofs. I scrambled onto the back fender of one heading to Miraflores." Ale had started crying, and Bob tucked her inside his jacket.

At the end of the day we located a miners' station on the shortwave, a rebel radio program broadcast underground from somewhere in Siglo xx. That was the biggest tin mine in Bolivia, south of La Paz, and the most combative. The miner explained what had happened. Alberto Natusch Busch, a member of the cabinet during Hugo Banzer's dictatorship, had taken power through a bloody coup, ousting Walter Guevara and halting any chance for the 1980 elections. Committed to returning the country to a Banzer-like dictatorship, Busch was determined to keep the neo-liberal economic order of Bolivia intact. There was well-organized resistance in the streets of La Paz, the miner announced, and the Central Workers' Union, banned for a decade, was calling for a general strike. School was suspended, and everything else was closed.

On the morning of the coup in Chile, my mother and father had called Ale and me into their bed. Together, we'd listened to President Allende say goodbye over the radio as warplanes flew above La Moneda Palace. "Compañeros, surely this will be the last opportunity for me to address you. My words do not express bitterness but disappointment. May there be a moral punishment for those who have betrayed their oath: the soldiers of Chile... The only thing left for me to say is to the workers: I am not going to resign. Placed in a historic transition, I will pay for your loyalty with my life. And I say to you that the seeds we have planted in the good conscience of thousands and thousands of Chileans will not be shrivelled forever... Social processes can be arrested by neither crime nor force. History is ours, and people make history. Workers of my country: I want to thank you for the loyalty you always had, the confidence that you deposited in a man who was only an interpreter of great yearnings for justice... At this definitive moment, the last moment when I can address you, I wish you to take advantage of the lesson. Foreign capital, imperialism, together with the reactionary right, created the climate in which the armed forces broke their tradition... I address the youth, those who sang and gave us their joy and their spirit of struggle. I address the worker, the farmer, the intellectual, those who will be persecuted, because in our country fascism has already been present for many hours... History will judge them."

There had been a whistling, then the sound of bombs exploding. My parents, who had joined the student movement in the sixties, had sobbed quietly as they held us, and when we tried to speak, they pressed a finger to their pursed lips and whispered, "Listen. Compañero Allende has something important to say, and no matter what happens to us, you must always remember this moment." And so we'd sat and listened. "I will always be next to you. At least my memory will be that of a man of dignity who was loyal to his country. The people must defend themselves. The people must not let themselves be destroyed or riddled with bullets, but they cannot be humiliated either. Workers of my country, I have faith in Chile and its destiny. Other men will overcome this dark and bitter moment when treason seeks to prevail. Go forward knowing that, sooner rather than later, the great avenues will open once again where free men will walk to construct a better society. Viva Chile! Viva el pueblo! Vivan los trabajadores! These are my final words, and I am certain that my sacrifice will not be in vain. I am certain that, at the very least, it will be a moral lesson that will punish felony, cowardice and treason." That voice and its message had been burned into my core forever. We'd listened on that bed in our yellow wooden house in Valdivia as if we were on a vessel lost at sea.

Two weeks later, Natusch Busch was ousted by popular resistance in Bolivia. Many people had fought in the streets, and the whole country had responded to the Central Workers' Union's call for a general strike, paralyzing Bolivia for fifteen days. Soldiers in U.S. helicopters had shot at protesters in La Paz, and the crackdown on street protests had resulted in over two hundred dead, hundreds of injured and over one hundred disappeared. People had resisted in spite of the repression, and Natusch Busch had agreed to step down as long as the power was not handed back to Walter Guevara. It was agreed that the new provisional president would be Lidia Gueiler, the leader of the House of Deputies. She would be Bolivia's first woman president, and she was a feminist and social democrat who'd spent a lot of time in exile, most recently during the Banzer years. Elections were still to be held in 1980, but as per Natusch Busch's condition, the transition would not be entrusted to Walter Guevara.

School began again, but the celebratory mood in my classroom changed to fear when a soldier in fatigues arrived to teach the first class of the day: art. Señorita Flores whispered that the teacher had disappeared. The soldier made us do jumping jacks and march around our desks while he yelled: "Left, left, left right left!" He looked uncomfortable in his helmet. He wasn't much older than we were, and, like most low-ranking soldiers in Bolivia, he was a poor Indian. Young men with the means to do so bribed their way out of military service, so the army was made up of poor brown men made to kill their own people. The army provided them with meals and shelter, though, Señorita Flores said, and when you were starving, you took what you could get. Natusch Busch may have been ousted, but it seemed that the military still had all the power.

At recess in the courtyard my classmates talked excitedly, mostly in hushed voices, and the boys who had fought, including Eugenio Aguirre, were treated like royalty. Kids lined up to hug and kiss them, and stories of heroism spread like wildfire through the school. The teachers were quiet, avoiding the topic of politics at all costs. They'd all taken part in the general strike, and though everyone was proud to have participated, they knew it wasn't the end. Anything could still happen, and it probably would. Would they lose their jobs, accused of breaking the law that had prohibited unions and strikes for a decade? Would they be placed on a blacklist? Would they too disappear into thin air, replaced by some poor kid from the rural highlands wearing fatigues?

That day, Ale and I came home to a quiet house. My mother explained that Lucas and Trinidad had gone somewhere else for a while. Tears stung my eyes, but I knew it was probably safer for everybody this way.

A month later, the school year came to an end. Things had gone back to normal, with the teachers yelling at us every chance they got and the principal ruling the school with an iron fist. We had a new art teacher, who drew pictures on the board for us to copy. On the last day of class, we danced to the Beatles and the Doors in the courtyard. Then the girls ran off to their maid jobs, kissing Ale and me goodbye. Valentina was indeed pregnant, and she wouldn't be back in March, when the new school year began. Eugenio Aguirre waved from the fender of a bus, shoeshine box strapped to his back. As I walked home alone along the cobblestones, I prepared myself for a journey Mami and Bob had described to us late one night, while most of the city was asleep.

6

IT WAS SIX in the morning at the La Paz train station, and already the first-class section of the train heading to the border was crammed with well-dressed ladies, families from all walks of life and the odd businessman in suit and tie, fresh newspaper in hand. Christmas was only a few days away, and many people were travelling.

Bob and Mami had instructed us on the details of the journey Ale and I would be making without them. One of our instructions was to pretend we didn't know Trinidad, who'd be accompanying us part of the way. She'd been back sleeping on our floor for the past week, acting as if she'd never left. This time around, she had gotten up early every morning and readied herself to go downtown, where she was "picking up some papers," she said. Her morning ritual began by taking a curling iron to her frizzy head. Once her hair was in ringlets, Trinidad would powder her face and apply red lipstick, blue eyeshadow and mascara. Skin-tight black jeans and a red paisley shirt completed the look, with a black corduroy blazer to keep her warm in the cold highland mornings. She'd carry out her ritual while smoking one Gitane after another and listening to the miners' radio on the shortwave. Low, so the neighbours wouldn't hear.

The four of us had taken a cab to get here. Trinidad was going to meet us on the train. Inside our brown carry-ons, stuffed with clothes, cheese rolls and grapefruits, was a typewritten letter my mother had given us, which we were to read, memorize, then burn and flush down the toilet shortly after the train left. The fifty-dollar bill at the bottom of my bag was all the cash we had.

Following Bob's lead, we were speaking English. When we arrived at our seats to see that a cholita, an urban Indian woman, had taken them over with five sacks of onions and seven children, Bob shouted at her to move, waving our tickets in her face.

"Señora! As you can see, I have paid good money for these seats so that my daughters can travel in comfort."

"Who cares about your tickets, Mr. Gringo? I got here first," she responded, sitting like a large oak tree rooted to the ground.

"Listen, Señora, don't make me call a policeman to have you forcibly removed."

"Just try it!" The woman crossed her arms.

"Police!" Bob yelled at the top of his lungs. The lady grabbed her onions and her children and moved, swearing under her breath.

We could have shared our seats with the lady, but Bob was acting like the big-city guy he'd argued with on the bus back in Peru. It was a soul-destroying tactic, but as my mother had explained, if we were to keep people safe and transport goods across borders without being caught, we had to hold our beliefs inside. I could see that it cut Bob to the quick.

Trinidad arrived a few minutes later, carrying a small white Samsonite. She looked tired, maybe because she had spent a good two hours in the bathroom in the middle of the night. Trinidad had some health troubles because of the concentration camps, my mother told us; that's why nature rarely called. When it did, she had to heed it. Speaking in a perfect Mexican accent now, Trinidad greeted Ale and me and indicated she'd be sitting in the seat facing us. Bob made a huge show of asking her to keep an eye on his two daughters, who were going to Chile to visit their grandparents. That part was true.

Then it was time to go. Ale and I pressed our faces to the window as the train pulled out, leaving Mami and Bob standing on the platform with tears running down their faces. Their girls were going back to the beloved country they were not allowed to enter, and that was difficult to bear.

We gazed out the window in silence as the train climbed in circles up the bowl of La Paz. In the poor neighbourhoods on the hills, ladies lined up with kettles at outdoor faucets and chickens scratched in the dirt. The highlands stretched all around us as the train travelled west. We read for a while, and then I nudged Ale. She hesitated for a moment before grabbing her bag and coming with me to the bathroom.

I made sure the door was securely locked behind us before pulling out my copy of Mami's letter, written in English. I read to Ale in a whisper. "Girls: Please read this letter very carefully. I know you have memorized your instructions, but here they are anyway, in writing. Your passports say you were born in Santiago, Chile. If the border guards ask you, you must tell them that you left Chile for Canada in September 1970, because your parents are in the mining sector and had some work to do with Noranda. The guards will understand this to mean that you come from a right-wing, pro-Pinochet family. You will tell them that your parents are in Bolivia on business at the moment, and that you are going to visit your grandparents, who live in Iquique. Remember that you met Trinidad for the first time on the train. Never *ever* answer any questions from a stranger, and don't offer any explanations to the border guards unless asked. If Trinidad is taken away at the border, stay calm and get back on the train. Once you reach Arica, watch out for a young, well-dressed couple at the station. They will be waiting for you to approach them and will take care of you. If the couple are not there, or if you think it's not safe to approach them, use your fifty dollars to take a taxi to the bus station and buy tickets to Santiago. Your grandmother will be waiting for you there at the station. Do not under any circumstances tell your grandparents about this letter. We know your first trip back from exile will be an incredible experience for you both. Keep your eyes and ears and hearts open at all times, and in that way you will learn about life. We love you. Mami and Bob."

Ale was leaning against the wall of the tiny, disgusting bathroom, holding her nose. She didn't say a word as I rummaged through her bag, then set both copies of the letter on fire, using the lighter Bob had given me. I dropped them, still flaming, through the hole that served as a toilet onto the tracks.

My hands were trembling. Ale refused to meet my gaze. "You've gotta make sure you remember everything in the letter," I said.

"I do remember it, you fool. Let's go."

I made us both brush our hair before we left the bathroom. If anybody was wondering what we'd been doing in there, they'd think we'd gone to primp. Walking back to our seats, with the letters gone, I felt a million pounds lighter. Trinidad was lost in thought, watching the landscape go by and leaving red lipstick marks on her cigarette butts. She was probably steeling herself for the border crossing into Chile, which Bob had told us was twenty-four hours away. All I knew was that soon, very soon, I'd get to see my grandma Carmen again.

Four years earlier, my grandma and grandfather had come to Vancouver to visit us. I'd sat with Abuelita at our dining room table every afternoon while she knitted sweaters for us kids, and I savoured every scrap of her news. After the coup, she and my grandfather had moved to Limache, a small town an hour inland from Valparaíso. There my grandfather had built a yellow wooden house, and they'd succumbed to the quiet life imposed upon them now that two of their three children and half their grandchildren were exiled. As she wondered aloud how the watermelons and peaches and apricots in her orchard were coming along, my heart ached for that place I'd never seen. Their yellow house was the stuff of legend, the place we'd all go when Pinochet fell and Chile was socialist again.

Ale had pulled a deck of cards from her bag and was shuffling them like an expert. "Señora Zamora, do you know the game Mao-Mao?" she asked Trinidad. I froze, because Ale had just put her foot in it. Mao-Mao was a game Trinidad had taught us, and anybody in the know would recognize it as one of the games, like Ho Chi Minh You're the Bomb and Run Ché Run, that had been invented by political prisoners to pass the time in concentration camps. This train had to have at least one informer on it. But Trinidad simply stifled a laugh and shook her head no.

AS NIGHT FELL, the temperature on the train dropped to freezing. People hugged their knees to their chests. It was too cold to sleep, and by morning my whole body was numb.

It was almost noon when a guard yelled out: "Everybody off the train with your belongings! Stand in line for inspection!"

The small border station quickly filled up with passengers. Everybody stood nervously silent, the only sound an occasional baby crying. People had pulled combs through their hair and passed wet hankies over their faces. The ladies wore fresh lipstick. Border guards with machine guns walked up and down the lines. Directly above the head honcho, who sat at a wooden desk, hung a massive portrait of Pinochet, captioned "The Saviour of the Fatherland." Pinochet was wearing a grey cape in the photo, and his eyes followed you wherever you went. My knees started to shake. Their accents, their impeccable uniforms had brought on the Terror. I'd been scared lots of times since we'd left Canada, but this was the kind of fear that felt as if a rat was walking up and down your spine, from your tailbone to the base of your skull. It was the kind of fear that gave you a sick, cold feeling in the pit of your stomach and made you sweat—only the sweat was ice. And the ice got you trembling like a leaf in a storm.

A wailing baby brought me back to the border station. I looked over at Trinidad, who was standing stock still, holding her white suitcase. The head honcho shouted at a group of Bolivians. "Indians! Swine! Filthy pigs! You are a disgrace to a civilized country such as ours. Step aside."

A great fury strangled me. But then I remembered; my sister and I were escorting Trinidad into Chile so she could fight for a revolution that would change all this. This was her first venture back, and Ale and I were her cover. I stood straight and still just like her.

I remembered the conversations I'd overheard many times among the adults. The thing was to hold on to any information you had for at least twenty-four hours after you were picked up, they said. The thing was not to break in the first twenty-four hours. How would you know when twenty-four hours had passed, though, I worried? How long had we been standing there in the border office? The head honcho's eyes landed on Trinidad, Ale and me in the throng.

"Señora, I did not see you and your lovely daughters there. Please, come forward."

The three of us left our place in the silent lineup and laid our passports down. Within seconds he had stamped all three, and we were waved back to the train.

All the Bolivians who were not dressed like Indians were let back on the train. Some of the cholitas had managed to get through, too, and they were beside themselves with joy. Now they would be able to sell their onions at the Arica market the following day, trek back to Bolivia and do it all over again. As the half-empty train pulled out of the station, I saw a crying baby in her mother's arms, left behind on the platform. The mother didn't look much older than me.

A river of tears started in my gut and was moving up my body. My throat stopped it with a tight knot. I thanked God for that knot. Otherwise, I might have wailed the way the Bolivian ladies did at wakes and funerals. Their wails were so loud that sometimes on Sundays it felt as if the whole city of La Paz was in mourning.

THE NEXT DAY, Ale and I boarded a bus at the Arica station. Final destination Santiago, twelve hundred miles away. Trinidad waved goodbye from the curb, her chest heaving as she cried behind her sunglasses.

Sometimes the road ran alongside the Pacific Ocean. Sometimes we could see the towering Andes right outside our window. The Atacama Desert stretched on for the entire first day, like a gigantic bowl of brown sugar. Being back in Chile had unleashed a herd of wild horses deep in my chest. I sat quietly in my seat, ankles crossed, hands folded in my lap, swallowing jagged stones as my eyes took everything in. The bus stopped in every major town and city. A drunken man got on at the bus station in Antofagasta and passed out in a seat in front of us. He snored like a walrus as the bus pulled back onto the vast stretch of highway, lit only by the star-filled sky.

In the photo album we'd left with Papi in Vancouver, there was a series of family pictures taken on the beach in Antofagasta. I'd been only a year old, wearing a white undershirt and a little white sunbonnet. My grandfather Armando was holding me in one photo, my father in another. In one shot I was reaching for my mother, who looked hilarious in cat's-eye glasses with her hair in a beehive. Aunts, uncles and cousins sat on nearby blankets, chewing on crab legs. My first cousin Chelito, the oldest of our generation, was a beautiful boy with a luminous smile and twinkly eyes.

We were the only exiles among our friends lucky enough to have personal pictures from Chile. My grandparents had brought them when they came to visit us that time in Vancouver. They'd brought Chile with them in their pockets, their suitcases, their eyes and voices. I'd smelled a country on them when we greeted them at the airport, a country that still clung to my own skin and hair. It was something fierce, that country. My abuelita had taken my hand, interlocked her fingers with mine and stuffed both our hands into her grey coat pocket. I'd discovered gold: a stick of bubble gum. As the coating dissolved in my mouth, I'd been on the streets of Valparaíso again.

The bus continued along the highway at top speed. The Southern Cross led the way in the pitch black. I sat motionless, legs like noodles, skin tingling. Brief bouts of sleep took me on adventures filled with bullets, torrential downpours and snowy peaks. The sound of flapping wings, like an eagle taking flight, woke me with a start. The bus had pulled into a station, and passengers clogged the aisles, ready to exit.

"Last chance for La Serena," the bus driver yelled on the platform. "We depart in three minutes."

As we wove out of La Serena, a great boulevard displayed its name prominently: Aguirre. Seven years ago, I'd spent a summer here. This was the region where my father was born, and his parents, and their parents, all the way back to the Conquest. In our photo album there was a picture of my parents, Ale and me on the beach here, too, sharing Popsicles.

The streets of Santiago were jammed with buses, taxis, ice cream vendors walking through the traffic and hundreds of necking teenage couples. The heat had rotted the garbage, and the smell was unfathomable. This city was the most beautiful, dangerous and exciting place I could imagine, the place where my mother had carried me in her womb in the student days of the sixties and where a midwife had pulled me into the world.

A weary-looking woman was standing on the station platform, purse clutched to her chest. Our eyes met hers. It took a split second for her to realize who we were, but once she did, she leapt a foot off the ground. Her face broke into a smile, bringing a dancing light into her eyes. She ran alongside the bus, yelping and laughing. My palms pressed hard against the glass, leaving their imprint behind. The doors of the bus flew open, and we ran down the aisle. The woman stood at the bottom of the steps, a hanky in her fist. She was wearing her Sunday best: a flowery dress, knee-high stockings and black shoes, her grey coat nestled in the crook of her arm. Her thick hair, cropped close to her jaw, was freshly combed. I smelled Coral cologne as we were enveloped in Grandma Carmen's embrace.

7

MY GRANDMOTHER'S VIRGIN sisters lived with their mother in a mini-Parthenon in Santiago's Barrio Alto. A set of marble steps led to the entrance, which was framed by marble columns on either side. The floors inside were marble, as were the walls. Even the twenty-foot-long dining room table was gleaming white marble. Every surface in the house was adorned with crocheted white doilies, and upon every doily sat a glass poodle. From the top of the second floor, a real poodle barked at us.

My great-grandmother Dulcinea had suffered a stroke, and the left side of her face was frozen solid. She ignored this weakness, pride being her staple diet. Bisabuela sat at the head of the table, flanked by her four daughters, two great-granddaughters (Ale and me) and my grandfather Armando, her hated son-in-law. Even though he later became a school principal, my grandfather was the son of a nitrate miner and a seamstress, both of whom had died young. He'd earned his keep shining shoes from the age of four and was now the sole survivor of a brood of thirteen. My grandmother Carmen had run away with Armando from her family's big locked-up house in the north of

Chile. Her father, now dead, had been a brutal military man. Those who'd suffered most at his hands had been his own wife and children. He beat them regularly, and he'd leave the house for days on end, locking the door from the outside and leaving his family to starve.

My great-aunts Milagros, Remedios and Perlita had made a blood pact back then to remain virgins, so that no man would ever control their lives. Their pact also required them to make a fortune, which they had done: while still in their teens, the three sisters had moved to Santiago and become smugglers of precious jewellery and fine leather goods from Argentina. Now they owned a mini-mall in the Plaza de Armas, facing the back of the seat of government, La Moneda Palace, from which they operated a boutique that sold crystal poodles. The factory that made these poodles belonged to them too. They were prepared to defend their riches at gunpoint, as long as they didn't have to do the actual shooting. They supported Pinochet through an organization called Fatherland and Liberty and masturbated to the portrait of him that hung in their house. Mami had explained all of this to me, including the masturbation part.

Lunch was served by two maids in embroidered aprons and "el maestro," a handyman, butler, waiter and man about the house. Two military men had joined us at the table, still wearing their guns. When Gerardo, my grandmother's younger brother, had drunk himself to death on skid row, my great-aunts had taken his two sons away from their mother and enrolled their nephews at military academies. Now here they were, sitting at the table with their buzz cuts and decorated jackets. Nobody was saying what had happened to their mother, though Mami had heard whispers of the great-aunts locking her up in a state-run loony bin. There was so much I wanted to know but dared not ask. Mami had warned us to be careful what we said in Chile. Remember that the enemy is most likely in the heart of your family, she'd told us.

Before lunch, the youngest and most stylish great-aunt had taken Ale and me on a tour of the house. Trying to make small talk, I'd said, "Tía Perlita, your white pantsuit is just like my Mami's." "Your *mami?*"

she'd responded. "I thought that Commie liked to dress like the Indians. Why is she dressing in pantsuits now?"

"I don't know. Has anybody ever told you you look just like Kate Jackson from *Charlie's Angels*?"

My great-aunt was not to be diverted. "Please shut your mouth. My nerves are frayed enough listening to my own blood talk like the cholas who relieve themselves in the street. Why can't you speak proper Chilean Spanish? And what is your family doing in Bolivia, anyway?"

Then she'd freaked out at Ale, who'd stroked the head of a porcelain doll that sat in an armchair by Auntie Perlita's bed. As we walked back down the stairs, I looked at Ale and whispered, "Tick-tock-tick-tock-ding-a-ling-a-cuckoo."

Milagros, the oldest great-aunt, dominated the conversation at the table, bragging about some new medals the military nephews had received. My uncle Boris had described the great-aunts with such accuracy that I felt as if I'd entered a fairy tale, vivid and terrifying. The poodle, called Preciosa, was now poised on my great-grandmother's lap. Dulcinea held a fly swatter in her right hand, punctuating the conversation with rhythmic swats at the fruit flies that threatened to land on the starched white tablecloth. She governed the table in steely silence, her thick white hair held back in a bun. She wasn't scary, though, which surprised me. At times I even caught a mischievous twinkle in her eye.

As the nephews held forth on national security, my grandmother feigned interest by raising her eyebrows or murmuring softly. My grandfather kept his head down. There was no sign of the boisterous, storytelling duo I loved so well. We were here out of duty: it was the day before Christmas, and my abuelita couldn't leave Santiago without visiting her mother. Finally Ale interrupted one of the nephews with an inopportune question.

"Have you killed people with that gun?"

"Shut your mouth, mini-hippie," Milagros snapped.

My bisabuela winked at Ale as my grandfather announced that it was time for us to be going.

IT WAS MORE beautiful than I'd imagined, this home my grandparents had created in Limache after the coup. Beams of sunlight entered through the tall windows to shine on the dark wooden floor. A white gas stove was the centre of my grandmother's universe, and the large kitchen table was where she rolled out dough, beat eggs, sliced fruit fresh from the orchard and decorated cakes. The back rooms of the house, built for the exiles' eventual return, were a treasure hunter's paradise. I spent hours going through my parents' boxes of books, notebooks and photo albums. Even their clothes lay intact in a trunk, along with some of Ale's and my old drawings, clothes and toys.

The orchard was a magic place, and at the end of it was a shrine to the Virgin Mary. Chickens laid their eggs in a coop and, when special occasions called for it, were killed, plucked and cooked by my grandmother. The sky was clear and blue, the air filled with the scent of fruit and flowers. It was idyllic. After we'd all gone to bed, I could hear the shortwave playing in my grandparents' room. Radio Moscow wasn't popular with Pinochet. Everybody listened to it, though, because it was the only way to find out what was really going on in Chile.

One morning as I sat on the toilet, about to pee, the doorbell to my grandparents' house rang. There were loud hellos, and I could hear my first cousin, Chelito, being escorted into the kitchen, where a pot of tea, apricot jam and fresh-baked bread awaited. My heart started pounding in a way I'd never experienced. I twisted and turned on the toilet, too embarrassed to pee until I finally reached over and turned on the taps.

I scrambled to the mirror and took a good look at my face. For the first time in my life, I saw that I wasn't pretty. Mami had always told me I was the most beautiful girl in the world, but mothers lied, I realized now. My teeth were bigger than a horse's, my lips were chapped, and I had a unibrow and a moustache. The Cousin's voice moved up the back of my neck, causing my toes to curl.

My grandmother was knocking on the bathroom door, demanding that I come out. As I did, I was hit by a sight that shook me from soles to crown. Chelito was sixteen, and he glowed like a circus tent in the night. His eyes were green; suddenly, the whole room was emerald.

68

There was a flash of white teeth and dimples, and a smooth bronze chest revealed itself through the undone buttons of his crumpled shirt. The Cousin was perched on a wooden stool, his palms pressed on strong thighs. His pelvis reached out and up, with the force of an orca parting the waters, and then his arms were around my back, his pelvis jammed against my belly.

"Cousin, cousin, exiled cousin!" His breath smelled like condensed milk and tobacco.

He set me down, and I stood swaying. "The typhoid's hit me," I said faintly.

The Cousin stuffed a piece of buttery toast in his mouth as my grandmother's hand landed on my forehead. She shook her head; there was no fever. "Hurry and eat before the tea and bread go stone cold," she scolded.

That afternoon the Cousin leaned next to the round wooden radio in the living room, searching for the perfect station from Viña del Mar, the one that played "Mama Maremma" and "Boogie Wonderland." He hummed along to the music, his pelvis a corkscrew. My disco dancing classes in that musty church basement in Vancouver were paying off now. The Cousin smiled as I did a kick ball change around him, never forgetting to snap my fingers on the kick.

From then on, wherever he went, I followed. If he was lying in the orchard surrounded by exploding watermelons, I sat cross-legged next to him. If he was on his bed leafing through old magazines, I leaned against the door frame. At first Ale trailed after me, asking if I wanted to play cards or dice. But eventually she got bored of bringing up the rear and spent her afternoons with our grandmother, watching talk shows or fetching the eggs the chickens laid.

I stayed up late so I could sit at the dining room table with the Cousin and my grandfather. They smoked cigarettes, played cards and talked about loose women. They thought I didn't understand. But I did. I understood everything now.

When siesta came each day, Ale dozed in her bed. My grandfather dreamed in his. My grandmother snored at the dining room table as a Brazilian soap opera blasted from the TV. The Cousin would slide on his motorcycle jacket, slip a cigarette into the corner of his mouth and sneak out the front door. Only after I'd seen him walk all the way down the sidewalk from my station at the kitchen window did I enter his room and begin the feast of smells and textures. I would inhale the armpits of his lifeless shirt and the crotch of his empty jeans until I was light-headed. One afternoon, as he pulled his black jacket on, he looked back at me over his shoulder and moved his head in the direction of the outside world. I followed him into the forbidden universe of Limache at siesta.

He led the journey to the plaza in his tight jeans. Every so often a tiny flame would travel from his hand to a fresh Lucky Strike. The match flew into the gutter as a stream of smoke left his generous mouth. I stayed two steps behind, matching my pace to his.

I'd strolled around Limache before, with Ale and my grandparents. It was a sleepy town with one general store along the main strip. The store was owned by Señor Perez, a kind, gentle man who was also a Pinochet supporter. He let my grandparents use the store's phone whenever they called Canada collect, but politics was never spoken between them. The plaza was beautiful, with a yellow fountain at its centre. The buses from Santiago arrived there, and the plaza was where the cathedral stood, with its ancient bell.

Today, the colours were so vivid it hurt. The voices that surrounded us belonged to creatures beyond beautiful. There was a bearded lady strumming her guitar outside the Jehovah's Witnesses Hall. Two Mormons, unmistakable with their buzz cuts, blindingly white shirts and American drawl, sipped orange Fantas as they strode by, Bibles held to their hips. Señor Perez, in his smock and spectacles, was heading home for siesta. We passed my grandmother's neighbours, the ones she'd warned us were informers. We passed the fortress on the corner that everyone whispered was one of Pinochet's weekend getaways. The hot breeze in the trees, the smell of raw sewage and dirt, the doe-eyed girl who sold the bread, the shoeshine boys resting on their wooden boxes, the ice cream man singing out "Chocolate, strawberry, vanilla and chirimoya" in his lazy tenor: it was as if I was discovering it all for the first time.

The pinball arcade, our destination, was dark and smoke-filled, a cacophony of whistles, bells, steel marbles crashing and the hoots of wild boys. I was the only girl in a sea of them. The Cousin, the king of them all, stood at a machine crowned by a tiny-waisted mermaid with massive boobs. Her nipples lit up whenever a marble hit a trigger point. The Cousin placed his palms on my waist and steered me in front of him. He took my wrists and showed me how to play, his pelvis in the small of my back. His laughter reached me from very far away.

On the seventh day of his visit, hoping the Cousin would ask me to the pinballs again, I checked my buck teeth in the bathroom mirror and brushed my frizzy hair a hundred times. I perched on the toilet to pee, but as I got up I noticed something alarming: the toilet water was crimson. My underwear was already soaked. I knew what this was, thanks to my mother. If she had been there, she'd have marched me to the general store, holding my hand in hers, and demanded maxi-pads at the top of her lungs.

The Cousin was waiting at the front door when I peeked out of the bathroom. He gestured for me to join him, but I shook my head. He shrugged his shoulders as he left, the screen door clicking behind him. *Isaura, the White Slave* climbed to its crisis on TV. My grandmother had missed it all, her head thrown back, her mouth wide open, snoring so loud the trinkets in the cabinet trembled.

"Abuelita. Abuelita!"

Her eyes popped open. It took her a moment to place me. "You startled me, Carmencita. What is it?"

"Abuelita, I just got my period."

She fumbled for her Coke-bottle glasses. She was always losing them, mumbling, "Incredible. It's gotta be Uncle Mario's ghost that took them," only to discover that they'd been on the top of her head the whole time. As I explained about the period situation again, she raised her index finger to her mouth.

"Shhhh."

She got me to sit on the edge of the tub, then pulled my dress up and the stained underwear down. Glasses perched on the tip of her nose, she peered between my legs and made thinking noises. After a few moments she emerged, announcing that I was to wait in the bathroom.

My grandmother reappeared, holding a few old undershirts of my grandfather's and a large pair of scissors. She cut the shirts into long strips that she turned into little pads. Once she'd finished, she produced a fresh pair of underwear from her pocket. They looked like a beige girdle. She pinned one of her homemade pads to the crotch of the heirloom underwear, and as she helped me pull them on, she explained how things were to be done.

"When a strip gets stained, come to the bathroom and lock the door behind you. Then wash it in the sink with very hot water and soap. Wring it out, roll it into a ball, and take it in your fist to the armoire. Hang it at the back. Keep blood out of sight at all times, because men are squeamish."

Abuelita took me by the hand, and together we made our way to the back of the orchard. There we kneeled before the Virgin, who was surrounded by rusty old horseshoes. A lone red flower rested in a blue vase.

"Dear Virgin," my abuelita prayed, "it has been six years since I quit smoking, on the day my children and grandchildren went into exile. I made a promise that I would no longer smoke if you kept them safe and brought them back to me. Thank you for bringing two of my granddaughters back to me, Virgin, and for making one a woman while in my presence."

Her voice cracked and she cried and cried, kneeling like that. I squeezed her hand and rested my head on her shoulder.

MY UNCLE CARLOS, Chelito's father, was my mother's oldest brother. He was married to my aunt Vicky, a Chilean of German descent, and they lived in Concepción, a coastal city a day's drive south of Limache, with the Cousin and his siblings Mario, Elena and Gaston. Before the coup, we'd been like any other Chilean family, a clan. But now we greeted each other as if we'd never met, nervous and excited. My aunt and uncle had come to take Ale and me back to Concepción. My grandfather came along at my grandmother's insistence. She'd taken to giving me chores that kept me by her side and away from the Cousin.

My aunt and uncle's house was airy and modern. Uncle Carlos worked for a major bank, and my cousins went to private school. Mami had warned us we were not to talk politics with him. This household did not tune in to Radio Moscow late at night.

Here in Concepción, the Cousin was nowhere to be found. He was always out with his friends, and on the third day he brought his girlfriend home for lunch. She was pale, like Snow White. Jet-black hair tumbled around her face, and her body was like the mermaid's on the pinball machine. She chatted with the adults while the Cousin fell all over her, offering her seconds, playing with a strand of her hair.

My uncle's family had a maid, a woman who arrived at the crack of dawn every morning and didn't leave till late. She would not allow me to wash my own cup or to set the table, and neither would my aunt. As the maid placed the dessert flan on my placemat, I understood something: I didn't exist. I didn't exist in the Cousin's life, or in this country, or in the exile countries of Bolivia or Canada. I didn't exist anywhere anymore. It was that simple.

During siesta, on the second-floor veranda outside the guest room Ale and I shared, I wept the way Dorothy had in *The Wizard of Oz* as the flying monkeys surrounded her. When the balcony door slid open, I straightened up and slapped the tears off my face, keeping my back turned. I felt a hand on my shoulder, and when I turned around, I met the emerald eyes that belonged to the Cousin. Something had shifted between us, and he moved in for the kill.

"Motherfucker! Where did you learn to kiss like that, exiled cousin?"

I shrugged. Pierced him with my eyes. And we kissed again. On our third night at my uncle's house, a touch on my cheek woke me with a start. My sister slept heavily beside me.

"Exiled cousin, let me into bed with you," the Cousin begged.

His naked body glowed like an ember in the half-light. A pod of dolphins leapt out of my solar plexus. We were already kissing as the Cousin climbed in beside me. Lifting my nightgown, he pulled down my grandmother's 1920s underpants. I pulled them up. He pulled them down again. I pulled up.

"Come on, exiled cousin, please let me see you."

I shook my head no, holding on to the underpants with all my might.

"Don't be afraid, cousin. It'll only hurt for a moment, then it'll be like having my soul inside your secret place. Te amo, cousin. Te amo."

My mother had said I could make love anytime I wanted to, but there was one condition: I had to be on the Pill. All I had to do was say the word, she told me, and she'd take me to the women's clinic.

"No. I have my period now, and I'll get pregnant. I can't until I'm on the Pill."

We made out all night long, with my grandmother's underpants-turned-chastity-belt firmly in place.

Every day, my aunt Vicky took us to a private club where there was an enormous swimming pool, a golf course and a fancy restaurant with a large patio. Waiters in starched jackets scurried around serving pisco sours, the Chilean national cocktail, to club members lounging on deck chairs. People talked about their trips to Disney World, about the new malls being built in Santiago's Las Condes neighbourhood. Ale and I were witnessing the lives of Chile's new elite, those who benefited from and supported Pinochet's free market economy.

For the rest of our visit, the Cousin arrived at my bed every night like a loyal husband, after having spent the day with his girlfriend. We'd make out and then fall asleep with limbs entwined, the underpants like a second skin between us. As soon as the house began to stir in the morning, he'd tiptoe back to his room. The only person who knew about our nights together was the maid. She'd glanced at me after washing, starching and ironing the sheets one day. I longed to talk to her, to ask her for her help in making sense of so much ecstasy and sorrow. But I didn't dare approach her. I remembered my classmates in Bolivia talking about what a burden it was being confidante to the women of the house when you still had a floor to wax and a toilet to disinfect.

On the last afternoon our hosts drove my grandfather, Ale and me to the train station. We lingered on the ramp as the train tooted one last time. Every possible configuration of hugs had occurred, except the hug between the Cousin and me.

"Come on, Son, hug your cousin, for God's sake! Can't you see the train's leaving?" my aunt Vicky ordered, curlers rolled tightly under her Hermès scarf.

He opened his arms. I took a step. And then another, and his arms enveloped me. That night, as the train aimed north along its tracks, and my grandfather and Ale slept in the seat across from me, I cried myself dry.

When the bus from Santiago finally pulled into the Limache plaza, the grocery boy from the general store was waiting. We piled our bags into the giant basket on the front of his bicycle, and he rode on ahead while the three of us walked to my grandparents' house. My grandmother was waiting with a hot lunch. Before my grandfather retired for siesta, they spoke in whispers in the kitchen.

"I kept my eye on Carmencita day and night. He never got a chance to lay a hand on her."

"You sure about that? If that scoundrel took advantage of her, he'll have to deal with me. My kidneys may be shot, but I still have a heavy hand."

I sat with my grandmother during the soap opera. She snored through most of it, as usual. If she only knew it was her underpants that had protected me. As I remembered the girl I'd been at eleven, back in Vancouver, lolling on tree branches, riding my banana-seat bike through rainforest trails, sucking on jawbreakers and eating Revellos four at a time, I felt small and alone.

8

"I AM DEEPLY HURT and disappointed by the letter I received from you. How do you think a mother feels when her daughter tells her that she would rather live with her grandparents?"

I peered down at the Andes from the window seat of the plane, Mami's words tumbling around in my head like clothes in a dryer.

Halfway through our visit, my grandparents had asked Ale and me if we wanted to stay on in Limache with them. I couldn't believe our luck. At their house, we weren't expected to be brave and mature and revolutionary. We could just be kids. Pinochet might be in the fortress on the corner every weekend, but it didn't matter, because the most important thing was us, and my grandparents would do anything to keep us out of harm's way.

The invitation made Ale sullen. She withdrew into herself and spent her afternoons in the orchard. She figured our parents were trying to get rid of us. Nonetheless, unbeknownst to her, I had written to Mami from Concepción, telling her Ale and I wanted to stay in Chile. My grandfather and I had walked from my uncle's house to the post office together to send the letter express. On the way back, he'd held my hand and whistled and asked me to challenge him with an arithmetic question. So I'd said, "What's three hundred and twenty-five plus sixty-seven minus twelve plus thirty-three times eleven?" He'd put his thinking face on and answered: "Four thousand four hundred and fifty-three." Abuelito had taught himself to read by looking at the newspapers of the men whose shoes he shined. One day, while he was shining the priest's shoes, he'd decided to show off his reading skill. The priest was so impressed that he turned my grandfather into the bell-ringer at the cathedral and put him through school. One of his favourite pastimes now was to tell us stories about his decades as a school principal. At the busy station in Santiago, a man had stopped him and said that my grandfather was the best teacher he'd ever had. My abuelito walked proudly after that and whistled even louder. He got his shoes shined and bought Ale and me some cotton candy before we caught the bus back to Limache.

Mami's reply had reached me at the yellow house. She'd sent us to her beloved Chile even though she herself could never set foot there again, she wrote, and this was how I was rewarding her. So now here I was on the plane back to La Paz, Ale at my side. The plane crossed above the highlands, into Bolivian territory, and just like that, the last summer of my childhood was over.

Before we left Chile, Ale and I had spent a few days back in Santiago visiting our paternal grandmother, Lourdes, three aunts, an uncle and two cousins from my father's side. My grandmother had given us some money to buy shoes, and my aunts had urged me to buy cork platform sandals, now that I was a young woman and all.

"Get the highest ones," my aunt Lola advised. "They flatter the legs."

Aunt Lola had been Miss Paihuano, 1965, so she knew a lot about ladies' shoes. Paihuano was my father's village in the Andes' enchanted Elqui Valley. Magic things happened there, Papi had told us, involving ghosts and hidden treasure. I had been conceived in Paihuano during carnival, when my mother was eighteen and my parents were penniless newlyweds. Before the coup we'd spend part of every summer there, at the big Aguirre house with its courtyard in the centre and tall adobe rooms. During carnival women in bikinis rode in the back of trucks while cumbia bands played and people followed through the streets, dancing and hooting and drinking locally made wine and pisco.

Now my aunt Lola was a high school history teacher with perfectly plucked eyebrows, feathered hair and large sunglasses tinted in a purplish hue. Even though she was a self-proclaimed perpetually single gal, she had loads of boyfriends, and she was an expert on all things feminine. On the bus back from shopping, I'd started telling her about the Chile solidarity work we had done in Vancouver. Since the Aguirre side of the family lived in Maipú, a working-class suburb of Santiago, and the bus was full of poor people, I'd thought it was okay to mention that, but her eyes darted around as if they were going to jump out of her head, and her manicured finger shot up to her lips, as she mouthed "Shhh." Once we got home, I put on the pastel denim jumpsuit my aunt Vicky had bought me in Concepción and stepped into my new platform heels. Aunt Lola was satisfied. "Impeccable. Now you look like an Aguirre girl."

This outfit was my plane gear. My mother didn't approve; I could tell that as soon as we spotted her in the waiting area at the La Paz airport. Neither did Bob. But they didn't say anything. None of us mentioned the letters, either, as we hugged and kissed. Mami wrapped her arm around my shoulder as we walked outside, and I realized how much I'd missed her.

The airport taxi spit us out into a brand-new life. We sped along El Prado, the main avenue in the central part of the city, but instead of turning left at the university, en route to Miraflores, the taxi kept going until El Prado turned into Arce Avenue, lined with luxury apartment buildings and the president's residence. At the bottom of a very steep hill we turned right, up past 6 de Agosto Avenue, and then left onto a cobblestone lane. Halfway down we stopped. The four of us climbed out and stood facing a large beige house.

"This is our new home," Mami announced, as if it were the most normal thing in the world to land in a neighbourhood you'd never seen before, no explanations offered.

Trinidad was waiting for us inside, with the table set for tea. We leapt into each other's arms as Bob carried our suitcases to the new room Ale and I would share at the back of the house. Once we were all settled in the dining room, Mami said she had something important to tell us: she was pregnant. She beamed as she delivered the news, and Bob's eyes shone with excitement. I adored babies. I jumped up to feel my mother's belly, anxious to dispel the tension between us. Ale's jaw dropped open, but she didn't say a word. Later, in our new room with the light off, she hissed that it was crazy to have a baby underground.

At the end of our new lane, steps led down to a series of narrow pedestrian-only alleyways. The steps were the invisible border between San Jorge, our new neighbourhood, and the lower-class, nameless neighbourhood below. A concrete wall with broken glass cemented into its top separated San Jorge from the shantytown that hung off another adjacent hill. The first thing you saw when you turned into our lane was snow-covered Mount Illimani, watching over the city like a jagged jewel in the blue sky.

Carnival was in full swing, and that meant La Paz was one big water fight. Water balloons flew from passing cars, buses, trucks and bicycles. Buckets were overturned from balconies. Ale and I were taking a rest at our gate, soaking wet after a dash to the corner kiosk, when a group of girls passed by discussing strategy. We introduced ourselves amid a flutter of hugs and kisses, and soon Ale and I were in the thick of a girls-against-boys water fight that involved all the children in the lane.

When we'd had enough of fighting, the girls convened at Lorena's house for tea. From the outside, her house didn't look like much, just a squat brick building surrounded by a security gate, but on the inside it was palatial, decorated with Louis xiv furniture. The parquet floor, draped with rugs, made a nice sound under your shoes. Lorena was the oldest sister of a clan of six, and her mother was young and cheerful. Her father arrived soon afterward in a red Mercedes-Benz. Apparently he worked at the Palacio Quemado—called the Burnt Palace because it had been set on fire during the war of independence—advising

Bolivia's president on legal matters. After that, I went to Lorena's house every afternoon, and we lay on her bed reading her grandmother's romance novels from the forties.

Our new house was fully furnished. Its two large bedrooms, dining room with french doors, windows all round and back porch off the kitchen made it a mansion compared with our two-room bungalow in Miraflores. The owners were an old Nazi couple. That was a good thing, according to Bob, because it made our cover better than ever. The Nazis came around once in a while to make sure we were taking proper care of the place. On those occasions Trinidad hid on the back porch, puffing on her Gitanes. Once when we were downtown Bob pointed out Club La Paz. That was where the Nazi couple hung out with their friend Klaus Barbie, a German war criminal who'd been living in Bolivia for years.

One afternoon I came home from Lorena's to discover a new person in our house, sitting in a cloud of smoke at the dining room table with Trinidad and my mother.

"This is the Swede," Mami said.

The Swede had long baby-blond hair and wore a tunic from India. From then on, the dining room became his bedroom after dinner every night. (Trinidad slept in the living room.) He'd unroll a small mat and work on wooden carvings with his Swiss Army knife or draw in his sketchbook. Ale and I liked chatting with him about all sorts of things. I asked him if he'd ever met ABBA, since he was from Sweden, but he said no. He had such nice hair and luminous skin that we wondered if he'd let us do makeovers on him. He said yes, so Ale would pull out the curling iron and create a do while I applied his makeup.

The four adults talked late into the night. From listening in, I learned the plan. The Swede and Bob were supposed to find a way to enter Chile on foot, via the Atacama Desert. One of the leaders of the resistance was exiled in Mexico, and he needed to be smuggled into Chile as soon as possible, as did his second-in-command. The Swede would do an initial scouting expedition by himself, entering Chile legally on a bus as a backpacker, since he was not on the blacklist.

My mother had enrolled us in a new school for girls only. It was the only one she could find that wasn't run by nuns, she said, even though it was still Catholic. There was only one shift: 8:00 AM to 1:00 PM. On some afternoons we went back after lunch for physical education and dance classes. Almost everyone at San Miguel Ladies' School claimed to be either full-blooded Spanish or German. The most popular girl in my class was Pinochet's niece, who sat on the teacher's desk, legs crossed, holding court with stories of the summer she'd spent in Viña del Mar in Chile with her uncle.

Now I understood how Mami felt when she got home from the American English Centre every evening. Head down on her arms, she'd cry while she raged that she had to hold it all inside at work, that her colleagues were a bunch of racist, classist, right-wing pigs who assumed she was like them. The five of us sang the secret songs to cheer her up: Inti-Illimani's "The People United Will Never Be Defeated," Violeta Parra's "Grateful to Life," Pablo Milanés's "I Will Walk the Streets of Santiago Again." We danced to ABBA's "Voulez-Vous," the first cassette I'd ever owned, bought for me by my grandmother Lourdes on our last day in Chile. I missed Papi, my aunts and uncles, my cousins and all the other Chileans in Vancouver. I missed my old Vancouver school, where my best girlfriends came from hippie homes. None of them complained about the dirty Indians or the cholas or the backwardness of their fucking country.

Lorena was a student at the Northern Institute, a coed private school structured like a U.S. high school that was all the rage among Bolivia's rich; but we'd meet up every day after school to roam the neighbourhood, up 20 de Octubre Avenue to Plaza Avaroa, which had a monument to Eduardo Avaroa at its centre. He was the biggest hero of the War of the Pacific, a civilian who had defended a Bolivian bridge from the Chilean army to his last breath.

As the oldest girl in her family, Lorena was in charge of the house and her younger siblings much of the time. Her parents didn't have maids, which was unheard of for people of their class, and I noticed that Lorena never asked questions about my family, either. The teeny old Indian lady we often encountered in the kitchen was her abuelita. Lorena uttered racist remarks against the Indians just like everyone else, but I simply admired what I considered to be her best qualities: down-to-earthness and a directness that left you stammering. She was short and round and never swore, preferring expressions like "Jeepers!" Her philosophy of life, quintessentially Bolivian, was "Anything can happen. And it will."

At dusk, boys would play soccer in the lane. Two social classes met during these games: the private-school boys who lived along the lane itself, and the public-school boys from the narrow alleys that began at the bottom of the stone steps. The lane families were business people, or at least that's what the kids answered when you asked what their fathers did. The alley families were working people with white-collar jobs: secretaries, schoolteachers, bank tellers. The alley kids were not invited to the rich kids' homes. When tea time came, the two groups went their separate ways. But once the sun had gone down and darkness overtook La Paz, we'd all meet again at the top of the steps, telling stories, making eyes at each other and cracking jokes until our parents called for us to come home. The 100-per-cent Indian kids never mixed with us. The wall succeeded in making them invisible, even though some of them lived in makeshift houses propped up against the concrete, inches away from our world.

One day Rolo, a public-school boy, took me behind the front gate of my house and kissed me. Other boys followed suit. Before long I was the kissing queen of the lane and alleys. With each kiss came the possibility that the Cousin might be replaced in my heart. His memory was like a shard of glass that moved through my bloodstream.

El Camba, at sixteen the oldest boy in the neighbourhood, was Rolo's cousin. Sporting a perpetual leather motorcycle jacket and baggy jeans, he had jet-black hair, pale skin and brilliant blue eyes. El Camba was from Santa Cruz, a province southeast of the highlands whose men were renowned for being irresistible. Santa Cruz was also known as cocaine cartel central. Brand-new Mercedes-Benzes, shipped directly from Germany, were deposited in an open field there five hundred at a time, sold for cash only. Every last one went within the hour.

El Camba lounged on his motorcycle while kids gathered to listen to his adventures. He'd disappear for days and then come back covered in dust, telling stories of Bolivia's deserts, mountains, jungles and mines. The lane boys were being groomed by their parents to have a shot at becoming the next president of Bolivia, the next commander-in-chief of the armed forces, the next minister of economics. The money for their U.S. Ivy League education was already set aside. But the alley boys were free to pursue any dream they wanted; they had nothing to lose and no one to impress. The lane boys hated El Camba.

At school, my favourite class was etiquette. It involved lots of role-playing, which I loved. In Vancouver, I'd taken acting classes from the age of eight, having announced my calling five years earlier after seeing the circus in Valdivia. I'd written, directed and acted in dozens of plays, the most famous being *Revolutionary Cinderella*, which starred Ale as Cinderella and featured my cousin Macarena as the Clock, the Guerrilla and the Mouse. We'd performed it for years at solidarity benefits and for the international speakers who'd stayed at our house. Etiquette class was taught by Señorita Karina, a fancy lady who wore cream-coloured lace dresses, white gloves and a lovely hat decorated with plastic flowers and a fake canary. She talked in a soft, high voice as she perched on the edge of her desk, hands resting daintily in her lap. Beneath her hat, her hair was always pinned into a bun.

In etiquette class we learned that girls must always laugh with their lips creating a perfect O, to avoid getting laugh lines and crows' feet. For the same reason, you were supposed to avoid moving your face when you talked.

"If a gentleman is taking you on a stroll around the plaza, and he looks up at the sky and says, 'Amor mío, isn't the moon wondrous this evening?' how do you respond?" our teacher would ask us.

One of us would raise her hand. "Señorita Karina, one must always respond by agreeing with said gentleman. For example, one can say, 'Yes, the moon is magnificent tonight, isn't it?'"

"You are correct, señorita. But ladies, you must also remember that you are as much a part of the courtship as the gentleman is. So if he speaks of the wondrous moon, you might add something like: 'Yes, the moon illuminates your face so that I can see your passionate eyes, my dear.' Now you have given him the tools by which he can proceed to steal that kiss he so fervently desires."

We all wrote furiously in our notebooks.

There were Indians on our school grounds, construction workers who toiled twelve hours a day building the new gymnasium with no breaks, no bathroom access, no water, for slave wages. They were visible from our classroom window, and the teachers referred to them by pointing their lips toward the outside. "In today's speech lesson," Señorita Karina would say, "we will learn to speak in a quiet, articulate voice, unlike those illiterate, uneducated Indians out there who yell, swear and have no use for proper Spanish grammar." Our science teacher called them dirty Indians, though I knew it was they who'd taught the Europeans about washing. She informed us the answer to the "Indian problem" in Bolivia was mass sterilization. In Catholicism class, the Indians were accused of practising black magic, casting spells and giving people the evil eye. My heart was sick by the end of each day.

The Niece was always surrounded by the German contingent. I was much too dark to be accepted by them, and fear gripped me when I was around these girls. But the Niece was nice to me because I spoke English. She'd ask me about Canada and inquired what my family was doing here. I was afraid she must know about us, but Bob advised me to play it cool. Having the Niece as a classmate was a fantastic opportunity to learn more about what the hell *her* family was doing in La Paz, he pointed out. It was rare to be so close to the enemy, so I must seize the day. From the shortwave broadcasts and the newspapers the adults devoured, they were convinced something terrible was brewing again in Bolivia. New elections were scheduled to be held soon, but surely it was only a matter of time before a new and bloodier coup took place. All of South America was under right-wing military rule, installed by the CIA, funded by multinational corporations, with the IMF and the World Bank doling out billions of dollars in credit. There was no way Lidia Gueiler could hang on much longer.

When the Swede disappeared for two weeks, I worried about him. One day after school, I was thrilled to see him walking down the lane with his backpack. I ran to catch up with him, and his eyes lit up when he saw me. He ate like a starving man when we served up the special dinner we'd cooked in his honour. That night, listening from the door of my bedroom, I heard him tell the others that he'd been intercepted in Chile and taken in for questioning. When his bus was surrounded by the military on a desert road, the Swede had used a razor blade to slice open his seat cushion and had slid the documents he'd been carrying inside it. Two plainclothes cops had ordered him off the bus, then loaded him into the back of a military Jeep, and he'd spent the next few days in jail in a small town, sweating bullets. He'd played the "me no speak Spanish" card, even when the secret police agents told him they knew all about the Return Plan, including that many gringos were involved. But they'd found nothing on him, so they'd let him go with a warning. I wondered if the documents were still stashed in the bus seat and if so, what would happen when they were found. With Ale snoring softly in the bed beside mine, I lay awake for a long time.

9

IT WAS A regular July morning in La Paz. The radio was playing, coffee was on, and the adults were huddled around the dining room table speaking about Very Important Things. Except that Bob wasn't in his requisite corduroy suit, ready to go to work at the computer company. Mami, hugely pregnant now, wasn't in one of the two dresses she wore to teach at the American English Centre. Also, both the shortwave and the regular radio were on. The Swede kept turning and turning the dial on the regular one, but all he could get was static. That was the military intercepting, Mami said. The shortwave was still working, and from the miners' radio we learned that General Luis García Meza, commander-in-chief of the armed forces, had just staged a coup against Lidia Gueiler. There was a curfew, a state of siege and a state of emergency. Tanks and Jeeps had taken over 6 de Agosto Avenue, just a block down from our house. We kept the curtains closed.

I'd seen Lidia Gueiler just two days before. There had been a parade on El Prado to commemorate Bolivia's martyrs in the war for independence from Spain, and she was marching with a red, yellow and green sash draped across her chest, the colours of the Bolivian flag. Flanked by men in suits and officials in military garb—had Luis García Meza, who the miners' radio said was her cousin, been one of them?—she'd held a bouquet of flowers in one hand and waved with the other. In her heavy makeup, she looked like an old beauty queen.

Maybe Lidia Gueiler was dead by now. According to the announcer on the miners' radio, the situation was very bad. "Comrades! Luis García Meza's right-hand man is Klaus Barbie himself, that Nazi war criminal who walks our streets with impunity. Top advisers and torturers have been brought in from Argentina's Videla dictatorship. García Meza has declared that Pinochet is his idol. The military and the right wing are afraid of the ongoing congressional investigations of human rights abuses and large-scale corruption. This coup is funded by the cocaine drug lords and is, of course, part of a much larger plan by the United States to neo-liberalize Latin America. We miners, we peasants, we workers of Bolivia denounce this attempt to stop the democratic process. The Central Workers' Union is holding an emergency meeting and will likely call for a general strike. Stay at your posts, comrades, for further instructions."

We hid out in our house for the rest of the day, listening to our windows rattling from the low-flying airplanes and the nearby machine-gun fire. All I could think about was the cholitas and their babies who lived on the streets, the mules, the peasants just arrived in the city with nowhere to rest but the plaza. What would they do? There was an overnight curfew, and no one was allowed in the street, but what if the street was your home? Ale played with her Barbie dolls, but I stuck by the adults at the table, their worried faces sending chills up my spine. Operation Condor would go into even higher gear now that García Meza was in place, and that would mean stricter security measures for us. I wondered if we were hiding any documents or goods right now. There were certain nooks and crannies in the house that were off limits to Ale and me, and we both knew not to ask why.

At some point during the afternoon, the announcer on the miners' radio station began yelling. "The military has raided the Central Workers' Union in La Paz and has shot and taken Marcelo Quiroga

Santa Cruz, our renowned socialist leader, with them! Two union leaders have been killed on the spot! Chaos has ensued. The military is here, comrades, there are jets flying above." And then there was a huge explosion, right on the air. After that, only static. The miner reporting from the Siglo xx region had just given his life to keep us informed. Mami's glasses steamed up, and the Swede's eyes filled with tears. Bob pulled me in close to his chest, his jaw clamped tight.

Our lane was patrolled all day and into the night by Jeeps, and once by a passing tank. Sometimes there was shooting right outside our gate, setting the stray dogs howling. Whenever we heard gunfire, we'd all drop to the floor under the dining room table, a difficult thing for Mami to do with her huge belly. Once we were huddled, she'd be overtaken by a laugh attack and pee her pants. "It's the nerves, it's the nerves," she would say, wiping her eyes. We were used to it—certain things struck her that way. Sometimes the rest of us started laughing, too.

The adults decided we should all sleep in the bedroom at the back of the house. That would make it almost impossible for a bullet to hit us through the window. My mother climbed into my bed, and Ale into hers. Bob, the Swede, Trinidad and I stretched out on the floor. It was kind of fun having everybody take up residence in our room like that.

When curfew lifted at six each morning, I went out to buy black-market bread, sold from one of the alley doors by the cutest little grandma. The whole neighbourhood was buying bread there. People walked with their eyes glued to the ground, looking up only when a plane crossed the sky to see whether to run back home or dive down flat. Conversations took place in whispers. The stores were closed indefinitely, so everybody's new diet was this hard bread washed down with coca-leaf tea, which miners, peasants and the poor of La Paz drank constantly to ward off hunger. There was no school, so the neighbourhood kids huddled on the stone steps, unseen from the lane, swapping coup stories until curfew descended again at nine in the evening. According to one boy, Jose Luis, the military had been practising their aim on the stray dogs in the lane. I'd been wondering where they'd vanished to; now I knew.

El Camba and Rolo reported that the national soccer stadium, up the street from where we had lived in Miraflores, had been turned into a concentration camp. Thousands of people were being held there. Jose Luis said that was communist propaganda, but El Camba nailed him with his blue eyes. No, he said, he had been there himself. The coup had caught him on the way back from the salt mounds of Uyuni, and he was picked up for riding his motorcycle into a city under siege. We all went quiet. Only two people from our lane had gone to work on the day of the coup, and they had continued to go every day afterward: Lorena's father and Jose Luis's father. Theirs were also the only two families that still had a steady supply of food. According to Lorena, her father was a political adviser to the new president. She refused to use the word *dictator*. Jose Luis's father ran some kind of business. In Bolivia at that time, that meant he was probably into cocaine money.

When school began again ten days later, my classmates seemed ecstatic about the new government. The teachers nodded their heads in agreement. The Niece's status was even higher now, and the teachers tiptoed around her. Curfew was still in effect, and one evening we were at the stone steps when the little bread-selling lady staggered down the lane, hanging on to passing walls for support. Some of us jumped up to help her, and she told us she'd been caught in the curfew the night before, on her way home from selling seeds downtown. She'd been taken to the national stadium, where she'd witnessed things she never thought she'd live to tell. Beautiful young students being beaten, entire families held under arrest, intellectuals in blindfolds and handcuffs. Street kids and mules had been forced to run around the track all night; soldiers shot at their bare feet whenever they slowed down. Most of them collapsed into unconsciousness after hours of that. As for the old woman, they'd placed her in front of a mountain of soldiers' dirty socks and kept her up all night washing them. Whenever she dozed off, they'd shoved her hard with a rifle. They finally let her go with a warning to never break curfew again. It had taken hours for her to get to San Jorge from Miraflores, since the bus was a luxury she could not afford.

I waited for everyone to fall asleep when I got home. Then I snuck out onto our back porch. The porch hung above 6 de Agosto Avenue, but it was not really visible from the street; from below it got lost in the array of balconies running up the side of the hill. I'd stolen the Swede's special whistle from his backpack. He'd explained it was so loud it could be heard from very far away, especially useful if you were lost in the bush. I crouched low, so that I was entirely concealed, and started to blow it. The whistle pierced the wall of sound made by the Jeeps, tanks, helicopters and planes, and the shooting that rang through the night. It was perfect. Each blow of the whistle stood for something: this one's for what you did to the old lady, this one's for what you did to the miner on the radio who gave his life, this one's for all the maids, mules and shoeshine boys of Bolivia.

I heard soldiers yelling at each other and the sound of their boots on the cement. I stopped for a minute, slowly got up and peered down at the avenue. Sure enough, they were running this way and that, trying to figure out which of their superiors was blowing the whistle and what he wanted them to do. I blew again, hard. This one's for all the children who die every day of hunger, diarrhea and other curable diseases. The soldiers raced around like a bunch of idiots. They'd blackened their faces with shoe polish so they could commit their crimes without being recognized. My uncle Boris always said you couldn't have a dialogue with the enemy when the enemy was pointing a gun at you. You just had to defend yourself and take the power, by any means necessary. The whistle was a good start, as far as revolutionary tactics went for a twelve-year-old. I blew it for a long time.

I WAS NO LONGER the kissing queen of the neighbourhood, because I had a boyfriend. Camilo was Rolo's cousin; he and his mother and his three siblings were Bolivians who had moved back to La Paz after a few years in Brazil. Camilo's fifteen-year-old sister, Katushka, and I also became fast friends. They knew what it was like to leave everything behind and start anew. The whole clan, Rolo's family and theirs, lived simply—no maid, no fancy clothes, one pair of shoes each. Camilo and his brother slept on the living room floor, and their mother and sisters shared a double bed.

Camilo and I kissed in the alley more furiously than ever after the coup, heading home just in time for curfew. One afternoon I noticed a bunch of kids rushing into Jose Luis's house. Lorena told me that Jose Luis's mother had called an emergency meeting, and that everyone from the lane was attending except her family and mine.

"They say you're a filthy whore," she explained.

"Who?" I asked.

"Well, everyone."

Tears sprang from my eyes, gushing like a waterfall. Lorena handed me her embroidered handkerchief and caressed my arm. It began with the indiscriminate kissing, she explained. Also, I had kissed both lane boys and alley boys, and that was a no-no. Now my hour-long kissing sessions with Camilo, an alley boy, had the lane ladies up in arms.

"Carmen, I love you, you're my friend, but you've got to understand that this is Bolivia. If you act like a boy you will pay."

No, I thought to myself. This was not Bolivia. This was rich, mestizo, right-wing, sexist, hypocritical, Catholic Bolivia. This was the ruling class, but not for long. Rich Bolivia was where my family was for the moment, though, and I knew we must live by its rules.

I hurried home to prepare Mami and Bob. I'd barely finished speaking when the doorbell rang. Sure enough, Jose Luis's mother and a bunch of the other lane ladies, with their bouffant hairdos, heavy pancake makeup and tight girdles, were standing at the gate.

We agreed that Bob would deal with them, playing the stupid-gringo card. I spied from the window as Jose Luis's mother handed him a letter at the gate, gesturing wildly at the houses surrounding ours. Bob simply nodded at first. But then he got his back up, because the lady wouldn't let him get a word in edgewise. As he opened our front door to come back in, I could hear Jose Luis's mother yell: "Every family on the lane has signed this letter, including your downstairs neighbours. And I've already contacted your landlords. I'm sure they will not be too happy to learn about the whores and hippies they're renting to."

Bob punched the wall as Mami sank into a chair at the table, her head in her hands. Ale rolled her eyes at me. She agreed with the ladies, and she'd already told me so. Trinidad and the Swede called me into the living room. I'd done nothing wrong, they assured me, but I cried anyway, until my heart was squashed like a piece of fruit lying on the market floor.

Two mothers stood by me after that: Lorena's and Camilo's, kissing and hugging me every chance they got. But the neighbourhood girls started to cross the street when they saw me, and the boys watched from afar, elbowing each other in the ribs and laughing.

One afternoon, as I reached the top of the hill, I spied some boys at the end of the lane examining a banana-seat bike. I stopped in my tracks, because that was an unusual sight. Vendors rode around downtown La Paz on huge tricycle-type bikes from the 1940s, carrying mountains of merchandise in their massive bike baskets, but that didn't count. This bike was meant for a kid to have fun on. Jose Luis yelled at me to come look at it. His invitation was obviously a truce, I thought, and they might even apologize for shunning me. I realized how pathetically lonely I'd been without them.

The bike was a gift brought from Miami by Jose Luis's father. The boys begged me to teach them to ride it. I dropped my school bag and jumped on, whizzing down the lane. I felt free as I bumped along the cobblestones.

"Go down the hill to 6 de Agosto Avenue!" Jose Luis yelled.

The boys were running after me, egging me on. A tickle filled my belly, because the hill was steep and I was flying high. As I sailed along,

I was back on the forest trails in Vancouver, riding with my cousins, leaping on our bikes over fallen trees and protruding roots, covered in mud and rain, leaving all my problems behind.

Busy 6 de Agosto was coming up fast. But when I stepped on the brakes, nothing happened. That couldn't be, because the bike was brand new, with its shiny yellow seat and brilliant chrome. Then I was standing on the brakes, but still nothing. So I jumped. It was either that or smash right into a bus full of people.

The bike crashed against a wall, and I rolled along the gutter to land spread-eagled on the sidewalk, with skinned palms and knees but no real injuries. I looked up at the sky and, like a true La Paz girl, crossed myself, kissing my right thumb loudly. I got up, brushed myself off and walked the bike back up the hill, to where the boys were standing. The colour had drained from their faces. I handed the bike to Jose Luis, gave him my dirtiest look and kept walking.

A few nights later, Ale and I went for a walk with Trinidad and my mother. We strolled along the narrow downtown streets, where the sidewalks were so skinny there was room for only one person at a time, the four of us wearing alpaca ponchos to stay warm in the highland night.

A group of rich boys drove by in a Mercedes-Benz, hurling obscenities at the women as they passed. When they saw my mother with her big belly, they yelled: "Hey, look at that one! She got good and fucked!"

My mother gave them the finger. "Váyanse a las conchas de sus madres, huevones culeados!" she yelled back. (Go back to your mothers' cunts, motherfuckers!) It was the most Chilean insult anybody could use.

The boys shouted: "Oooh! Four Chilean whores! Go back to where you came from, putas!" Then they floored it and drove their car right up onto the sidewalk.

A lady opened her door and yanked us into her house an instant before the car would have hit us. She gave us tea to calm our nerves. On the way home afterwards, Mami said she shouldn't have yelled like that; we were doing too many stupid things to draw attention to ourselves these days. "You mean like Carmen being a slut?" Ale said.

Back at home, I opened a tiny silk change purse I'd bought in Vancouver's Chinatown so long ago. Inside I kept my Virgin of Copacabana, given to me by my classmates in Miraflores on the last day of school. La Grandma had handed it to me, with the rest of the class standing at her side. "May the Virgin keep you safe," she'd said, "whichever road you're on." Then we'd all held hands, because nobody knew where life was going to take them. It couldn't hurt, I thought, to thank the Virgin for taking care of us.

ICE CASTLES, a new figure-skating movie, was playing at the 16 de Julio Theatre on El Prado. Lorena and I had gone twice already, and Bob wanted to see what all the fuss was about. I knew he was probably going to lecture me about cultural imperialism and how Hollywood exported ridiculous versions of middle-class North America, but I didn't care—Robby Benson was cute, and I wanted to swoon over him again. When the movie stopped abruptly, right at the moment the blind ice-skater was bending to pick up the roses people had thrown at her feet, the audience moaned and whistled. It was common for the projectors to break down. But this time the lights came up, and an older woman in a business suit walked down the aisle and climbed the stairs to the stage.

"I am Dr. Vergara Emerson, pediatrician at the German Clinic and professor at San Andrés university," she began. "I am here to denounce the heinous crimes being committed by the dictator Luis García Meza. Hundreds of people have been killed. Hundreds of others have been imprisoned and are being tortured. Many have been forced into exile, and there are dozens of disappeared. We miners, peasants, doctors, students and teachers have resisted from the first day of the coup and will continue to do so. I ask each of you to stand right now and observe a minute of silence for Marcelo Quiroga Santa Cruz, leader of the Socialist Party, award-winning writer and university professor, and all the others who have fallen. García Meza has bragged publicly about torturing Comrade Quiroga Santa Cruz himself and disposing of his body so that it would never be found. We denounce this terrible crime. We demand the expulsion of Klaus Barbie and his Nazi cronies from our country, and the expulsion of the CIA."

I was shaking hard, but not just from fear. From excitement. I could tell Bob was excited too. The theatre was jam-packed, and everyone was waiting for someone else to make the first move.

Dr. Vergara Emerson looked out at us all, a strand of pearls trembling on her chest. Finally some young people got to their feet. The rest of the audience followed. No one walked out. Bob and I stood in silence with the others. After the minute was over, Dr. Vergara Emerson said, "Thank you, my compatriots." She climbed down from the stage and walked back up the aisle to where a small group of well-dressed people were waiting for her. They'd probably go on to another theatre and do it all again. People had started to clap and chant, and Bob and I got out of there fast.

On the bus home, I asked Bob if Dr. Vergara Emerson would be killed. Colonel Luis Arce Gómez, the minister of the interior, had announced on the radio that all Bolivians opposed to the new order should walk around with their wills under their arms.

"I don't know," Bob said. "But you will remember her, Carmencita, because what that woman did is the definition of courage."

PART TWO

THE
FALL

10

FIREWORKS ERUPTED ALL over La Paz, celebrating the kiss I'd been dying for. It was midnight on Christmas Eve 1981, and Plaza Avaroa was a little piece of paradise, its benches and grassy slopes home to the courtship of every kid in the neighbourhood.

Not that I was a kid. At fourteen, I was a veteran kisser, smoker and dancer, and I'd been witness to some very bad behaviour during my first year of high school back in lonely Vancouver. My classmates there had made a habit of alcohol poisoning. Bush parties were the name of the game. You'd crash through the forest to arrive at a clearing containing the moonlit bodies of thirteen-year-olds trashed on booze, pot, mushrooms and acid. I vowed never to drink or do drugs, no matter how much I wanted to dull my pain.

As the kiss continued, I flashed on my father, left behind to celebrate Christmas without us. Midnight had yet to arrive in the far North Pacific, I knew, and I wondered if it was another rainy night in Vancouver. The place had seemed so sedate and sterile after La Paz. Most of my adopted aunts, uncles and cousins had departed from Vancouver, leaving no forwarding address, no doubt responding to the Return Plan. I was still devastated by the image of Papi standing at the end of the airport tunnel, hand on his heart as my aunt Tita held him up.

The boy I was kissing was Ernesto, born and bred in Sopocachi, our new neighbourhood. We lived in a narrow two-storey row house with "Sunnyland" engraved on a plaque above the door. It boasted a palm tree in the front yard, a garage in the back and a tile courtyard where our laundry got washed and hung. The music of our own mortar and pestle joined all the others in the lunchtime symphony of chilis being crushed. Ale and I had been back in La Paz for just three weeks, because my parents had a new deal: the two of us would go back and forth between them until we came of age.

My mother explained the arrangement like this: "Your father misses you." But I knew it was more than that. As Mami had explained that day at LAX, most women who had responded to the Return Plan sent their kids to live with Cuban families who'd volunteered to raise them or with grandparents somewhere else. My mother had insisted on bringing her daughters with her, and not only that, on having another baby while living underground. As far as she was concerned, a woman shouldn't have to choose between motherhood and revolution. She wanted both. But Trinidad, I'd come to understand, was Mami and Bob's superior, and she'd argued that the current situation was too dangerous. If García Meza had fallen after a brief time in power, it would have been different. But six weeks after the coup, the dictator's boast that he would govern Bolivia for twenty years looked as if it might come true. Mami and Bob were in deep, and García Meza and Pinochet were soul brothers.

"Well, if you are ordering me to get rid of them, the best thing would be to send them back to Canada. But I feel absolutely that my girls belong with me. I am their mother, and I will not give them up just like that." Mami's voice broke.

Listening from my bedroom door, I knew that Trinidad would have the final word.

Before we left, my mother took us to the black market, where we talked her into buying us the white Bata clogs that were in fashion. When she reached for her wallet, however, she discovered a hole in the bottom of her purse, where it had been sliced open by pickpockets.

"Well, my precious girls, your memento of Bolivia from your mother will be the anecdote of this hole in my purse." Mami laughed till she cried. She cried and cried as we walked hand in hand all the way home. Ale couldn't stop sobbing. I cried silently, my teeth chattering.

Papi, who had just completed his PhD, was penniless, and the cheapest tickets he could get for our return to La Paz required a two-day stopover in Miami. We stayed with a Cuban family who still grieved the U.S. defeat at the Bay of Pigs; the driver pressed the gas pedal to the floor when forced to pass through black neighbourhoods. The Cubans were related to Julio, our Colombian friend in Vancouver, though they had no idea that Julio had defected to the left. They showed us around Miami, even giving us a tour of their "freedom farm" on the outskirts, a small sugar plantation where a couple dozen black men worked the land and were housed on the premises in huts. The men had been "saved" from Cuba by this family, they told us. They helped smuggle people out on a regular basis. The evening news on their TV was filled with images of Cubans scrambling out of speedboats, dropping to their knees and kissing Florida's shores.

The stopover was good practice for the Bolivian reality of having to nod and smile and keep our political views to ourselves. No more wearing painter's pants covered in buttons reading "El Salvador Sí, Junta No" and "Boycott Chilean Goods." In Vancouver I had officially joined the Rebel Youth Brigade, run by my uncle Boris, so I was now a card-carrying member of the resistance youth. (Not that we had actual cards; that would have gone against security measures.) After being sworn in, I was given the task of politicizing my high school. That involved showing documentaries on Latin America at lunch times, bringing in speakers and raising my hand in class to give my revolutionary opinion on whatever was being taught.

My button campaign had begun with me going up to random kids in the hallways and saying: "Hey, do you wanna wear this button? The red will coordinate nicely with the hats on your Devo button."

Random kid: "Well, what the fuck does it say?"

"Farabundo Martí National Liberation Front."

Random kid: "What the fuck is that?"

"It's a revolutionary guerrilla organization fighting for justice and bread in El Salvador."

Random kid: "No fucking way, man! Gorillas are taking over? Get the fuck outta here!"

"Totally. And they need our solidarity."

Random kid: "Like, how many are there?"

"Oh, thousands. Urban, rural, rich, poor, intellectuals and workers—"

Random kid: "Get the fuck out!"

"Yeah, so do you wanna wear one of their buttons?"

Random kid: "Hey, Yotto! Get a load of this! Gorillas are taking over Africa and they even have their own buttons! It's like *Planet of the Apes*, man!"

On our swearing-in day, I'd chosen my political name: Tania. Uncle Boris had handed me a red star, and I'd pinned it to my heart. The youth cell members were Ale, me, my cousins Gonzalo and Macarena, and eight other kids from the exile community. We met once a week to discuss the writings of Ché Guevara, Fidel Castro, Lenin, Marx, Ho Chi Minh and Tania the Guerrilla. We studied the history of Latin America from the people's point of view.

I'd had to leave my red star behind when we returned to La Paz, of course, along with a vintage copy of Ché's diaries presented to me by some visiting Cubans. A precious card from Laura Allende lived in its pages. Sister of Salvador Allende, mother of the resistance leader Andrés Pascal Allende, she had stayed at our house when I was eight, while she was on a cross-Canada speaking tour. I couldn't believe that a woman of her stature was sitting right at our table, drinking from our cups. At night I'd hear her weep. My mother explained that not only had Laura lost her brother, her country and the dream we all shared, but her son Andrés was underground in Chile and had barely survived an ambush. What's more, the cancer she'd had for several years was advancing quickly, and Laura was in great pain. At her speaking engagements in Vancouver, I'd admired her grace, elegance and strength. She'd handed me a card on her departure, which read: "Carmencita, never forget my brother's words: other men will overcome this sad and bitter moment in Chilean history, and the great avenues will open once again, where the free man will walk." When she committed suicide in May 1981, my uncle Boris dedicated a youth brigade meeting to her memory.

In Plaza Avaroa, someone cleared his throat, but Ernesto and I just kept kissing. Loud coughing followed, and when we disengaged I saw Bob.

"Carmencita, time to come home."

Bob took a few more steps and then did the same throat-clearing and coughing manoeuvre on Ale, who was lip-locked with Claudio, Ernesto's younger brother. They were the most beautiful boys in La Paz, and, as of tonight, they belonged to Ale and me. The brothers lived up the street from us, in a house decorated with hand-carved leather and wood furniture and Inca-inspired gold artifacts. Their father was a high-ranking military man, something we didn't discuss. García Meza's reign had lasted only a year, ending in August 1981, but his successor, General Celso Torrelio, was another extreme rightwinger financed by the cocaine cartels, the IMF and the World Bank.

Lalito, my new baby brother, was fourteen months old, all apple cheeks and big brown eyes, golden curls framing his cherubic face. Mami and Bob had brought him to meet us at the airport in a little woven poncho. Our new life began with no mention of Trinidad or the Swede.

We had a maid at Sunnyland. Nati, a woman in her fifties, did all our laundry, cleaning, cooking, dishwashing and grocery buying. A decrepit old Aymara man referred to as "el maestro" came by once a week and wheezed his way around the house, waxing every last inch of floor on all fours. The whole situation made me sick, but I understood the rationale. People gossiped about moneyed families who didn't have servants, wondering what they were trying to hide. And now Bob had ties with the ruling class. He'd been promoted to head honcho at the computer company, and the firm was pleased that he'd become the go-to guy for the Bolivian government, selling computers to the military, the cocaine cartels and the politicians. Having a computer system installed was very First World; when the guy in charge of the installation was a real-life gringo, you knew you'd made it. The computer company's building was on the corner of Plaza Avaroa. Directly across the street stood the Ministry of Defence. On another corner overlooking the plaza was the United States Embassy. Bob and Mami, who was now the director of the American English Centre, went to cocktail parties there. The minister of defence had Bob over to his office for tea and sweets every week.

There was a white car locked in the garage at Sunnyland. Nobody ever mentioned it, but two other voices joined Mami and Bob's out there some nights, one female, one male. Our new house also had a darkroom, where Mami and Bob photographed documents and developed the rolls of film that arrived on a regular basis at a post office box downtown. Over lunch one day, they revealed that both of them had been having fainting fits over the past year. We were not to call a doctor if we came across one of them sprawled on the floor, though; we were simply to pour ice water over their faces. The fainting spells were due to stress, they assured us, not anything medical. Then they filled us in on what had brought them to Sunnyland.

Soon after Ale and I were sent back to Canada, the lane house had been dismantled. Trinidad and the Swede had moved to an undisclosed location, and Mami and Bob had gone to live in a small apartment close to Plaza España, a lower-end neighbourhood, with newborn Lalito. One day, after picking up Lalito from daycare, they got home to find the apartment had been raided. Papers, books, pictures and the contents of overturned drawers and closets littered the floor. Nothing had been taken, but the message was clear: we're watching you. García Meza had already had a thousand people killed. Political prisoners filled the jails, thousands had gone into exile, and nobody knew how many people had disappeared. But instead of leaving the country, Bob and Mami had simply stepped up security. This meant, among other things, making sure they looked middle-class and mainstream.

But then Bob had made a mistake, they told us. He bought his daily pack of cigarettes at a kiosk across the street run by an old couple, and one day he'd purchased an expensive silver lighter as well. When he presented it a couple of months later for the free refill he'd been promised, the woman had called him a fucking gringo who wanted to take advantage of Bolivians. Bob lost his temper and started yelling. The woman jumped up and lunged at him. Then her husband came out and accused Bob loudly of molesting his wife, at which point a cop had been summoned. The cop had arrested Bob on the spot, and he was thrown into the clandestine jail in the basement of the ministry of defence, a mere block away. My mother had waited and waited for him at Sunnyland.

Bob was beaten at the jail referred to as "the dungeon" by the guards. Surrounded by political prisoners in different states of pre- or post-torture devastation, he had spent the night listening to horrific howls and desperate pleading. The next morning the minister of defence himself had done his daily inspection of prisoners. Upon seeing Bob, he had chastised the guards, apologized profusely and taken Bob up to his office for coffee and cheese rolls. If Bob hadn't already befriended the minister, no doubt they'd have done a background check on him, and that would have been the end of it all.

These stories were meant to remind Ale and me that we were not back in Bolivia just to make out all day with the beautiful brothers, dance with Lorena—whose house I'd run to as soon as we arrived—to the B-52s and have our jeans ironed by Nati, even though she was paid triple the going rate, had weekends off and worked only half days. We were in Bolivia doing serious, perilous work, and two new people were going to take Ale and me under their wing, my mother informed us. Ale and I glanced at each other, not daring to ask what that would entail.

I ANSWERED THE DOOR the next morning, and there was Rulo. Rulo, who'd driven us to the airport the day we first left Vancouver and been gone by the time we returned. Rulo, who'd shown me his scars and sung the old protest songs in a quavering voice, his eyes squeezed shut. Here he was. On the doorstep of Sunnyland, hands in his pockets, a big smile plastered on his face. My heart almost jumped out of my chest. He winked at me as he came in, followed by the most beautiful woman I'd ever seen. Her cheekbones were the highest ever created, and she moved like a panther.

Soledad looked to be in her early twenties. I deduced as we sat around the table that she and Rulo, who was now called Leo, were a couple and that the voices I'd heard in the garage late at night belonged to them. Now they'd also be educating Ale and me. Our work together would be twofold, Rulo outlined. We'd continue to learn about the history of Latin America, and we'd hone our underground skills. With a nod, he turned things over to Soledad, who launched into a lecture on beauty. It had taken her years to accept the way she looked, she began, because of the racism in her country of Bolivia, where standards had been set by the invaders. Indian was ugly, Spanish was beautiful, gringo was downright gorgeous. It was still hard for her to claim her Aymara blood in certain circles.

Ale stifled a yawn while she stared at the ceiling. All I cared about was the two whistles coming from Plaza Avaroa, signalling the arrival of the brothers and their posse. By now, Soledad had started in about our petit bourgeois concerns. Rich boys were mentioned, and our repeated trips to see *Endless Love* at the cinema on 6 de Agosto. The fact that Ale liked to take the curling iron to my head before we went to house parties was another example of our shallowness. My pants were too tight, my lipstick too red, and the couple from the kiosk across the way—who were friends again with Bob—had reported that Ale and I were wasting our summer days sitting on the front steps of our house with gangs of kids. This obsession with popularity and Hollywood standards of beauty was unrevolutionary, Soledad scolded, and was causing our parents great concern. There were far more important things to worry about in this world than looking like Brooke Shields, such as universal medical care. Anger flashed through me, but then I glanced over at Rulo, with his broken body and his concentration camp eyes. He and Soledad were giving their lives for the revolution. If they could do it, so could I.

Tomorrow, Ale and I were to meet Rulo and Soledad at Plaza Murillo. For now, we were released into the Plaza Avaroa sun, where the brothers waited for our afternoon make-out session to begin. Once outside the door, we dove for the gate and, together, broke into a run.

11

RULO'S HANDS STEERED ME from behind. Climbing cobblestone steps was a feat at the best of times. Doing so when you were wearing dark glasses *and* your eyes were closed upped the ante. Add to that the carsickness from driving in circles to lose any possible followers, and it was a miracle I wasn't rolling down those steps, head clunking at every landing. Ale and I had arrived at Plaza Murillo with five minutes to spare. We'd stood on the assigned corner, and before we knew it Rulo and Soledad had pulled up in a nondescript Brazilian car. The back door flew open, Soledad yelled at us to get in, and the car merged again into the heavy afternoon traffic. Soledad handed each of us a pair of dark glasses with orders to put them on and keep our eyes shut for the entire ride.

"Just a little farther," Rulo said now. "Good."

I kept my poker face on, turning this into an acting exercise. Since returning to La Paz, I'd been taking classes with a teacher who was also a respected theatre director. I never missed his twice-weekly sessions, where I was the only teenager in the bunch. I'd given up on my earlier dream of becoming an actor, since that would be too bourgeois and self-centred, but I could put my skills to use in this kind of situation. I pretended my eyes were open for the benefit of any onlookers, moving my head from side to side occasionally.

Finally, after leading us through a door, Rulo said it was okay to remove our sunglasses and open our eyes. We were in the tiny living room of a small house. Every wall we could see was covered in newspaper. As we settled onto an old couch, Rulo updated us on the struggle in Chile. It was the beginning of 1982, and the movement of the masses was picking up, he said. Thank God I knew what he was talking about. Back in Vancouver, I'd made a fool of myself at a Rebel Youth Brigade meeting by proclaiming, when quizzed by Uncle Boris, "The movement of the masses is when the workers are transported on buses."

The generalized repression of the 1970s in Chile had slowed down to the more selective practice of picking up resistance members in the middle of the night and doing away with them quietly, Rulo continued. "Overt violence has been relegated to underground detention centres and shantytowns. But we must remember, comrades, that the definition of violence is much wider than beatings, torture and assassinations. Is it not violent to starve people to death? To deny them the basic human rights of health care, shelter and clean water? Is it not violent to have an official unemployment rate of 30 per cent, to privatize schooling and deny the right of a huge part of the population to education, to privatize hospitals and clinics and allow children to die of the flu, to destroy national industry, giving free rein to the multinational corporations that have taken over Chile?" Rulo/Leo was leaning in close, his brow furrowed. He was treating us like adults, and it made me miss the old Rulo, the one I'd taught the hustle to.

Soledad took the reins. "We must remember, little comrades, that Pinochet is part of a much larger military and economic plan being orchestrated all over Latin America, with firm roots in the North."

Ale rolled her eyes. "Uncle Boris already told us all this stuff at our youth group meetings in Vancouver."

Soledad looked stern. "I'll pretend I didn't hear that, little comrade. You must remember not to mention the names of people or places."

I nodded furiously, trying to compensate for Ale's indiscretion. Soledad went on.

"The twenty-five Chilean economists who were offered scholarships at the University of Chicago have implemented a brand-new economy in Chile, referred to as neo-liberalism."

"The Chicago Boys," I interrupted.

"Yes, the Chicago Boys. These devout followers of Milton Friedman's teachings hold powerful positions as ministers of economics, finance and labour. They run the national pension plans, advise the central bank and direct the national budget. In short, they have privatized the Chilean economy." Soledad pushed her shining mane of hair out of her face and reached for her pack of Camels. Unlike other capitalist systems, she said, in which the state held some power over corporations, this new kind of capitalism was free from government regulation, and Chile had been chosen as the first country in the world to put it into practice.

Rulo jumped back in. "The social cost is huge, and the model is run almost entirely on giant amounts of credit doled out by the International Monetary Fund and the World Bank. That has raised Chile's foreign debt to exorbitant heights while multinationals make a killing, answering to no one. Pinochet and his cronies hold the country in a perpetual state of martial law while pocketing millions in government funds and building a $12-million bunker for themselves in case the Russians drop the bomb. The unlimited amount of credit that suddenly became available has driven thousands of Chileans into bankruptcy. But people are still lining up for credit cards at the brand-new department stores selling imported goods. Allende's socialist Chile—where top-notch university education was free, where there was universal health care, great pension plans, a model literacy campaign, nationalized natural resources, agrarian reform and a huge budget for arts and culture—has been completely destroyed and replaced with an all-out consumer society. According to the propaganda campaign, Chile will now join the First World." He made quotation marks with his fingers around the term.

"But the South *has* to be exploited for the North to maintain the standard of living it has. People are being tricked into believing some of this massive corporate profit will 'trickle down' to them."

My uncle Carlos's new-found wealth in the late seventies made sense to me now, as did the fact that he'd recently lost everything: his house, his car and the private school educations for his children. Mami had told us this, with worry in her voice, and I'd wondered how the Cousin was handling it all. The previous fall, one of my father's brothers had made a desperate call to Vancouver after being threatened with jail if he didn't pay his debts. His wages as a high school teacher (under five hundred dollars a month, with prices in Chile not much different from those in North America) would never be enough to get the creditors off his back. Could my father send him some money? Clearly, my uncle was among the many Chileans who refused to believe that most First World exiles were janitors and lived hand to mouth.

Add to all this Chile's new constitution, Rulo expounded, which gave Pinochet unprecedented powers and included anti-terrorism clauses that legalized the abduction, torture, murder and disappearance of dissidents—usually the poorest of the poor, simply demanding their basic rights—and the situation presented itself as difficult on the one hand, but perfect on the other for a revolutionary outcome. The regrouping of the resistance movement was leading people to mobilize. In spite of martial law, protests attended by thousands in Chile were on the increase, and a general strike was no longer an impossibility. People's desire to rise up was becoming stronger than their terror. But this time, Rulo said, there could be no mistaking that the people must be armed. The ruling class had a U.S.-backed army to defend its interests, and the people had the right to an army of their own. Allende's experiment had been the best thousand days in Chilean history, but the coup had proven that the peaceful way to socialism was not possible at this time in Latin America. If the peaceful way were possible, Simón Bolívar's dream of a united Latin America, in which there was bread and justice for all, would have been realized a long time ago, Soledad chimed in. Bolivia was named after Bolívar, she reminded us, who'd led the South American wars of independence from Spain in the 1800s. Revolution was still the only way to achieve Bolívar's vision. And for us, that meant being underground.

Our instructors were finally getting to their point. Although Ale and I lived in a privileged neighbourhood, Rulo said, and hung out with a bunch of rich kids in order to hide our beliefs and our reason for being here, we had to be careful to not let our bourgeois tendencies get the better of us. This was all very different from the meetings with Uncle Boris in Vancouver. He'd tell jokes and praise us for how incredibly revolutionary we were, and then reward us with trips to McDonald's and Playland, the local amusement park.

"Why do you decorate your walls with newspaper?" Ale must have spent the entire time waiting for an opening to ask the question.

"Little comrade, we have covered the walls with newspaper for security reasons," Soledad replied. "If any of us were to fall into the hands of the secret police, how would you describe this house?"

"Huh?"

"Exactly. You can't describe it. Not its whereabouts, nor what it looks like inside or out."

"Oh," said Ale.

She had no clue what Soledad was talking about, I could tell. Yet Ale was great at keeping secrets. Our rehearsed lies rolled off her tongue like the latest rock lyrics. As for me, I'd decided I didn't like Soledad. She was condescending. Also, I wondered many things. Why were we holding our meetings here, when they knew where we lived? We could have met at Sunnyland, doing away with the whole Plaza Murillo/dark glasses/newspaper-covered living room rigmarole. Wasn't it dangerous that they knew our address and names? What about the car they came to work on at night? Bob was away often now, sometimes for weeks on end, as was Mami, though she left for shorter stretches. I was suddenly exhausted by how much work a revolution entailed.

A SCRAWNY BOY in a leather jacket and Ray-Bans inched his desk up next to mine and stuck his hand out by way of introduction. He was a classmate at my new school: the Northern Institute. Having pulled many strings to get us in, Mami had finally enrolled us, a few days into the school year. So now I went to the same liberal school as Lorena, a few blocks up from the Higher University of San Andrés, where there were protests every week. My other classmates had introduced themselves via notes and winks while the mathematics teacher filled the board with formulas.

Now this boy was shaking my hand.

"Luis García Meza Jr."

"What?" I said.

"Luis García Meza Jr."

The teacher saved me from having to reply. "Mr. García Meza Jr, I understand that your dark glasses are of utmost importance to you. However, I suggest you have them off by the time I turn around." She tapped her long burgundy nails on the blackboard for effect.

At first recess I found out from Félix, a flamingly gay guy I already loved like a long-lost brother, that yes, Luis was indeed García Meza's son, and that Torrelio's daughter was in our class, too. Torrelio, as in the dictator himself? "That's right," Félix said. "She's the fat one who dresses like her mother. But don't call her dad a dictator in these circles," he corrected me. "And don't worry about the bodyguards—you'll get used to having them in the class." Oh, so that's what the four men with guns sitting in the back of the room had been doing. Guarding the dictator's and the ex-dictator's children.

The father of our classmate German was Luis Arce Gómez, Félix confided, the former minister of interior renowned for carrying out García Meza's dirty work. The most gorgeous guy in the courtyard, Juan Jose de la Cruz, was the son of one of Bolivia's biggest cocaine men. Juan Jose clearly came from millions, and his shiny, brand-new motorcycle proved it. "He's cramming in all the good times now," Félix explained, "because as soon as school's done he'll marry the daughter of another Santa Cruz clan. It's already been arranged."

Lorena and her posse joined us in the courtyard just as Silvio Rodríguez's song "El Rey de las Flores" (The King of the Flowers) started to blast from a loudspeaker placed on a top-floor windowsill of the school building. I looked around, flabbergasted. Rodríguez, an international superstar and one of the founders of the Cuban New Song Movement, was banned in Bolivia. Everyone listened to him at low volume in the privacy of their own homes, but this was a different matter altogether. The last time some young members of the New Song Movement had played in La Paz, they'd been arrested mid-concert and held for two weeks before being deported.

As the song ended, two guys wearing black berets with red stars stuck their heads out of the window. One of them spoke into a megaphone while the other dropped pamphlets.

"Comrades, welcome to the Northern Institute 1982, and to our Rebel Radio program, which will transmit every day from this very windowsill."

He paused for effect.

"General Torrelio, U.S. puppet and state terrorist, does not scare us. We will continue to resist the ferocious censorship campaigns by exercising our freedom of speech, whatever the cost may be."

Some kids continued with their regular courtyard lives, talking and necking, but most were listening intently, and some people clapped and whistled. I glanced over at Luis. He stood chewing his gum with his arms crossed, flanked by his bodyguards, sunglasses still covering his eyes.

"And now, comrades, to finish off this recess, we will play one of Silvio's more recent hits, 'Vamos a Andar.'"

I picked up one of the dropped pamphlets on the way back in. In it, the two beret-wearing guys referred to themselves as the Altiplano (Highlands) Kings. The pamphlet included the words to several of Silvio's songs and a call to join the San Andrés university students at an upcoming protest.

"Do you prefer artsy politico types like the Altiplano Kings or rebel rich boys like Juan Jose de la Cruz?" Félix asked me as we climbed the stairs to our classroom.

"Oh, Juan Jose de la Cruz. By far."

"Yeah, me too. But look, darling, if you want any guy's attention we're gonna have to do something about your nails. There's no excuse for a girl walking around with nude nails. We'll go to the pharmacy after school and get you some pink polish. I'm an expert at applying it."

I loved my new school, with its cacophony of sounds and smells drifting into the classroom: diesel, tear gas, the spray of water cannons, protest songs, slogans and drums reaching us from San Andrés university and chili peppers being ground in nearby courtyards. We held hankies over our noses as we took dictation. Ale and I attended the morning shift. Our classmates were mostly ruling-class kids, but the school handed out full scholarships to dozens of lower-income students as well; one of my classmates was a full-blooded Aymara Indian boy who worked as a servant at a mansion the rest of the time. This was the school where artists with money, intellectuals, doctors and lawyers sent their kids, and there were also the children of politicians, ranging from the outlawed Communist Party leaders to the Revolutionary Nationalist Movement (which, despite its name, was largely right-wing). The afternoon shift was public, so working-class kids passed us on our way out.

The courtyard was where it all went down: hookups, breakups, make-out sessions. The Altiplano Kings played banned music and took requests for romantic ballads while Luis Jr. compiled his list. Rumour had it that during García Meza's rule several left-wing kids had been picked up thanks to Luis Jr. Some of these kids had never come back to school; others had returned with harrowing stories of torture. These stories reached me as a murmur here, a whisper there. Some claimed they were a bunch of lies, others swore they were true. At recess, vendors came into the school courtyard to peddle their wares. Cholitas made the rounds selling salteñas, four-year-olds peddled Chiclets, Aymara Indian gentlemen fresh from the highlands sold packages of roasted peanuts. We bought ice cream from young guys carrying Styrofoam coolers on their backs. Lorena, Félix, my new friends Liliana and Fatima, and I held court arm in arm as Roberto Carlos crooned in Portuguese over the loudspeakers.

I'd broken up with Ernesto during carnival, after a girl knocked on our door at Sunnyland and told me he'd been necking with someone else at one of the many parties happening around town. He'd denied it, unable to believe I'd trust a stranger's word over his, but I broke up with him anyway. For the rest of carnival I'd turned into a slut again, kissing boys who came by the house to throw water balloons at us, then breaking up with them after a week. Why bother with the everlasting-love thing? If I'd been meant to have eternal happiness, I'd have been in Chile living a homeland life, fighting for my rights with the other teenagers who shook Chilean high schools and were a force to contend with. If I'd been meant to have it all, I'd have been someone else, not this girl who was told every two seconds that what she wanted was petit bourgeois. Rulo and Soledad had grown more and more critical of us. Now every meeting opened with a self-criticism session, in which Ale and I were supposed to condemn our behaviour. Mami and Bob seemed at their wits' end having to deal with two teenage girls, a toddler, their full-time jobs and their underground activities. It was hard to look them in the eye, knowing we'd let them down so badly. The least I could do, I figured, was walk around with a broken heart.

12

"**THIS IS JUST** like London."

The pronouncement came from Liliana, who had never been to London, or anywhere other than La Paz, until now. The four of us huddled in our ponchos on the plaza bench, Lorena, Fátima, Liliana and me, enveloped in the evening fog that had just rolled into Coroico.

It was mid-June, winter break, and Lorena had invited us to her family home in this jungle village, where a band played in the plaza every night and the kerosene street lamps were lit by torch. Leaving La Paz before dawn, we'd settled in the back of the bus and sung along to Radio Chuquisaca, which played all the number-one hits: the Police's "Every Little Thing She Does Is Magic," Loverboy's "Everybody's Working for the Weekend." My assertion that Loverboy was from Vancouver had been met with sidelong glances among my friends. My school friends in Canada had reacted the same way when I talked about stadiums being used as concentration camps in Chile and Bolivia. No matter where I went, my friends thought I was a liar. That was true, though not in the way they believed. But Lorena and Fátima also came from homes where secret things happened, and this recognition, never spoken, made us fiercely loyal to each other.

Tiny brick-and-cobblestone Coroico was one of a bunch of towns in Los Yungas, a stretch of forest that was basically a paradise on earth. Butterflies the size of your hand, flocks of bright yellow and red birds, bursts of fuchsia flowers, the jungle so green that it made your eyes hurt. To get there, our bus had had to navigate the Highway of Death, a dirt road so dangerous that one wrong move would send you careening into the abyss below. We'd been covered in sweat like the rest of the passengers when we arrived, having come from the freezing highland dawn to the tropics, the scenery changing from snow-covered purple peaks to banana-tree forests and coca-leaf plantations within the span of three hours.

The passengers had inexplicably started running as soon as they got off the bus, leaving their bundles on the roof. The four of us followed. After a few blocks, winding passageways had opened up to a valley that blinded us with its beauty: an explosion of green and cobalt blue. At the bottom of the valley was a dirt field with basketball hoops at either end. Everyone had gathered around the edges, craning to get a glimpse. Led by Lorena, we'd elbowed our way to the front.

A man carrying a machete stood at the centre of the field. Young and muscular, he wore a white undershirt that exposed his powerful arms. He'd walked in a circle, taking us all in, then raised his machete to the sky. My heart pounded in my eardrums. Clearly, basketball was not the name of this game. A sound broke the silence, and a furious bull came running out, raising a cloud of dust. Another man with a machete had appeared behind the bull. Just like that, he grabbed its tail and cut it off. As he spun it in the air like a lasso, blood gushed from the wound, turning the dust into crimson mud. In one swift move the first guy slit the bull's throat, then stuck his hand deep inside the animal's chest to pull out the heart. He'd held it high, like an offering, blood dripping down his arm. People gasped in admiration as the bull lay down to die. Once the trance was broken, the spectators had started talking and stretching, yawning and kissing friends on the cheek while they formed a line, old newspapers tucked under their arms, waiting for their ration of meat.

We'd trudged back up to the bus, pale as ghosts. Lorena nodded her head at the villagers sitting out on their stoops. A lot of them were black. It was confusing, because they were dressed like Aymara Indians and they spoke in Aymara, but Lorena explained that their ancestors had been slaves. I'd had no clue there had been African slaves in Bolivia.

I'd heard Lorena speak so much about the Coroico dwelling where her mother was born and raised that I was taken aback when I saw it. After the butchering of the bull, we'd retrieved our bags and walked down narrow passageways just off the main square, stopping at a makeshift door hanging off a frame and bordered on both sides by dense foliage. Lorena had knocked once, then let herself in, and we'd followed. A girl about eighteen was baking bread in a clay oven. The large cement floor was sheltered by a tin roof held up by four posts, but there were no walls. Way at the back I could see an outhouse. To our right there was a sink. In the open air stood a long wooden slab that served as a table, and some stumps and old chairs. A dozen barracks-style cots had been lined up in two rows under the tin roof, some bare, the rusty metal uninviting, others topped by burlap mattresses stuffed with hay. I heard a voice in my head say, "Not up to your middle-class standards?" It belonged to Bob, and it cut me to the quick.

The freckle-faced bread-baking girl came running with kisses and hugs. In her straw hat and dungarees, she was a dead ringer for Mary Ann from *Gilligan's Island*, her smile all dimples. She was Lorena's cousin Dunia, who'd lived here all her life. We dropped our bags on our cots and used the outhouse and the sink; an hour later we were eating fresh bread from the oven with slabs of cheese. Before falling into a deep siesta, I'd watched Dunia wash her hair in the sink, rebraid it, then pack her bag with books of poetry by Gabriela Mistral, Alfonsina Storni and Sor Juana Inés de la Cruz, reaching the door just as her boyfriend arrived. Over lunch, she'd explained that she was a poet who had great admiration for other women writers. She was also one of the village schoolteachers. She planned to finish writing her third book of poetry over the holidays.

By now, halfway through our visit, I was an old pro at washing in a basin carried out behind the outhouse. You had to pray that nobody was watching, because there was only the foliage to shield you. Anyway, the neighbours were too busy tending to their coca-leaf plants—watering them, trimming them, laying the leaves out to dry in the sun—to care about some city girls learning their way around personal hygiene without showers. For grooming, we made do with a minuscule hand mirror nailed to a tree. Ironing, a must in Bolivia, was done on the wood-slab table using a hundred-year-old iron filled with hot coals.

A torrential storm that night had us huddled three to a cot in our highland ponchos, the house full to bursting now with the arrival of Lorena's parents and younger siblings. We pulled all the cots to the centre of the room, which was lit by a couple of kerosene lamps. Two five-litre bottles of chicha were being passed around. I didn't drink any, faithful to the vow I'd made back in Canada. The rain pelting the tin roof sounded like ancient drumming in this magical place.

Dunia regaled us with the story of a mermaid she'd once seen. It took me a moment to realize she was referring to a woman who'd been able to swim; the roaring white rivers there were used only for laundry, which we did every few days, laying out our jeans to dry on the rocks. Lorena's father recreated the night he'd danced with the devil. I knew he was talking about the carnival devil dance. And Lorena's mother recounted the Second Coming of Christ.

It had happened in a remote village to the east, where she'd gone to visit relatives. She was still a teenager, innocent as could be.

A couple of her male cousins had taken her to hear Him speak in a secret jungle location. She'd noticed His followers first, men who'd walked with Him for many miles, with their long hair and beards, rifles slung over their shoulders. And then she'd seen Him, mane of black hair framing his pale face, tall, strong, eyes on fire as he spoke in a soft but powerful voice. Goosebumps had risen on her skin and her heart had sped up, for His presence was like a light.

"What did he say?" Liliana asked, eyes wide like saucers, jaw slack.

"He spoke of freedom and independence. He spoke of the brotherhood of this continent."

"Aaahh..." Liliana nodded, a little puzzled.

"They killed him later, because they said he was a terrorist, but I know he wasn't. No terrorist could have had that aura."

With that, she got up from the cot and poured some chicha right onto the earth, where it mixed with the pounding rain.

"For the pachamama, our Mother Earth. Amen."

Nobody said aloud that the man in the jungle had been Ché Guevara, who was killed in Bolivia in 1967. Lorena's mother had probably seen him when he'd first arrived in 1966.

Unexpectedly, we got to stay on in Coroico for an extra week. The storms had washed out the Highway of Death and torn down the telephone lines, cutting off Los Yungas from the outside world. I secretly wished it would stay that way forever. It was incredible to feel happy-go-lucky for a change, far away from the compartmentalized life of the underground. Mami and Bob would be beside themselves with worry, I knew, but now maybe they'd understand what it felt like for Ale and me to have our parents disappear for days or weeks on end, with no clue about when they were coming back, scared they might be dead or were being tortured somewhere.

My last night in Coroico was spent in the arms of Raymundo, a handsome private-school boy vacationing in Los Yungas with three buddies. It was Saint John the Baptist Day, and Coroico was overrun by La Paz teenagers. Free of parents and schoolwork, the teenagers rambled around town all day and met up at the plaza at night. Bonfires burned everywhere in the village, and the chicha flowed freely. Music played constantly, and the party went on all night. My friends and I had spent our last day at the river washing our clothes, drying them in the sun, breathing in the clean air that came with the passing of the storms. After the moon rose, we made our way to the plaza, for tonight was goodbye. Strolling arm in arm, we saw them after a couple of circuits: four La Paz boys in tight jeans. There was no time to waste.

As dawn broke, we girls set off for home, surrounded by revellers and small children. Lorena's parents and siblings were still sitting around the bonfire at their door. When they saw us, lips swollen, collars turned up to cover the hickeys, they elbowed each other and giggled.

Our bus left from the plaza an hour later. Our new beaux ran after us as the bus pulled away from the curb. I revealed Raymundo's gift to me for the journey: a Snickers bar, imported from the North, a rare, coveted gem in Bolivia. The four of us shared it, making it last all the way back to La Paz.

13

A COUPLE OF WEEKS after winter break, Mami made an announcement over lunch.

"Bob, Lalito and I are going away for a week," she said. "We're not at liberty to say where we're going, but Adriana's going to come stay with you girls. It'll be fun!"

A fellow teacher at the American English Centre, Adriana was my mother's friend. She was also, I'd gathered by now, a "helper." She hailed from Santa Cruz, and I'd heard Mami tell Bob one night there were whispers at work about Adriana having been held and tortured as a political prisoner during the Banzer dictatorship. I assumed that's why my mother had felt safe in approaching her. I loved Adriana, because she never talked down to us. I'd noticed she treated everyone with the same respect. The first night of her stay, we lingered at the table after Ale went to bed, chatting over tea.

"I did my master's in Boston, and I almost died of homesickness while I was there," Adriana confided. "I cannot imagine being expelled from my country and never being able to return. I cannot imagine being raised in exile."

We both had a little cry after that. Adriana had cut through the facade so swiftly that I was split open, guts hanging out, knowing that if I didn't gather up my insides and stuff them back in I'd cry so long and hard there'd be nothing left of me.

There were other helpers too, like Deirdre, who also worked at the American English Centre. I knew Deirdre was a helper because she'd drop by to "visit" sometimes when Mami and Bob were out. She'd pretend to be marking papers, but she'd twitch whenever there was a sound at the door. She'd agreed to be at home with us three kids at certain times, I figured, in case the shit hit the fan. I'd caught the tail end of a conversation once, when I'd walked into the kitchen while Deirdre and my mother were standing at the stove. Conversations at the stove happened a lot between foreigners in La Paz, what with having to boil water for half an hour every time you wanted a cup of tea. "You know I'm Chilean," my mother was saying. "You know I'm in exile. I'm sure you wonder what we're doing."

Deirdre's eyes had held fast to my mother's until the penny dropped, causing a little sound to come out of her mouth.

"If anything happens to us, will you look out for my kids?" my mother whispered. Her voice cracked.

"It would be an honour," Deirdre responded.

Deirdre was from Northern Ireland, she'd told Ale and me. She had brilliant blue eyes and round cheeks. She always wore jeans and woven Aymara tops. The last time she'd just happened to be in the neighbourhood (that was her standard line), she and I had drunk coca-leaf tea together, to ward off the altitude sickness that still hit her sometimes, and talked for hours about love and life. Mami had shown up a few hours later, covered in sweat, carrying a guitar case that obviously weighed a ton.

Then there was Mario, Bob's ex-boss at the computer company, who'd resigned to start a company of his own. Bob had not only taken over Mario's position after he left; he'd recruited him in the first place. Mario had a Harvard education, and he liked to tell stories of his boyhood visits to his grandfather in rural Bolivia. The old man had owned half a province, and thousands of peons would line up at the end of each month to receive their pay in food stamps from their master, who sat on a throne made of carved wood. Mario had vowed at that age to support the revolution, he said. I understood from the hushed conversations he had with Bob that he was involved in revolutionary activity in Bolivia and beyond, and that his connections in high places had allowed him to help us out when it came to certain paperwork. Mario had spent a lot of time around Sunnyland whenever the car was getting loaded for deliveries.

We didn't live at Sunnyland anymore, though. We'd moved right after I'd got back from Coroico to a high-rise on Arce Avenue, overlooking Plaza Santa Isabel, a few blocks down from Plaza Avaroa, but a million miles away from that life. Our secret political meetings were over, and we no longer saw Soledad and Rulo, with no explanation for that. The move had been sudden, and until we got there Ale and I had no idea where we were going. Afraid we were leaving Bolivia, I'd sobbed uncontrollably into my pillow. I loved the country now as if it were mine.

Adriana stayed with us for the whole week, as planned. Every morning we awoke bracing ourselves for the military marches we might hear on the radio or the tanks we might see rolling down Arce Avenue from our twelfth-floor window. Torrelio was so unpopular that Bolivia was on the brink of another coup or civil war. Repression was fierce, and the country faced an economic crisis because of corruption in the military.

One night as we lay in bed, Ale informed me that Torrelio was preparing to hand over power to General Guido Vildoso, his second-in-command, who had recently returned from training at the School of the Americas. "Vildoso will be in charge of returning the country to democracy," she whispered in the dark. "Before things get too out of hand. The Yanks have given an ultimatum, and no one wants a revolution on their hands. Not with what's happening in Argentina, what with the idiotic military there losing the Malvinas War to the British and letting the population get out of control. Soldiers are standing up against their superiors and calling the masses to the streets. Not to mention the terrorists gaining strength in Chile. Any chance of an uprising in Bolivia will be quelled when people get the chance to vote and feel as if they are involved in the future of their land." She swore me to secrecy before putting on her headphones and tuning in to "Tainted Love" on the Walkman we shared.

Ale spoke like this only since she'd started to date Luis García Meza Jr. Every morning she and I emerged from our high-rise to find Luis waiting to take her to school in the back seat of a bulletproof black car. I walked with Fátima, who lived in a high-rise just off Plaza Santa Isabel, and my new boyfriend Fermín, who waited religiously on the corner and always offered to carry my books. When Luis and Ale drove past us on the street, Luis always lowered his tinted window and shouted: "Hey, sister-in-law! Get in! I'll give you a ride! I'll even give your Commie boyfriend a ride!"

At which I'd shake my head, and the three of us would keep walking. At first recess Luis would tell me again how lucky Fermín was to be dating me, since that had saved him from getting on Luis's special list.

Fermín was one of the Altiplano Kings, the one in charge of running the record player and dropping the pamphlets. He and his friends loved to go on about Simón Bolívar and José Martí and Tupac Amaru and Tupac Katari, but all they did was intellectualize. They never referred to the blood and guts of the situation. I nodded and smiled, nodded and smiled. Fermín had been my boyfriend for the past month, and I was tired of being told how great the revolution was. I knew if he really was a revolutionary, he wouldn't walk around in his black beret with the red star quoting Ché Guevara for all to hear. He'd be underground, like Bob and Mami. Soledad and Rulo had explained that people like the Altiplano Kings were necessary for the revolution; unwittingly, they were spokespeople for the likes of us. But it still bothered me that the people who were risking their lives had given up the right to speak while mestizo, middle-class, artsy-fartsy people claimed the title of revolutionary for themselves.

Of course it wasn't so simple. The Altiplano Kings *were* taking a risk by speaking out and playing their music. And Fermín came from a lower-middle-class home. It showed in his only pair of school slacks, washed and ironed so many times they shone. He wore a silver airplane pin on his sweater and dreamed of being a pilot someday. He'd declared himself to me at the Montículo, the lovers' lane of La Paz. I'd said yes because he was nice and he loved me. But the truth was I was still in love with Ernesto.

Ale had started dating Luis for the fame it brought, but I knew it wouldn't last. She was still in love with Claudio, Ernesto's brother. They'd broken up and then made up a dozen times already. In the meantime, her dating situation was top secret, never to be shared with Mami, Bob, the helpers or the revolutionary cast of people we lodged. Like Kiko, the British twentysomething anarchist punk rocker who had stayed at the high-rise a few times, with his shaved head and steel-toed workboots. "I come from the north of England, from a line of coal miners," he explained to Ale and me. "Times are tough now there, very, very tough. England is next in line for neo-liberalism. But we're putting up a fight, and we've always admired the miners in Bolivia. The miners here have balls of steel, and they fight for their rights to the bitter end." Kiko carried his precious collection of punk tapes in a little black case, each tape carefully labelled. He'd learned how committed he was to being an internationalist revolutionary when Chilean resistance leaders in London ordered him to shave off his neon purple two-foot-high mohawk and take the studs out of his ears. In La Paz, he mixed in like a regular European tourist in his brown alpaca sweater, *The South American Handbook* peeking out of his dusty backpack. The last time he'd stayed with us he'd popped a tape out of his Walkman and given it to me. It was his favourite, *Sandinista!* by the Clash. I'd tucked it into my special hiding place for treasures, because I knew this could only mean goodbye. We wouldn't see him again.

On July 21, as Ale had forewarned, General Vildoso was handed power by Torrelio. It was a quiet changing of the guard, with no jets, no shooting, no curfews. Now it remained to be seen what Vildoso would actually do with the task at hand. It seemed obvious that the presidency would go to Hernán Siles Zuazo, who'd been elected twice already, the last time in 1980, without having the chance to govern. There was a tangible feeling of hope in the air.

One morning a few days later, Bob handed Ale and me an envelope, with the instructions that we were to take it to Plaza Murillo and pass it on to a woman who would ask us for directions to a charango stand on Linares Street. I was supposed to wear my rainbow suspenders, and Ale would be in her baby-blue Adidas sweat top. She was a preppy sort of girl, which was one reason she was so in love with Claudio. He dressed in matching alligator shirts and socks with a pastel frat sweater thrown over his shoulders. I preferred Ernesto's scuffed black motorcycle boots, faded baggy jeans and just-got-laid hair. I saw him sometimes at the bowling alley on Arce Avenue. Our eyes locked, but he never approached. The woman in Plaza Murillo would have dark glasses and a red scarf around her neck, Bob told us. Our evacuation plan, once the envelope was handed over, was to go for a leisurely stroll down El Prado, stop to watch the matinee showing of *The Cannonball Run* at the Monje Campero movie theatre, then go to a friend's house for tea before heading home. This was called losing the tail, in case you were being followed.

Ale and I arrived at Plaza Murillo on the M bus. Just as on every other Saturday at midday, the plaza was crazy with activity. Standing on the corner by the cathedral, we tried to look like a couple of normal teenagers hanging around talking. I remembered my acting teacher's constant exhortations for us to stop playing the emotion and start playing the action. Just as I'd come up with an action—I'd play the verb *convince*, as if I was trying to persuade Ale to do something—an older, elegant lady wearing large sunglasses and a red silk scarf stopped right in front of us. "Señoritas, would you mind telling me where Linares Street is? I've been told it's around here somewhere, but I can't seem to find it. Apparently the best charangos in the world are sold there."

Ale and I looked at each other, deer caught in the headlights. The woman waited, a little smile playing on her lips. "Over there," Ale pointed.

"Thank you," the woman said.

I gave her the envelope in an underhanded way, and before I knew it, Ale had disappeared into the crowd, walking toward the statue of Pedro Domingo Murillo, a martyr of Bolivian independence from Spain, at the centre of the plaza. The presidential palace stood directly in front of us. I dashed after her, eager to spend the coins Bob had given us. We were surrounded by ice cream vendors, laughing children and cholitas selling shelled and baked broad beans, but I purposefully avoided the shoeshine boys, for fear of seeing one of my old classmates.

"Carmen!"

I jumped out of my skin. What if it was my first Bolivian boyfriend, Eugenio Aguirre, shining shoes while he whistled, hair combed perfectly to the side? I couldn't have my two Bolivian lives collide, not now, not ever. Not here, when the woman with the envelope was just a block away. General Vildoso was probably sitting in the presidential palace at this very moment. I wouldn't have the nerve to look into the eyes of a boy who worked from dawn to dusk, biting into life with a hunger never quenched, and have him see what I'd turned into: a bourgeois, Northern Institute brat.

"Carmen!"

It was Fermín, only today he was wearing an orange tunic and a carnation necklace. Clapping his hands, he danced with his comrades.

"Hare Krishna, Hare Krishna, Krishna Krishna, Hare Hare."

One of the other Altiplano Kings was with him, beating on a drum that hung around his neck. They were with a dozen other people, chanting as they moved through the plaza.

"Fermín! I had no idea you were a Hare Krishna!" I said, trying to make it sound as if I'd just discovered he had an appealing hidden talent.

"Oh, yes. I believe there are many ways to counteract the age of Kali, and I've been meaning to talk to you about—"

"Oh, shit, where's Ale? Sorry, I have to go. I'll talk to you later."

"Wait! Let me introduce you to Swami—"

And with that I took off. Ale was waiting for me, laughing her guts out as she leaned against a post. As the opening credits for *The Cannonball Run* lit up the screen, I realized I was going to have to break up with Fermín. Dating a Ché wannabe who played banned music was foolhardy from a security perspective, I told myself. But I knew the real reason was that I would never be able to erase the profoundly unsexy image of Fermín practising his religion.

14

"**H**ELP!!!"

I choked out my plea a split second before I was dragged under the water again, my body forced into impossible contortions. Eyes open, I twirled like a whirling dervish in the deafening hum of the Atlantic. Yemaya, goddess of this ocean, had put me on spin cycle.

Sugar Loaf Mountain, the hill that was a trademark of this city, came into view. I reached for it, but a wave the size of a house slammed into my skull, and the undercurrent grabbed me by the feet. As my mouth opened to let out a scream, my lungs flooded with water. And then I let go. I'd have thought a life-or-death decision would take deliberation, but this was a split-second choice, made with conviction: I was dying, so I might as well go along for the ride. No longer mine to punish or please, my body was a sand-filled sack rolling around at the bottom of the world. My corpse would be washed up on shore, bloated and dull-eyed. As for my soul, it was already rocketing down a fibre-glass tunnel toward a very bright light.

Two minutes earlier, when I was still alive, it had been August in Rio de Janeiro. Copacabana Beach was peopled with only a few locals and the odd tourist on this off-season morning. The sun had burned quickly through the clouds as pineapple vendors wound their way around the towels. Ale and I had contemplated the towering waves for a while before deciding to dive under them to reach the calm waters on the other side. The red flag flapping furiously in the wind had been our invitation to rebel, not an order to obey. We'd grown up swimming in Chile and at Long Beach on Vancouver Island, so we were experienced. A few Brazilian waves? Please.

As I shot along the tunnel like a cannonball, I was surrounded by voices: Mami, Papi, Bob, Ale, my grandparents, my cousins, my friends and Lalito's little-boy words. I travelled right through the faces that materialized in front of me, as if they were made of smoke.

We'd been in Brazil for a week, but as usual this was not a mere vacation. Mami and Bob had disappeared for hours at a time while Ale and I entertained Lalito in our hotel room and ignored the constant knocking of a middle-aged room service waiter who'd grabbed my crotch the one and only time I'd answered the door. That morning Ale and I had woken up early and come down to the beach on our own. The last time I'd seen her, she was being pulled farther and farther away from me, her face seized by fright, her arms grasping at the air.

I had almost reached the bright light when white noise exploded in my eardrums.

Someone was rubbing sandpaper on my left cheek. A hand had grabbed my right ankle. The white noise—static—was replaced by animated voices. When my eyes cracked open, I saw wet sand covered with tiny pebbles and shells. Somebody flipped me onto my back, and a dozen faces peered down at me, yelling in Portuguese. Two muscular men stood among them, panting and dripping with water: my saviours. I realized suddenly that I was naked. Gasping and coughing, I covered my privates with one hand as I yanked at my bathing suit, which had rolled down around my ankles. It took me a good five minutes to pull it back on. To think it took more time to cover your exposed vagina than it did to reach the gates of Heaven, assuming that's what lay waiting at the end of the tunnel.

I ignored the chiding voices and looked around for Ale. Down the beach I could see another group of people huddled over a shaking body. Somehow Ale managed to get up and stumble toward me. We looked at each other without uttering a word and collapsed onto our towels. Within seconds, we'd passed out.

Two hours later, I woke on the beach from the deepest, deadest sleep I'd ever had. Ale and I walked in silence back to the hotel, just in time to join Mami, Bob and Lalito for brunch in the dining room.

"There you are! How was your swim?" my mother asked.

I shrugged. "Okay, I guess."

Ale and I peered at each other over our coconut shakes.

On our last night in Rio de Janeiro, Bob stayed with Lalito while Mami took Ale and me to the movies. Although my mother convinced the ticket seller that I was twenty-one, nothing—not even an attempted bribe—would get thirteen-year-old Ale into the restricted movie playing inside. After sending her back to the hotel in a cab, Mami and I settled into our seats to watch the film that was banned in Bolivia and the hottest black-market video in Chile right then: *Missing*. The Costa-Gavras docudrama about the coup in Chile showed the stadium, the involvement of the United States, the repression in the streets, with Hollywood stars playing the lead roles. We were shocked to see our lives depicted on the big screen. The members of the sold-out audience sobbed and gasped aloud at a story that had been so intimately ours until now. On the way home in the cab, Mami and I talked in broken voices, gripping each other's hands.

BOLIVIA WAS IN a state of joy when we returned from Brazil. General Vildoso had announced at last that Hernán Siles Zuazo would take over as president in October. The streets were jammed with people celebrating Bolivia's imminent return to democracy. Political debates raged on every street corner, now that people felt it was safe to speak out loud. There were countless rallies and parades: to honour the incoming president, to grieve the thousands who'd been killed during the years of darkness, to welcome the returning exiles. Add to that Bolivia's win in a major soccer championship in Europe, and these were the happiest times the country had seen in the last three decades. The day of the win, people ran out of their houses screaming to hug absolute strangers. Drivers pounded on their horns or abandoned their vehicles to jump in the streets. Fireworks, blaring music and outdoor dancing went on through the night. When Tahuichi, the junior soccer team, arrived in La Paz bearing the trophy, it was as if God himself had come down from the heavens.

I would be turning fifteen in October, and we planned to celebrate it with a simple gathering. My grandma Carmen arrived from Chile carrying an enormous cake. It had taken her two days to bake, she told us excitedly, and she'd been able to get it through Bolivian customs only by slipping a bottle of wine to the officer. Mami had sent her the money for the trip, so that she could fly to La Paz, and I ran to greet her as she walked toward us across the airport tarmac. In the taxi on the way home, she lamented my grandfather's lousy back, which had kept him from coming along.

Once we got home, we served Abuelita some coca-leaf tea. That was the traditional way to receive new arrivals in the highlands.

"So, where's the quinceañera party?" she asked with a twinkle in her eye.

"Right here," I answered.

"Here? In this tiny living room? No!" She tapped me gently on the forearm, smiling.

My mother took over. "We're not joking, Mamá. Carmencita's having an intimate gathering of her close friends. She's decided not to go all out."

"You mean to say you've brought me all the way here and you're not having a quinceañera party?" my grandmother demanded. She scanned our faces, hoping she'd misunderstood.

Parents spent years saving up for their daughters' quinceañeras. They were wedding-like ceremonies involving ball gowns, live bands, hundreds of guests, a five-course meal, speeches and a throne for the girl being honoured. Fifteen was seen as the threshold of womanhood, and quinceañeras had been celebrated for centuries in Latin America, long before the arrival of the Europeans.

"Ay, Mamá, it's so bourgeois—" my mother started to say.

My grandmother cut in, her eyes flashing. "Don't give me that. Carmencita is turning fifteen. That happens only once in a girl's life. I don't know when you became so bullheaded in your beliefs, Daughter, but being as arrogant as a cat is deadly. Throw your daughter a decent party, for God's sake."

"It's okay, Abuelita. I think quinceañeras are kind of dumb anyway," I lied. There was no way I was going to let Mami and Bob down by asking them to be a princess for a day.

"Mamita, don't cry," my mother implored. "Please. You're tired, and the altitude is exhausting. Why don't you go lie down?"

"I don't know what's happened to you, Daughter," my grandmother mumbled through her tears. "There are things in this life that are important. I was the first daughter of my generation, and my mother called me Carmen. You were the first daughter of your generation, and I called you Carmen. Carmencita is the first daughter of her generation. Our line of women must be celebrated. And when Alejandrita turns fifteen, we'll hold a quinceañera party for her, too."

"We'll have a good time anyway, Abuelita. We will," I reassured her.

The last time I'd seen my grandmother, she'd been trying to protect me from the Cousin's advances. Now here I was, a bad girl in a blue suede tube skirt and rust-coloured cowboy boots. Despite the tea, she spent most of her time asleep over the next few days, bedridden with altitude sickness. I wondered if her illness was really caused by grief, the bitter pain of having her grandchildren grow up in exile and reject the rituals she had so painstakingly devoted herself to. Not only had she spent days baking and decorating my cake, she'd built a special box that would transport it across the Andes intact, bribing her way in, all to be met with a girl she no longer knew.

The night of the party, Félix, Lorena, Liliana, Fátima, a dozen close male friends and I gathered to eat the dulce de leche cake Abuelita had brought "all the way from Tacna, Peru," as my mother made a point of saying. My grandmother didn't join us; she was still in bed. Mami had agreed to leave me alone with my friends, so she'd gone out with Lalito. I'd wanted my little brother to stay for the party. My friends adored him, and he loved being passed from arm to arm. But he'd become so traumatized by the constant disappearances of his parents that Mami had to take him everywhere she went. He clung to her like a little monkey, sitting on her lap even when she peed. When Bob was away, as he was now, Lalito walked from room to room calling "Papá? Papá?" and looking under the bed and in the closets.

Early in her visit, my grandmother had wondered out loud why Lalito was so scared he stuck close to his mother all day. Hands on her hips, she'd confronted Mami brow to brow. My mother shrugged, muttering something about my grandmother not understanding the choices the modern woman was forced to make.

"I know all about the modern woman," my grandmother had snapped. "Don't you forget it was I who forced you to finish your university degree after you had your girls. Don't you forget I moved to Santiago to look after your babies so you could continue your studies, get a degree and get a job so you would never have to depend on a man for money. Don't you speak to me about the modern woman. But do answer me this: at what point did the modern woman lose respect for motherhood and, above all, for the children of this world? Explain that to me."

My mother had gone into the bathroom, Lalito hanging off her skirt, and closed the door behind her.

I excused myself from the party and stepped out onto our tiny balcony. I contemplated my Plan B life, the one in which Ale and I had remained with our grandparents in Chile while my mother responded to the Return Plan. In that life, I'd be wearing a ball gown sewn by my grandmother on this day. I'd be dancing with my grandfather while a Chilean boy my age looked on. I breathed in the La Paz night and choked back tears.

Félix came to find me. "You're never going to believe who's here."

"Who?"

"Ernesto."

I'd swallowed my pride and invited Ernesto to the party a few weeks earlier, when our eyes locked as usual at the bowling alley. He hadn't committed to coming, but here he was now, his buddy Ramón by his side. Ramón strummed his ever-present guitar while Ernesto sang: "And the regretful dog is back . . ."

It was a silly number teenage boys sang to their girlfriends when they wanted to apologize for something. He performed it with mock conviction, clutching his heart and throwing himself on the floor à la James Brown. I laughed till I cried.

My grandmother left the next day, carrying the empty cake box. Her lonely, resigned figure made its way across the tarmac, and a steward helped her up the stairs. Just before she disappeared into the plane, she turned around and waved.

I FASTENED the silver chain around Ernesto's neck, with its dangling charm in the shape of the letter C. It was December 31, 1982, and we were in the emergency stairwell of the Plaza Hotel where my family and I were staying on our last night in Bolivia. It was three in the morning. I kissed the love of my Bolivian life for the first time in almost a year. In two hours I'd be leaving La Paz behind.

The goodbyes had been going on for a month. The school year had ended a couple of weeks earlier, and then Christmas had come and gone in a flurry of activity. I carried a stone of pain in the bottom of my heart, mixed with fear at what we would encounter next. As usual, Ale and I didn't know exactly where we were going, though we'd been instructed to tell people we were moving to Bahía Blanca, a navy port on the Atlantic south of Buenos Aires. Mami and Bob had put it like this, a month after we'd returned from Rio de Janeiro.

"We have to move away from Bolivia. We can go to either Brazil or Argentina. You girls decide."

Ale and I had received the news in silence. I'd looked out the window at La Paz shining in the night.

"When are we leaving?" Ale asked.

"At the end of the school year."

"Are we coming back?"

"No."

That *no* was like a machete. There was nothing more to say.

"Well, you two let us know as soon as possible which country you prefer."

All I knew about Argentina was the terrible war with England that the country had been waging. It was talked about incessantly in Bolivia, where solidarity rallies were organized and communiqués were read over the radio offering unconditional support to our Argentinian brothers and sisters. During recess, the Altiplano Kings had taken to playing Mercedes Sosa, the Argentinian superstar, and making pronouncements against the imperial British enemy. A friend of my mother's, an Argentinian with British ancestry and hence an English name, had been turned back at the border, even though she'd been born in Argentina, as had her parents. At our house, she'd repeated the border guard's words: "As a British subject you are an enemy of Argentina, Señora. You are not allowed in." She'd boarded the train back to La Paz, sitting in a state of shock for the twenty-four-hour ride, her suitcase of gifts intact at her side.

Argentinians were unbearable. That's the other thing I'd heard since I was a child. Absolutely insufferable, because they considered themselves better than other Latin Americans. Actually, they didn't believe they were Latinos at all. No amount of arguing would change their minds: you could pull out maps, refer to history, ask a self-proclaimed "European" Argentinian if he'd ever even been to Europe, and still there was no budging them. A favourite pastime at Latin American parties was exchanging Argentinian jokes. Like: "When an Argentinian wants to commit suicide, he hangs himself by his ego."

The few Argentinians I'd met were loud braggarts who never let you get in a word edgewise. So this was all I knew: the Malvinas War, Argentina's horrific dictatorship, the unbearable citizens of Argentina. No images of the country's landscape came to mind. We'd been to Brazil, but Ale and I saw our near-drowning there as a bad omen. Plus, we didn't speak a word of Portuguese. The prospect of learning a new tongue again on top of everything else was too much to bear. Within two days we'd announced that we might as well move to Argentina.

That night in the stairwell, I promised Ernesto I'd write to him as soon as we arrived in our new city. If he waited till I was eighteen— only three more years—I'd come back to Bolivia and never leave again. He confided in a low voice that his family was also leaving very soon. "Now that Siles is in power, people want to burn us at the stake. My father's high up in the military, he's dedicated his life to the service, he's studied good and hard at the School of the Americas, and there are certain people who would have him shot by firing squad. We will leave quietly, in the night. I don't know where we're going. But I will give you a post office box here in La Paz. Even if it takes months for your letter to reach me, I will write you back."

"Do you agree with what your father has done?"

"No. But he is my father, and I love him."

Bob poked his head into the stairwell. "It's five in the morning, Carmencita. Time to go."

Ernesto and I rode together in the elevator down to the lobby. The doors opened, he stepped out, and he walked through the front entrance of the building just as the elevator doors closed. He never looked back.

The previous morning, Ale and I had gotten up before dawn and tiptoed our way to the living room. Opening the curtains just a touch, we'd had a full view of Arce Avenue. Sure enough, the García Meza convoy appeared. Luis had confided to Ale that his father was fleeing the country to avoid being arrested and charged with corruption and crimes against humanity. They were flying to Buenos Aires, where the Argentinian dictator, Reynaldo Bignone, would welcome them with open arms. The three-car convoy drove quietly up Arce Avenue, the García Meza family in the centre bulletproof vehicle. Headlights turned off, they'd headed toward the airport to make their getaway before the sun came up. A jet awaited them at the top of the city.

As our own taxi climbed toward the airport, I bid farewell to La Paz, the crater city that touched the sky. La Paz, "Peace," was now a piece of me, a place so vibrant I knew I'd never experience anything like it again.

The previous afternoon, Lorena, Liliana, Fátima and I had dressed up in our pleated skirts and lace-collared blouses. We'd taken the bus to Plaza Murillo, where we planned to stroll together one last time through our old haunts. I surprised them when I whistled at the first hot guy who walked by.

"Hey Papacito, has anyone ever told you you're good enough to eat?" I yelled.

As the guy's jaw dropped to the ground, my girlfriends ran and hid behind a kiosk, legs crossed to stop them from peeing in their panty-hose as they giggled.

"Carmen! What are you doing? We belong to respectable society!" Fátima scolded.

"I'm doing what any feminist worth her weight would do: turning the tables so these sexist fucking pigs can know what it feels like to be objectified in the middle of the street, when you're just trying to get on with your day."

"Promise you won't do it again!" Liliana pleaded, slapping me on the arm.

"Okay."

Two beautiful guys were walking toward us. As they opened their mouths to say something, I beat them to it: "Hey, sweet cheeks, I'd like to dip you in chocolate and lick it all off!"

"Run!" Lorena ordered, and we ran like crazy to El Prado, my friends electrified by my shockingly bad behaviour.

Four more guys were about to pass us, already puckering their lips for the loud kissing sounds they planned to make.

"Mmmm. Hey, you hot things! There's four of us and four of you. How about us girls teach you all there is to know about the art of sucking?"

We'd raced down El Prado, doubled over with laughter, and jumped on a bus as it pulled away, leaving behind the four boys who'd started chasing us.

The Indian porters at the airport tripped over themselves to help us, their gaze lowered to the ground. It was a crisp morning, the quiet a perfect soundtrack for the vastness of the Andean highlands.

Bob pulled out our passports at the Lloyd Aéreo Boliviano counter. His was Canadian. Mami's, Ale's, Lalito's and mine were Bolivian. For the last few months, our red-tape guy had made a full-time job of standing in line at government buildings to get our papers in order. Anyone who had the money hired somebody like this. The red-tape guy would hand the clerk a wad of cash; the clerk would pocket it and then hand over the documents, on which the red-tape guy forged your signature. Documents were handed back and forth in this way until they were complete.

"Mr. Bob Everton. Your presence is required at the front of the plane."

The announcement came just as we were about to taxi down the runway. I reminded myself that death wasn't so bad. It was just a tunnel, after all, with the drone of voices and the light. If I hadn't been meant to die a drowning death on Copacabana Beach, then maybe I was meant to be tortured to death in the city that kissed the sky. As long as they let Lalito and Ale go, Mami, Bob and I could pay for our sins.

After an animated conversation with the flight attendant, Bob rejoined us, carrying a little box. He handed it to me. "This is from Félix. He stopped the plane so you could have it."

Inside the box was a porcelain poodle, parts of its face chipped away. At the bottom lay a letter.

"My dearest friend and sister Carmen: I'm so sorry I couldn't make it to the hotel last night to say goodbye. I found a way to get here, but I was too late for the airport, too. I adore you and will never forget you. Always keep a place in your heart for my country of Bolivia, the shining jewel of South America. This poodle is from my house. I hope my aunt won't miss it too much. Keep it always as a memento of me. Your friend and brother forever, Félix."

And with that, we were on our way.

15

TANGO PLAYED IN the taxi as we sat in a Buenos Aires traffic jam. Our driver hadn't shut up from the moment we'd got in his car at the airport. So far, his monologue had covered the Malvinas War, the last decade of dictatorships in Argentina, the economic crisis and, most importantly, how Boca Juniors would fare in the upcoming preliminary rounds for the Libertadores Cup. He'd yell "Go wash the dishes, little missy!" at the occasional female driver, methodically wiping a checkered handkerchief across his brow. It was hot and humid as hell, and I tried to digest this other planet we'd landed on. Who knew that the capitals of two neighbouring countries could be so different? First there were the women. Uniformly bottle-blonde, with towering frames, they paraded along the narrow sidewalks in stilettos and tube dresses. They were the whitest Latinas I'd ever seen. Then there were the men. Curly-haired and tall, light eyes contrasting with their olive skin, they glided along in perfectly pressed slacks that hung just so. It was a shock after the Bolivians, who were all five foot two with size four feet.

All of a sudden a torrential downpour of paper began. Not confetti: actual sheets of paper. By the thousands. Our driver pounded on his horn, stuck half his body out the window and shouted up to the gods: "Happy New Year, motherfuckers! Goodbye to 1982, the worst year ever! And by the way, you fucking Brits, the Malvinas are Argentinian!"

The honking of taxis and buses rebounded off the hundreds of buildings in the downtown core. As the storm of paper continued, I leaned out to see where it was coming from: office workers were throwing the pages out the windows. It was midday on December 31, work was over, and the new year had to be greeted with a clean slate. Big-band tango continued to blast from the car radio. The bandoneón, a kind of accordion, punctuated the voice of the tango diva Libertad Lamarque singing "Today you will enter my past," as we inched our way through the centre of the second-biggest city in South America.

The four of us fell into a dead sleep at the Hotel Rochester. We didn't wake up until the sun had set, and by then Buenos Aires was humming with the biggest celebration of the year. We found a table at the nearby Potato Palace. It seemed to be a typical restaurant around these parts, with a whole cow splayed over an open fire in its front window. In a room the size of a basketball court, people chewed on steaks so huge they hung off the plates. One wall was a mirror. Mirrors were everywhere in Buenos Aires, and everyone stopped to primp with no shame whatsoever. The yelling, laughing and joking of the families who surrounded us, ranging in age from newborns to great-grandparents, contrasted so sharply with the dead silence at our table that we had the waiters worried. Standing by in their bow ties, they'd dive every time the breadbasket needed refilling. We stared down at our plates, each lost in our own world of uncertainty and fear. I had no idea where the next stop was or how much trouble we were in. But Mami and Bob were worn out, that was obvious, and this time there was no pretending we were on some exciting adventure together.

We got back to our hotel at precisely midnight. The bellboys in the lobby sprayed champagne in our faces. Up in our room, Ale and I flipped on the TV, to be greeted by the sight of García Meza Sr. giving a news conference at the airport in Buenos Aires. Flanked by bodyguards and what appeared to be Argentinian secret police, he was thanking the local authorities for providing him with asylum. The camera moved from his face to a view underneath the table, revealing a revolver strapped to his right shin.

"Sweet father-in-law," I whispered.

Ale punched me in the ribs.

TWO WEEKS LATER, my new friend Griselda and I were sauntering down Mitre Street, the main thoroughfare in Bariloche. A ski resort in the Andes, frequented by jet-setters from around the globe, Bariloche was a day's trip from the Chilean border. We'd arrived here after spending a week in Buenos Aires, two days in Bahía Blanca at the home of an Argentinian doctor and his wife, and one night at a fancy hotel in the desert city of Neuquén. Bob had promised Ale and me we were headed to a beautiful place with snow-capped mountains, pine trees and endless forests, trying to chip away at our impenetrable teenage rage. We refused to be swayed. All I knew was this: I would never forgive them for plucking me away from Bolivia.

Griselda, fifteen like me, was our landlords' niece, visiting from Chile. Our landlords were a working-class family of German descent who had built four little row houses on their plot of land. Bob had rented the main house, on the edge of the plot, for us. The landlords lived with their two small daughters in one of the row houses. The father's mother, Griselda's grandmother, lived right next door. The other two houses were rented to a trucker and his wife, and a low-ranking military man.

We'd arrived in Bariloche on a grey January day, the town so dead the pit of my stomach had frozen over. As our taxi passed through an area of ramshackle dwellings on dirt roads, pulling up at a wooden gate held closed by a rope, I realized we'd left behind not only a country but a social class. There was nothing quaint or bohemian about our new home. The massive wood stove in the kitchen warned us that the winters were long and harsh. Stray cats screeched on the roof, and a layer of dust covered everything. Lalito ran around the place, excited that we were putting down roots somewhere.

Griselda was beautiful in a character-actress kind of way. The harsh Patagonian wind whipped her gold locks away from her face as we walked, her big blue eyes squinting in the midday sun. She'd gotten here two days after we had, and without her I would have died. We took a daily stroll down Mitre, window-shopped and then walked all the way back home for yerba maté, a special digestive tea drunk by the litre in Argentina, and butter biscuits made by her grandmother. Griselda came from a family of fishermen. Her class was evident from her one pair of jeans (flared, when drainpipe had been in for years now) and her only shirt (paisley polyester, when the fashion was satin with shoulder pads). It never occurred to her to look longingly inside the dozens of cafés, bistros and lounges offering steaming cups of hot chocolate and copper pots of cheese fondue. She'd never eaten out. She was waiting for the perfect movie to come to the town's movie theatre; she had enough money for one matinee.

I'd taken on the role of housekeeper in our new home. No one else seemed to notice that after years of having Nati clean up after us, we'd turned into a bunch of lazy pigs. Managing the house took a few hours of my day, what with all the sweeping, mopping, waxing, dusting, polishing and disinfecting. Bob suggested that Ale and I join the Andean Club, a hiking group, but something odd had happened to me since our arrival: I was afraid to meet people. The thought of putting myself out there was so frightening I'd end up hyperventilating on my bed, covered in cold sweat. I was ashamed to be mestiza in a country full of whites. But mostly I was tired of lying, of keeping up the facade, of living in fear that at any moment it could all come crashing down. So instead I kept the house sparkling and smelling of Pine-Sol. Bob started calling me the White Knight.

Griselda seemed safe. She accepted everything I told her—that I'd been born in Bolivia but raised mostly in Canada, and that we were here on business. Why would it cross her mind that was a pack of lies?

She came from Valdivia, the city where my family had been living when the coup happened, situated just across the mountains, and she talked in the delicious working-class Chilean accent I hadn't heard in so long, referring often to places I used to know: the Calle Calle River, the seafood market, the Spanish fort at Niebla Point. While I played the fool, she'd explain about the delicacies the sea offered: seaweed and kelp, urchin and abalone, salmon and sea bass. I reacted with the requisite retching when she described crudos (raw beef patties seasoned with onion, cilantro and lemon, a specialty introduced by the Germans in the south of Chile), never letting on they had been one of my favourite treats as a child. Griselda was Chilean to the core. Though she didn't know it, it was precisely her Chileanness that drew me to her. There was nothing to explain; all the social signals were understood.

Griselda believed, along with her family, that Pinochet was the best thing that had ever happened to Chile. They were typical working-class supporters of the dictatorship, people who backed him out of ignorance, not because it was in their interests. She was also a staunch supporter of another notorious dictator.

"Hitler was a very intelligent man. The thing about him is that he's misunderstood. People who hate Hitler haven't actually read his writings. Do you want to read him?"

We were crossing the lawn of the cathedral. It overlooked enormous Lake Nahuel Huapi, where the waves were crashing today.

"Who?"

"Hitler."

"Oh. Yeah. Sure."

"I'll bring over the wedding edition of *Mein Kampf* the next time I come to see my oma. It's an original given to a family friend when he got married back in Düsseldorf. Or maybe you can come visit me sometime in Valdivia. I can show you Chile."

"Sure."

"Chile puts a spell on people. That's why so many Germans went there and never left. It's a special place. I've been here only three weeks, and I have only one week to go, but I'm already dying of homesickness. You know, if it wasn't for you, friend of my soul, I would have left early."

"I feel the same way about you. But of course I have nowhere to return to."

"You can come home with me. There's still a month left before school starts. That's it! Come with me next week. We'll have so much fun!"

"I don't think my parents would let me."

"Let's ask them."

She entwined her arm with mine, and together we marched home, savouring the intoxicating aroma every time we passed one of the chocolate factories Bariloche was famous for.

JACQUES AND MARCIA were the local resistance contacts. He was French, she was Brazilian. They had a baby called Micaela, and Ale and I fought over who would get to hold her. Bombing around town in a four-by-four, they fit in perfectly with the many bohemian couples in Bariloche who lived in log cabins, strummed guitars by the fire at night and spent their weekends camping and hiking. Jacques was hilarious, and I enjoyed his spot-on impersonations of Shirley Temple singing "On the Good Ship Lollipop" and Tiny Tim's "Tiptoe through the Tulips."

Marcia would lend Ale and me books to read—Isabel Allende's *The House of the Spirits*, Eduardo Galeano's *Open Veins of Latin America*—and then we'd go over to her place, on the top floor of a typical downtown Bariloche house, to discuss them. Marcia's informal style contrasted so sharply with that of Rulo and Soledad that I didn't think Ale realized these were political meetings. Sometimes Marcia would take us to a movie. *Pixote*, about the street boys of Brazil, left all three of us a wreck.

"That movie is about survival," Marcia said. "Isn't it incredible that millions and millions of the world's children don't get to live life, but simply go through each day hoping to survive?" And with that, she pulled the car over to the side of the road, broke down and cried. "Nothing is sacred, for fuck's sake, nothing is sacred."

Ale rubbed Marcia's back until she calmed down.

"Girls, always know this: it's your human right to be happy."

I lay in bed that night in the room I shared with Ale, staring at the ceiling. I'd always thought revolutionaries didn't cry. At least not when they were in the role of revolutionary. And I'd never heard a revolutionary use the word *sacred*. That was a word reserved for religious fanatics and hippie dumbbells. But she'd used it to mean that children were sacred. That children shouldn't have to think about certain things, like survival. Did that mean children shouldn't have to think about revolutions, or safe houses, or being tortured to death, I wondered? Then there'd been her final statement: it was our human right to be happy. I'd known it was our human right to have food, health, shelter and education, but happiness? What would that be for someone like me? I thought back to those rainy nights in Vancouver when my uncle Boris and all us kids would end our meetings by gorging on Big Macs and milkshakes. And then, for the first time since we'd left Bolivia, I cried. Not just for Pixote and all the street children of the world, but for Ale and me. And I wondered, was it my human right to cry for us?

WE SPENT MUCH of that summer camping, setting up base at the bottom of a mountain while Jacques and Bob disappeared into the dense foliage for days at a time. Mami and Marcia, Micaela, Ale, Lalito and I held down the fort. Ale and I would be bored to tears by the end of these trips. The water in the mountains was too cold to swim in, so there wasn't much to do. The return of the men would be met with intense relief by Marcia and my mother, and once darkness set in, the four adults would huddle around the fire and speak in muted voices about maps, compasses, weather conditions, landmarks, rivers and streams.

That first night of the broken dam had led to many more like it. My eyes welled up constantly, but I'd hold back the flood of tears until I was safely locked in the bathroom or until night fell and I could let it rip in our bedroom till I was hollow, while Ale slept like a log. Griselda had gone back to Chile almost a month earlier.

Our food was rationed, since Bob had paid a year's rent on our house up front, leaving us cash-strapped. Neither he nor Mami had found work yet, but inflation was high, and Bariloche was outrageously expensive. Bob had always had temper tantrums, but now they were constant, explosive and unpredictable. Sitting at the kitchen table, he would fume so hard you could almost see his nostrils steaming. Often the eruption would fail to materialize, but the possibility had our forks trembling in our hands. When Ale and I were sullen, which was often, he'd jeer: "What's the matter? You poor little rich girls can't get used to living on the wrong side of the tracks? Your bourgeois tastes can't fathom this dirt road with these ignorant German fascists?"

He'd shake his head in disgust, darting accusatory glances at my mother. These days, she sat silent during his outbursts, lost in her own world. Lalito would play extra cute to diffuse the tension.

"Do you think Mami's in love with Bob?" Ale asked me one night in our room.

"I guess so. Why else would she put up with him?"

"Well, if I ever get married I won't call that love."

"Mami says we have to understand that Bob is depressed. That he's in a crisis. That he's tired and broken, and we have to understand."

"She should just leave him," Ale said.

"She'll never do that. They're revolutionaries together, running a safe house."

"Yeah, right. Here's a revolutionary thought: provide for your children and pay attention to them."

"Maybe Bob will fall off the side of the mountain on one of his treks and split his head open and die," I offered.

"Maybe."

One late summer afternoon I lay on the floor in the living room, exhausted after another bout of sobbing. Ale was playing in the yard with Lalito, and Mami and Bob were holed up in their bedroom at the back of the house. Someone knocked on the door. Three knocks, then a pause, three knocks, then a pause. I hauled myself up and staggered to the door.

Trinidad stood there with her beaten-up white Samsonite in her faded black jeans.

"Carmencita. How you've grown!"

I shook out my legs, unable to speak.

She smiled. "Are your parents here? I arrived a little earlier than expected."

I finally found my voice. "Oh, my God." We hugged each other. "Come in. Come in. I always wondered—"

"If I was still alive? I am, little comrade, I am. You really are a young woman now. But look at you. You're thinner than a ghost. Don't your parents feed you?"

It was true. My bones protruded all over the place. I ate only once or twice a day, and tiny portions at that. Sometimes I wouldn't eat at all and would just subsist on tea.

Trinidad slipped off her corduroy blazer and hung it on the back of a kitchen chair. As soon as she put out the cigarette she'd been smoking, I picked the ashtray up, dumped the butt in the garbage, washed out the ashtray, dried it and put it back on the table. Our house sparkled. Nothing was out of place. And it was all thanks to me. I took a teacup down from the cupboard—thank God I'd bleached them the day before—and put on the kettle, which I'd Ajaxed to a shine that morning.

"I'll go get Mami," I said.

The following day an American woman named Mitzi showed up. She and Trinidad seemed close, and for the next week the two of them slept on our living room floor. The meetings would go on for hours, while Ale looked after Lalito and I disinfected the bathroom and kitchen. One thing was clear: this Mitzi was Mami and Bob's superior. They seemed to be undergoing some kind of exam, because every time the living room door opened, I'd hear them being drilled.

"So: show me again where this trail begins, how wide it is and how long it would take fifteen people to reach the border," Mitzi would say in her Brooklyn accent.

"Well, as far as I can tell, the trail starts here—"

"Not good enough, comrade. I want *exact* locations."

"Okay, well, the trail starts here. You drive to Villa La Angostura, take a boat across this stretch of lake, get off right here, and then hike to the edge of this river. This is a good place to set up base camp. From there you cross the river and work your way up through the bush. After about five hours you will find the trail, which is really a sliver used by cattle smugglers."

"Good, good, comrade. Now here's the key question: is it possible to navigate this in the winter?"

"In the winter?"

"Yes, comrade, I've asked you to prepare these trails for winter crossing. Is it possible?"

"Well, it will be twenty degrees below zero. There will be two to three metres of snow."

"And that's when the enemy will least expect us to be crossing."

"Right."

"Good. We have to figure it out."

Sometimes Socorro, the trucker's wife from two doors down, would come over and ask to use our phone. Phones were a most coveted possession in Argentina, so hard to come by that even doctors spent years on a waiting list to get one. Miraculously, our house had one, and the neighbours would leave behind a peso after using it, the cost of a local call. Socorro was the resident gossip, and the phone was the perfect excuse to get past our door. We were the new family on the block, and a mysterious bunch at that. Socorro liked to look around our place, then report on what she'd seen at the corner store. Now that Mitzi and Trinidad were here, she needed to get an update. Whenever she knocked at the door, I'd let the adults know, and they'd quickly hide their maps and documents before Socorro came into the living room to dial the number.

"Hello? Hello? Yes, this is Socorro, Pancho's woman. Fine. Life treats me well. As for Pancho, he's working on his truck so he can go pick up a load of mussels in Chile. Yes, always on his back that one, all

I see is his feet, and at the end of the day the hands and face black from grease. Ayayay. Anyway, I better go now."

As she hung up, she'd nod at Mitzi, Trinidad, Bob and Mami, taking note that Mitzi was a Yank (*gringo* here meant Italian; North Americans were Yanks). Everyone exchanged niceties to make it all look natural.

One afternoon Socorro nonchalantly invited me over for tea, and from that moment on we had tea every day, demolishing a baguette and a whole block of cheese as we gossiped about the military man who lived alone next door—apparently he had the hots for our landlords' eldest daughter, who was attending university in La Plata—and about the landlords themselves: poor as church mice, but rich in land, since the man's brother owned prime property right on the lake out by Villa La Angostura, where he made his living conducting boat tours to the Arrayanes Forest. I was an agoraphobic fifteen-year-old skeleton with obsessive-compulsive disorder, and she was a stout, working-class housewife in her late forties. Once we'd found each other, we didn't let go.

16

I
T WAS FIRST RECESS, and my classmates were yelling at the sons
of the military from atop their wooden desks.

"*Where are they?!*"

The demand was punctuated by three stomps of their feet.

"*Where are they?!*"

Three more stomps. My classmates' blue school smocks created
the illusion of a choppy sea. Half of them were taking part in the
impromptu protest; the other half watched or looked out the window.
The military men's sons, three of them, leaned against the blackboard,
facing the onslaught. They lived on the military base on the edge of
town, which meant they came from low-ranking families. These boys
were mestizo, poor and destined to become military men themselves.
Irma Weiss was the first to jump down from her desk and walk with
menace toward the shrimpy boy in the middle. Six feet tall, all knees
and elbows, with eyes that bore down into his upturned gaze. "You
military pig. You've committed genocide in this country for the last
seven years, and you will pay, you son of a thousand whores. *You will
pay.*" Irma lived in a mansion overlooking the city. Her parents owned
a five-star chalet right on Cathedral Hill, which boasted the best ski
slopes in the country.

"Where are the thirty thousand disappeared? I'm sure your daddy knows, you little piece of shit." She spit in the shrimp's face.

"*Everybody off their desks! Now!*" The men in charge of monitoring the school hallways had raided our classroom. These warders had the authority to issue warnings, add your name to their list of bad kids and suspend or expel you if they caught you vandalizing school property.

"All of you troublemakers form a line. I'll take down your names, and you'll go to the principal's office to explain yourselves. But even if Madame Principal decides to go easy on you, rest assured: your names will remain in my book."

The twenty protesters formed a line, Irma Weiss standing defiant at the front.

"Hey, German! The thirty thousand disappeared you're so worried about? They're sunbathing in the Caribbean," the shrimp yelled, now that he had some backup.

"Aren't you going to take down their names, too?" Irma demanded of the warders.

"Mind your own business, Señorita Weiss. Those three have done nothing wrong."

"Right. Other than defend the dirty work of their genocidal fathers, who run the torture chambers."

"If it wasn't for their fathers, this country would have been taken over by Communist terrorists. You should be on your knees thanking them for defending the motherland."

I sat stock still at my desk in the back of the classroom, fingers braided, eyes focussed on a Charly García verse etched on my desk: "Don't bomb Buenos Aires, we cannot defend ourselves. The kids in my neighbourhood are hiding in the sewers, spying the sky... Today I'm afraid of a blond, tomorrow I don't know who I'll fear." That was one good thing about the Malvinas War: the ban on all things English had meant an explosion of national rock, with Charly García, one of Argentina's biggest rock stars, at the forefront. The conflict had also brought people into the streets en masse to demand freedom from the dictatorship that had led them into war in the first place. The fear that had gripped the country for years was still there, but people had had enough, and they were willing to speak out, despite the danger. It was halfway through the school year, 1983, and the shit was hitting the fan. Emotions ran so high that during the frequent protests in the classroom half the class would be crying with rage or sadness.

Protests were happening daily all over the country. Elections had been called for December, and my classroom, like the rest of Argentina, was a powder keg just waiting for a match to be thrown its way. The vast majority of Argentinians went to public school. So here at the National School, my grade ten class consisted of working-class kids who lived on the edge of the shantytowns, super-rich kids like Irma Weiss and everything in between. None of the twenty students staging the protests were poor. The poor kids knew too much was at stake for them to exercise this imminent freedom of speech they heard so much about. And despite their professed interest in democracy, Irma and the other protesters shunned the poor kids like the plague.

Being a flawless English speaker with a Canadian father made me royalty among the rich and middle-class kids. They considered my family's choice of dwelling a typical "eccentric North American on a Third World adventure" thing. These were the kids I hung out with, which made perfect sense for our cover. I was secretly relieved that living on the wrong side of the tracks, close to the Chileans, was so easily excused. As in Bolivia, the worst thing you could be here was Chilean, but for very different reasons. Being Chilean meant you lived with the poorest of the poor, the brownest of the brown, the dirtiest of the dirty. Chileans were considered even lower on the social scale than Gypsies, another hated group. Most of the Indians in southern Argentina had been massacred by the army in the nineteenth century, and the remaining few lived on reserves scattered around Patagonia. That left the Chileans, who were in Argentina illegally, crossing the Andes by the thousands after the coup, as the country's source of cheap labour. Those who lived in the shantytowns were actually lucky; many lived under the rosehip bushes that lined the road leading from downtown Bariloche to Cathedral Hill.

The maids in Argentina were Chilean, as were the construction workers and janitors. Chileans were reviled for "taking all our work," "using our hospitals" and "sending their kids to our schools," though no Chileans were at the National School, the only public coed school in the city. The majority of Chileans who'd fled here were Mapuche Indian. Under Allende, agrarian reform had begun the process of giving much of the land back to the Mapuches. Fighting under the banner of the Revolutionary Peasant Movement, many of them had resisted the coup for days, keeping the military at bay with a few arms. The resistance had joined them, and an internationalist referred to as the Swede (a different Swede from the one who'd stayed with us in La Paz) had been on the front lines. The Mapuches, indigenous to the land on both sides of the Andes, had retreated to the Argentinian side of Patagonia and ended up living along the border in shantytowns like the one in Bariloche. The Swede had made it out alive but been captured by the Argentinian military three years later. He'd been disappeared ever since.

It was winter by now, and Bariloche was in a deep freeze. My posse consisted of the privileged girls from my class. We spent our afternoons at the Old Munich Café drinking coffee and philosophizing, the most popular pastime in Argentina. My best friend was Dalia, whose father was a physics professor and researcher at the Atomic Centre, a nuclear research centre several miles down the road that wound its way along the lake. Beaten regularly by her mother while her ineffectual father buried his nose in his books, Dalia had the eyes of a woman who'd lived many tough years, not the gaze of a German-Italian teenager living in an immaculate middle-class cottage. She didn't know my real story, of course, but as a keeper of secrets herself, she never asked. She'd show up at school wearing scarves to cover the bruises left by her mother's attempts at strangling her. Heavy makeup took care of the black eyes and scratches, and a fierce dedication to schoolwork gave her a reason to live. We spent many afternoons on top of the hill across from her house, planning our future lives in Buenos Aires, where we'd share a studio apartment and go to medical school.

My mother was now the English teacher at the Atomic Centre. The post became available shortly after the school year began, just in time to save us from real hunger. Teachers' pay was only slightly above that of blue-collar workers, but at least our rent was taken care of and there was no middle-class facade to maintain. At the Atomic Centre Mami met Miguel and Cristian, researchers who'd moved here from Rosario with their young families in tow. Both these men, along with their wives, Lidia and Felicia, were recruited as helpers. Felicia's best friend, Judith, a pediatrician, was a Polish Jew whose family had barely survived the Second World War. She became a helper too.

Now Bob and Mami had friends, people they could speak freely with. Compartmentalization had stopped us from seeing Jacques and Marcia other than for resistance matters. With the Rosarinos, there were late-night dinners during which the end of the Argentinian dictatorship was discussed, the continued success of the Sandinistas celebrated, the resistance to Pinochet toasted. Mercedes Sosa singing Violeta Parra provided the soundtrack. I deduced that Miguel had started to accompany Bob on his treks through the Andes.

Bob's rages still kept our household walking on eggshells. I wangled sleepovers at Dalia's, and Ale spent every weekend she could at her best friend Vero's. There was no job on the horizon for Bob, though he gave private English lessons a couple of times a week. Stuck at home in the bitter cold, he spent his days studying documents as the snow fell outside, simmering and chewing over whatever it was that made him so mad. Whenever there was a window of calm, I seized the opportunity, but our talks about life made me sadder than ever. Sad because of how close Bob and I had once been, because I couldn't help him, because my mother was trying so hard to hold it all together. The rips and tears in the fabric of our little world seemed irreparable. There was no way for the four of us to talk about any of it. The only conversation acceptable to Bob and Mami centred on the misery of others.

Outside the house I was the carefree Canadian surrounded by friends. At home, I kept things so clean that even the insides of the cupboards were scrubbed weekly. Since money was still scarce, I got good at subsisting on two pieces of toast with cheese a day. Tea with five spoons of sugar kept my stomach full, energy up and palms warm. I secretly patted myself on the back, for all this meant one thing: I could survive in a concentration camp. Having mastered the ability to carry on backbreaking physical labour and hard mental work (there were fourteen subjects at school, with four hours of nightly home-work) while I was near starvation, I set as my next goal to conquer my terror of rodents. Horrific tales of torture involving rats and mice were shared at school, where chilling accounts of Argentina's many con-centration camps were making the rounds. My first step, facing the rodents, was easy. Hundreds of mice had invaded our house in deep-est, darkest winter, and a mouse often jumped out when you opened a cupboard. One had even hit me in the face. I had learned to control my shrieks; now I needed to suppress the initial jerk whenever I came upon one. Mami shared my phobia, but she too was determined to overcome it. "The enemy must never know about our fear," she'd mut-tered when we'd found ourselves on hands and knees on the kitchen table, screaming for Bob to get rid of a baby mouse that had scurried behind the stove. We had our work cut out for us.

"CARMENCITA?"

"Yes."

"It's your mother. How are you, my beloved girl?"

"Fine."

"How are things there?"

"Fine."

"I cannot tell you how much I miss you. I cannot tell you how much I love you, my dear girl."

"Me too."

"I have to go now. I don't know when I can call you again, but I love you."

Mami's voice broke as if someone had pressed a thumb into her throat. I was like a glass dropped from a great height, smashing into a thousand jagged pieces upon impact. My mouth opened, and I emitted a foreign sound. As I put the receiver back on the cradle, a ray of sunshine parted the clouds and pierced the window. The lake shone grey in the distance. Black clouds rumbled. I sucked in great gulps of air as I walked toward the cupboard. I opened it and saw that nothing had changed; there were still only two cans of food left. A can of kidney beans and a can of asparagus. I'd save them, I decided. I put the kettle on again and retrieved the soggy tea bag resting in a dish in the refrigerator.

It was weeks since they'd left: Mami, Bob and Lalito. There was no way to get hold of them, since their destination was top secret. A friend of Jacques and Marcia's had been hired to sleep at our house and watch over Ale and me. She thought our parents were in Canada, dealing with Bob's ailing mother. As the days wore on and their return date was repeatedly postponed, the woman went home, dropping by our place from time to time to make sure all was well. Ale moved in with Vero's family, owners of a local car dealership. By now, the food money had run out. Argentina's entire trade surplus went to pay the interest on the tens of billions owed to the International Monetary Fund, and the country's economy had collapsed after only a few years of the deregulated capitalist model installed by the dictatorship. Inflation was at 500 per cent, which meant the million pesos my mother had left us for groceries was worth almost nothing. I could have gone to Jacques and Marcia for help, but Bob had made it clear they were to be contacted only in an extreme-case scenario, and I wasn't sure this counted as one. I shunned the neighbours; it would be too dangerous for them to find out what was going on. So I stayed at home alone, keeping up the pretense of my parents' emergency trip, making up stories for my classmates about the regular phone calls from Canada. I was proud to know that I could survive on recycled tea bags dipped in boiling water, even though my diet had turned me into a chronic trembler.

Just when I concluded that I'd have to move to Dalia's house in order to be fed, Jacques showed up with some groceries. He cheered me up with his imitations, and though neither of us talked about Mami and Bob's whereabouts, relief flooded through me at being with someone who understood our situation. I didn't know then that this would be the last time I'd see Jacques. He and Marcia were transferred shortly afterward, leaving no forwarding address.

I unpacked the bags Jacques had brought, placing the cans of tomato sauce in a row next to the packages of spaghetti. The count-down began anew. Each can consumed meant one more day without Bob, Mami and Lalito. Each forkful was a ritual: this one had them in Canada, actually looking after Bob's mother; this one had them in Chile, delivering goods; this one had them in the Caribbean, not sun-bathing as the shrimp in class had said but receiving guerrilla training at a camp in Cuba. The odd one, which I tried to keep at bay, had Lalito being sold on the black market to a rich military family. The children of political prisoners were taken from their parents regularly for that purpose. He'd be worth a lot, with his golden locks and apple cheeks.

17

BOB RETURNED FIRST, so gaunt his face was sunken and bony. Lalito held fast to him. I kissed my little brother all over his face as Bob made some coded phone calls: "The company is doing well, and the delivery has been made." "New members have joined the company." "Look for correspondence in the next forty-eight hours." Mami appeared a week later, chest collapsed, holding me close for a good long while.

In Chile, they told Ale and me excitedly, monthly mass protests were now happening right across the country. Electrical towers were bombed periodically by the resistance, creating nationwide blackouts that allowed people to take to the streets, banging pots and pans while chanting against Pinochet: "Y va a caer!" (And he will fall!) Argentina was only months away from the elections called for October 1983, in which the front-runner was the centre-left candidate Raúl Alfonsín. Bolivia had ended years of dictatorial rule and was still celebrating its new president, Siles Zuazo. The international call to boycott all things Chilean was gaining momentum; exile communities around the world had spread the word, urging people not to buy Chilean grapes and wine. With the abolition of social services under Pinochet, hunger, homelessness and disease were rampant in Chile, and a hundred people had just been killed in a Santiago protest. But it seemed as if the end of the dictatorship was near. It was good to know what we were doing was not in vain, but I ached to join the Santiago high school students who rallied regularly in the streets. I craved the chance to yell and scream and fight the military out in the open—to leave the underground, to be myself.

Within a couple of days of their return, my mother and Bob retreated into their world of documents, meetings and plans. Ale continued to sleep over at Vero's most nights, coming home only to pick up more clothes. Bob joked that she'd turned into a ghost. But her absence made things more lonely for me. I'd written to Ernesto shortly after we arrived in Bariloche, reassuring him he was still the love of my life. As soon as I was of age, I promised, we'd be together forever, just as we'd pledged in the stairwell. A response had taken months to come, and one morning there it was, in the form of a note scrawled across the envelope stating that the post office box no longer existed.

I placed the unopened letter on my pillow, went to the kitchen and retrieved the final can Jacques had delivered. I'd left it untouched at the back of the cupboard for superstitious reasons, even through my last days of hunger. Now I opened it and took the jagged lid into the bathroom. Sitting on the edge of the bathtub, I turned on the taps and pulled my sleeve back. Then I sawed through the skin on my left wrist. The blood appeared immediately. I continued to cut.

"Bob!"

My voice was new to me, the cry of a wounded animal.

He appeared in the doorway and moved quickly through the steam-filled bathroom. He clasped my wrist tight as he let out a howl.

"I want to go home." Words I'd never spoken. Words that had been stuck in my throat since our long-ago stopover at LAX. Now that they'd finally come out, I couldn't stop saying them. "I want us to go home."

Bob rocked me, his face tight with pain. "We can't go, Carmencita." He didn't ask what I meant by home: Vancouver, Bolivia or Chile? I wouldn't have known the answer if he had.

166

When Mami got home that night, she came to sit on the edge of my bed, where I lay with a bandage around my wrist, drinking a fresh cup of tea Bob had made. He'd turned back into the Bob I used to know, before the constant rage and darkness, holding my hand all day, taking care of me like the child I was. Now it was my mother who was angry.

"Bob told me what you did. I don't think you really wanted to kill yourself. Otherwise, you wouldn't have called for him. We'll see what we can do about getting you some help, Carmencita. But don't ever try that again. Think of the consequences. Think of us. Suicide is a selfish act. In the end you're gone, but the others are left behind."

The help my mother promised came in the form of a few visits to the best psychiatrist in town. The doctor lived in a mansion with a stunning view of the lake and mountains. After giving me an IQ test, she verified what she'd already suspected, she said: I was below average in intelligence, which explained my suicide attempt and all-round rebelliousness. Since I couldn't tell her anything that was true, I stopped going, but I found some relief in knowing I wasn't the sharpest knife in the drawer. Now, if Mami or Bob accused me of being bourgeois, I could retort with: "I'm sorry, what was that again? Let me check the dictionary."

Bob and Mami were careful to ask how I was doing, and Bob took me to a couple of movies. Mami got a nice haircut, put on a conservative skirt and agreed to have tea with some of my girlfriends' mothers. She was trying hard to be more like them, for my sake, but eventually her resistance work drew her in again, and Bob disappeared back into his anger. I took refuge in Michael Jackson's *Thriller*, sent by my father along with fleece-lined jean jackets and off-the-shoulder sweatshirts for both Ale and me.

"I'M A VIRGIN and will make love only when I'm in love," I said.

"I'm in love with you."

"Okay. Let's go."

I'd known him for less than twenty-four hours. His name was Dante, and he'd asked me to dance the night before at By Pass, the newest nightclub in Bariloche. It was September 21, the first day of spring and the Day of Lovers. In my borrowed miniskirt, my look was cutting-edge. Being dark and curly-haired was all the rage, thanks to Jennifer Beals in *Flashdance*. And so it was that Dante, eighteen years old and the most coveted playboy in town, hadn't let me go all night. I found it shocking. I'd been invisible since our arrival in Argentina; no boy had even glanced my way, much less put the moves on me, until now. Dante and I made out on the seawall as the sun rose.

Now it was the following evening, and Dante leaned in closer. We were at the Stratus Café on Mitre, a place too swanky for the likes of me, but a regular hangout for him.

"Another Cinzano, ché!" he called, with a smile at the distinguished old waiter.

Three hours later, we climbed through his bedroom window and I spread my legs while his uncle snored in the next room. Afterwards, I shook so hard it was as if I'd had a seizure. At six in the morning, I climbed out the window and walked home along the icy sidewalks, an ache between my legs that reached up through my centre, filled my heart and beamed out through my toes and fingertips. The moon breathed over the lake.

Dante stayed in my life for the next two months. On weekends we'd go dancing at By Pass, the Brain or Grisu, which was right on the lake, and on weeknights he'd help me with my homework. He took it upon himself to fatten me up, and within weeks I'd gained twenty pounds, thanks to generous portions of gnocchi, french fries, pizza and grilled provolone cheese. Dante paid for it all. He'd walk me home at the end of the evening, have a glass of wine with Mami and Bob, and then leave, only to walk around the back of the house and let himself in through my bedroom window. With Ale at Vero's so much, I had the room to myself. Bob and Mami caught me once and grounded me for a month, but Dante just kept coming back. For my sixteenth birthday, he threw me a costume party. Spring draped Bariloche in red, yellow and orange flowers.

On October 30, Raúl Alfonsín, the Radical Party candidate, won the national elections in Argentina. My school was mayhem. Students and teachers cried for joy in the classrooms and hallways. Even the poor students joined in, adding their voices to the chanting. "Que viva la democracia! No mas vivir bajo la bota! Con la democracicia comeremos!" (Long live democracy! No more living under the boot! With democracy we'll eat!) The sons of the military men locked their jaws as they looked on.

Dante was beside himself with elation. Then the military service came calling, ordering him to report to a Buenos Aires base in mid-December. Before he left, I learned from my classmates that Dante had continued sleeping with half the town—locals *and* tourists—the whole time he'd been with me. To preserve my dignity I broke up with him, but the betrayal didn't destroy me, because Dante had saved my life. He'd fed me, loved me and showed me what it was like to have guilt-free fun. On the day he left, we met at the cathedral and made out on a pew one last time. I walked him to the bus station and waved as the bus pulled out. Hanging out the window, he cheered, clapped and blew me kisses.

At the kiosk on the corner, a crowd had gathered around a TV. Alfonsín was addressing a million people in the Plaza de Mayo in Buenos Aires. It was December 10, the day he officially took power, inheriting the biggest social crisis the country had ever seen and a harrowing financial collapse, thanks to neo-liberalism gone wrong. A third of the population was living in abject poverty and thirty thousand people had disappeared. An uneasy military was waiting to see how Alfonsín would respond to the clamour for trials for crimes against humanity and rumours about secret Swiss bank accounts, where millions in stolen state funds had been stashed by the top military men and their advisers.

"May democracy reign, goddammit," the kiosk owner muttered under his breath, tears welling up behind his Coke-bottle glasses.

The bus disappeared around a corner, and that was the last I saw of Dante.

18

I<small>T WAS FEBRUARY</small> 1984, and the Bariloche summer was coming to
a close. At the beginning of the holidays, I'd joined the local theatre
troupe as the lone teenage member. I hadn't acted in any plays yet, but
the director had taken me on as his intern. I sat by his side, drinking in
all I could during rehearsals for a scathing piece that exposed Argentina's class system. When the lead actress didn't show up for rehearsal
one evening, I figured I'd have to wander the downtown streets until
one in the morning, the time my mother was picking me up. My family
had moved to the apartment complex on the Atomic Centre grounds,
so I could no longer walk home. Just as I was about to head off, the
troupe's volunteer lighting designer called out to me.

"Hey, Skinny, let's go for coffee."

Over hot chocolate at the Saint Nicholas Café, Alejandro told me
he was from Córdoba and had moved to Bariloche to work at a nuclear
plant on the outskirts of town. He had done his military service during
the double-whammy times: under the dictatorship and during the war
with England. His lower-middle-class family had no means to bribe
him out of doing service, so he'd been stationed in La Plata, south
of Buenos Aires. Boys from all over Argentina had joined him, eyes

hollow with terror, mostly poor Indians from the northern provinces. The Indian boys were sent to the Malvinas first, and some had died of hypothermia and starvation, never having set eyes on an enemy soldier. Alejandro had been transferred to the Little School, he explained, a military training ground that also housed a concentration camp. Angel Face was there, a young military man notorious for infiltrating the Mothers of the Disappeared, using his cherubic face and a fake story about a disappeared brother to win their trust. After tricking them, he'd systematically had the members of the organization—mothers demanding to learn the whereabouts of their children—arrested, tortured and disappeared.

As for the military service boys, it had been all about breaking their spirit. Sent out into the freezing pampas with nothing but flimsy blankets, they'd been woken up by a whistle in the middle of the night and given three minutes to board a non-existent plane supposedly bound for the front lines. Anybody reacting with fear had been beaten.

"I'll tell you one thing, though, Skinny. I'm grateful to the military pigs for getting me into the best physical shape of my life and for teaching me how to shoot a gun. After walking across the pampas for days, with almost no food or water, carrying a forty-pound pack on my back and a rifle, I gotta thank those pigs for giving me the training to rise up against them."

"You believe in armed struggle?"

"Of course. How could I not? I'm a great admirer of the Republicans who fought in the Spanish Civil War. My father is a Spaniard who arrived on the boats landing in La Boca, among the great masses of immigrants fleeing fascism. My aunt was holed up in a Spanish convent throughout the war, and I never tire of listening to her stories. I'm also a fervent supporter of Cuba and Nicaragua."

"So you don't support Alfonsín?"

"I support real change. Alfonsín is no revolutionary. But I'll give him this much: our constitutional rights have been restored, and therefore I am exercising my freedom of speech and telling Skinny here that I believe in the revolution, that it is my right to believe in it, and it is my right to speak of it loud and clear." His voice was husky now, a hoarse whisper. "On weekends I go to the shantytown to work with a literacy campaign. You should come with me sometime. The people there are all Chileans, you know."

"Yes, I've heard that."

"You should see the conditions in which these people live. Truth be told, my comrades and I haven't been able to get our literacy campaign off the ground yet, because from the moment we arrive on Saturday morning till the moment we leave on Sunday night, it's all about finding food, bringing doctors in and fixing roofs."

"Who are your comrades?"

"I belong to the Intransigent Youth. But what about you? Tell me about Bolivia. Were you there when Ché Guevara was caught and killed?"

"No, I wasn't born until a week after that."

"I've never been anywhere. Only here. The vast country of Argentina. And I will never leave."

"I know what it's like to love your country that much," I said. "And I can see why you love this place."

"A sixteen-year-old immigrant actor who loves the shittiest country in the world. You're the last person I thought I'd meet at the Dramatic Arts Institute."

"I have to go now. My mother will be waiting for me by the library."

"I'll walk you there."

Just before I got into the 1950s olive-green Estanciera that Mami and Bob had been driving all summer, Alejandro pointed at the only tall building in the city.

"Apartment 901. Come by tomorrow night."

ALEJANDRO ANSWERED his door naked, as if it was the most normal thing in the world. Rubbing a towel over his wet hair, he invited me to make myself at home. I sat on the edge of his single bed, with my jacket on, and picked up a book from his bedside table: the collected poems of Miguel Hernández. Alejandro puttered around the studio apartment. Finally, he sat opposite me on his roommate's bed, our knees touching. He offered me some yerba maté from a Thermos, then cleared his throat.

"Listen, Skinny, you probably think I'm crazy with all that stuff I said last night. But for some reason I felt I could talk to you openly. It's something I don't usually do, because I grew up under the boot. To speak like that to an absolute stranger..." His voice cracked.

And then I did the impermissible, the inconceivable.

I told him my family was running a safe house. I told him we belonged to the resistance and that I was Chilean. It came out in torrents, like a waterfall crashing down the side of a mountain during spring thaw. I gasped for breath between sentences. I told him about growing up in exile in Canada, about the Return Plan, the trip back to Chile with Trinidad, the day we'd left Bolivia behind. I told him about the starvation, the fear, the return-to-sender letter, the suicide attempt, about how I'd spent the summer swimming daily in Lake Nahuel Huapi while my parents and their Rosarino helpers scoped out the Andes trails. And finally, since it was too late to turn back, I told him about the day I first felt the Terror, something I'd never spoken about before. Icy sweat broke out all over my body, and a rat clawed its way up my spine.

One afternoon in Valdivia, when I was five and Ale was four, we'd been at home with Lucha, our babysitter, when the pictures on the walls started to sway. The china in the cupboards danced. An earthquake, I thought. But no. Military Jeeps had surrounded our house, and soon boots were pounding up the stairs. As the soldiers stormed in, closet doors flew open, drawers crashed to the floor, beds screeched out of their corners. Two soldiers dragged Lucha into the kitchen. Where were my parents? they shouted. I could hear Lucha hiccuping the words. "I don't know. I don't know."

One of the soldiers reached for my doll. As he backed up, I followed, being careful not to step on the things strewn across the floor:

the pink dress made by my great-aunt Perlita, the picture of my grandmother and me at Santa Lucía Hill, the pencil crayons that were a gift from Uncle Jaime. The soldier looked me straight in the eye as he tore my doll's head off. He threw the body down and peered inside her head, as if he might find something hiding there.

Then he produced a chocolate bar. Hershey's, just like on the American TV shows.

"Do you like chocolate?" he asked me. I nodded. Drool poured down my chin. "Where do your parents keep their papers? Tell me, and I'll give you a bite." More soldiers had come into the room by now. Some of them were laughing so hard they had to lean against the wall.

"Everywhere," I said. It was true. My parents were teachers and bookworms, and there were papers all over the house. I could see he wasn't satisfied with my answer, though, so I took him to my parents' bedroom and pointed to a shoebox at the back of their closet. I knew there were things in there we weren't allowed to touch.

Ale whimpered in the corner as I devoured the chocolate bar the soldier tossed me.

I glanced up, ashamed, but Alejandro just nodded for me to continue.

"After the military had gone through our stuff, they took Ale and me outside. It was so quiet out there. I figured the neighbours must be lying on their bathroom floors, crouching in their bathtubs, saying their prayers. That's what they'd done when the police raided my friend Romina's house, across the street, and took away her father and her older brother.

"A few days earlier a soldier had knocked on our door and threatened to arrest my mother for wearing pants. In the days following the coup, as you know, a warning was issued that women would no longer wear the pants in Chile. There were already women in jail for not wearing skirts, and women in the street with their pants torn to shreds by soldiers. The soldier had ordered my mother to buy a flag and raise it on the post outside, to show our allegiance to Pinochet. She complied after he left, but she'd put it up only halfway, weeping as she explained to us that it was a sign of mourning.

"The soldiers pushed Ale and me up against the wall of the house, right by the rose bush. From the corner of my eye, I caught a movement in the upstairs window of the house next door. A girl my age, Veronica, lived there with her mother and grandmother. Since the coup, she'd stopped talking to me. My parents said that was because her family was on the right. That day it was an adult looking out the window, watching the scene. Surveying our house, which was surrounded by trucks and Jeeps. Ale and I quaked in the mud as the soldiers formed in a line in front of us, lifting their guns.

"The soldier who'd given me the chocolate bar laughed. 'Oh, well,' he said. 'I guess it's the firing squad for you two.' The other soldiers laughed too, as if that was the funniest thing they'd ever heard. 'Turn around,' he ordered Ale and me. I took her shoulders and turned her so she faced the wall. Then I did the same. 'Hands up. Both of you,' the soldier yelled. Ale raised her arms. I did too. An intense aroma of roses reached my nose, and all of a sudden I was cold. I heard my teeth chattering in my skull, and then the soldier's voice from very far away: 'Ready. Aim. Fire.' I was shaking so hard I thought I'd fall down. Ale and I stood there, swaying in the mud, as the soldiers got in their vehicles and drove away. We stayed there until Lucha ran out of the house to get us."

By the time I was done talking, hours had passed. My yerba maté sat stone cold in its gourd. I was still wearing my jacket, and yet I was frozen solid, shaking uncontrollably. After a moment, I said, "I'm scared."

It was a long time since I'd uttered those words, and now I couldn't stop. I repeated them like a mantra: "I'm scared, I'm scared, I'm scared."

Alejandro reached across the space between us to take me in his arms. When the shaking had calmed down, he flipped open the book I'd returned to his bedside table and read me a poem written while Hernández was fighting with the Republicans in Spain. It was about a starving peasant child, with the final lines, "Who will save this child smaller than an oak seed? Who will break the chain that binds him? Let it be the hearts of labourers, who were chained children before they were men."

Alejandro closed the book and looked me in the eye: "You are that child. I've been waiting for you all my life."

I'd met my first compañero.

19

I BUMPED INTO ALE after school on Mitre Street. She was wearing her smock, giggling with her friends, but she pulled me aside.

"Come home today. I need to talk to you. Don't worry, Mami and Bob aren't there."

I nodded and kept walking. I was with a Malvinas War vet, so everyone on the street was giving us dirty looks. It was June 1984, and I hadn't shown up at school for weeks. Soon after I met Alejandro, I'd basically moved in with him. I'd leave our family's apartment on the Atomic Centre grounds on the school bus every morning, then get off downtown and sleep the day away in his bed while he worked twelve-hour shifts at the nuclear plant. In the afternoon I'd take the school bus back home. For the past few weeks I'd rarely bothered to go home at all, spending the nights at Alejandro's. Mami and Bob had given up on me, shouting that I was the most stubborn, rebellious person they'd ever met. Their apartment was a disaster since I'd let my cleaning duties go.

Alejandro and the ten Malvinas War vets he'd taken in were my new family. Many vets lived on the street and were addicted to drugs. Bariloche had tried everything to get rid of them. They were in and out of jail for vagrancy. Business owners barred them from the sidewalks.

Public meetings called for their expulsion. Hanging out on Mitre, the vets harassed tourists for money and complained openly that there was no social safety net for them. I was the only girl at Alejandro's place, and the only teenager. We spent our evenings smoking black tobacco and passing the yerba maté gourd around while the vets swapped stories about the war. We passionately debated democracy, dictatorship and the explosion of pornography now that Argentina's censorship laws had been demolished. The big bang theory, nature versus nurture, the revolution and polyamory were also hot topics. Alejandro was the breadwinner for us all. I'd always considered it my destiny to be part of the revolution, but Alejandro was coming to that choice for himself. We dreamed of being urban guerrillas together.

A few hours after seeing Ale on the street, I took a bus out to the Atomic Centre. As I strolled toward our building, a sense of doom seized me. I made myself climb the stairs to the second floor. The apartment was a mess, as always. Ale was at the table doing homework. I sat down opposite her.

"Mami has disappeared."

I blinked.

"She left a week ago. She didn't say where she was going or when she'd be back, and obviously I didn't ask. Bob was in and out all week, so I looked after Lalito a lot. Then yesterday afternoon Bob took off, all serious, with Lalito on his shoulders. He said that Mami had gone off to the mountains to try out a trail they'd charted in the summer. She was supposed to meet him back on this side four days ago. But she hasn't come back. And there's no sign of her."

"Aren't the Andes under six feet of snow right now?"

"Yup. Bob said he's gonna wait at the agreed-on place for a while. Then he'll go in and start looking for her."

"With Lalito on his shoulders?"

"Yeah. I think Miguel was going to join him."

She closed her books and looked at me.

"They've agreed to adopt me."

"Who?"

"Vero's parents. And they'll take Lalito, too. I often take him there. They love him, and he loves them, too."

I nodded. I wasn't sure if Vero's parents had literally agreed to adopt Ale, or if she was reading that into their incredible hospitality. In any case, I wasn't about to burst her bubble. I lit a cigarette and watched the streams of smoke billow under the silver dome of the dining room light. There was nothing we could do. We couldn't go to the police, because then we'd all be dead. We couldn't tell any friends, because then we'd all be caught. We couldn't tell the other helpers; compartmentalization was such that no information could be passed on unless explicit orders had been left to do so. All we could do was try to act normal, so that the neighbours wouldn't suspect something was up.

I climbed into the top bunk of the bed I shared with Ale. The heater in our room wasn't working, and ice had formed on the inside of the windows. We shivered in the dark, tuned into every sound. On the bus the next morning I ran into Dalia.

"Where have you been, Carmen? The philosophy teacher asked me the other day if you'd moved back to Canada. I miss you, my friend. If you've decided to drop out of school, at least come over some time."

"I will. I promise." I couldn't look her in the eye, for fear I'd fall to pieces.

After Alejandro left for work, I wandered aimlessly around town, diverting my eyes from the Andes shining on the other side of the lake. Mami must be dead. I prayed she hadn't been caught but had died of hypothermia. People said it wasn't a bad way to go; you simply lost consciousness and then froze to death.

Alejandro and I hitchhiked together to the Atomic Centre grounds once his shift was over. Ale sat at the lone table in the apartment, poking at a plate of pasta. She nodded at Alejandro; they'd met many times on Mitre Street. After that, there was nothing to do but wait— we weren't sure for what. My body was so numb I had no sensation in the tips of my fingers. My heartbeat filled my ears. When we heard the door open, Ale glued her eyes to mine. Lalito's footsteps echoed in the hallway, and then there he was in front of us. I jumped up and wrapped him in my arms; his little-boy scent was like no other. Bob limped behind him, body stooped, backpack tattered. He seemed to have aged ten years since I'd last seen him. And behind Bob was my mother. It had to be her. She was holding herself up on the wall as she inched along, her breathing laboured. Her face was purple. And black. And blue. Her eyes were so bloodshot no white was visible. Her face was severely swollen, but not evenly; it was as if she had two hard-boiled eggs stuck to her cheeks. Her hands were purple, too, and some of her nails were gone. Her clothes hung in shreds. Her hair looked like straw. Mami's eyes reached for mine. I opened my mouth, but there was something stuck in my chest. Was it my childhood? A war? A lost country? Who knew? It wouldn't let me breathe or swallow or scream or speak. Ale was holding Lalito. Alejandro had collapsed onto the couch and I could hear Bob in the bathroom throwing up.

A voice reached me from a distance. I was so cold, as if I was trying to shake myself out of my old skin and into a new one. The heater still wasn't working, and it was twenty below zero outside. The voice got closer. My mother's. She was saying that she had died and then come back into her body because she knew she couldn't leave us alone.

I struggled to make sense of her words. For as long as I could remember, she had left us alone. During Allende's years in power, she'd gone to Mapuche land with a literacy campaign. During the exile years in Vancouver, she'd been out day and night organizing for the solidarity movement. After the divorce, she'd left us with our father. Since the Return Plan had come into effect, she'd continually come and gone. So why not leave us once and for all? But now she was talking about wild boars chasing her through the night, under the canopy of the winter forest; about her limp body being carried by a violent river and a male voice, distinctly Chilean, calling to her from the shore.

Mami asked us for help getting into her bed. I couldn't rid myself of the shakes, so Ale had to do it. Bob had left the apartment by now, and soon he returned with Judith and Felicia. As they entered the bedroom, I heard them break into sobs.

Throughout the night, Judith tended to my mother, asking for hot compresses, painkillers and rubbing alcohol. At one point she asked Bob for a glass of whiskey and gave my mother that too. The adults conferred, deciding that the three of them would take turns looking after Mami, while Ale and I kept going to school and Lalito went back to daycare. Bob had told the Atomic Centre Mami had the flu; now he would report it had turned into pneumonia.

At some point I went into the bedroom, and I stayed at Mami's bedside all night. She was drunk from the whiskey, or delirious from the fever, or both. She jabbered about life and death, and her story came out in pieces.

"I was gone, Carmencita. I'd fallen off the side of a mountain and banged my way down a cliff, landing on jagged rocks and tree trunks. Funny how the beating of my life came not from the military but from the Andes. I hit my head so hard I lost consciousness. When I came to, it was night, and I stumbled around the freezing cold forest in the pitch black. The boars nearby were sniffing, sniffing. Days and nights passed like that. I watched my fingers turn purple, the nails falling off from the cold, my eyes swollen almost shut. I could hear the crash of a river in the distance, so I followed the sound, knowing the river would lead me somewhere. I didn't know if I was still in Argentina or had made it to the other side. All I could think about was you, my big girls and little boy. I couldn't let you down. So I found my way to the river, but when I saw it, at the bottom of the world, I fell and landed in it face down. I knew that was it. So I gave in, letting that river take me, but then I heard a voice say so distinctly, 'Señora? Señora?' I knew he was Chilean, with that lilt. I felt relief that I was going to die back in the country I came from. But the boy wouldn't leave me alone, kept calling, and then there were other voices. Next thing I knew they were pulling me by the hands and feet toward the shore. They laid me down, and one of them left and came back with two women, a mother and a grandmother. Mapuche mountain people. The women carried me to their house, a shack, really, in the middle of the mountains. A fire was burning in the wood stove, and they laid me down on their hay mattress and kept me there, boiling water with herbs, cleaning the infections, trying to bring down the fever. I was in and out of consciousness. The boys kept a lookout, and on the third day, one of the women said, 'Señora, the police are coming. They come here every few days, and my oldest boy tells me they're only a couple of hours away now. You must leave. My boy will walk you through the cattle trail and leave you at the border.' They hugged me goodbye and gave me a walking stick and waved me off. I said to them, 'I'm from here.' And they nodded and covered their mouths with their hands to contain their emotion, and the boy took me along the trail and told me when we'd reached the Argentinian side and said to keep walking, Señora, just keep walking, and you'll reach the dirt road. So I did, and when I got to the road I saw Bob standing there with Lalito on his shoulders. And now here I am, my beloved girl, my daughter whom I love so much."

WITHIN A WEEK, my mother was back to teaching. She was our family's sole breadwinner, and she'd missed so many days at the Atomic Centre that she was afraid of getting fired. At the last minute the adults had decided the pneumonia story wouldn't hold water. Now the story was this: Mami had felt so much better after being bedridden with the flu that she, Bob and Lalito had gone for a little winter hike. She had slipped in the snow and fallen down a small cliff. Judith pointed out that any outdoorsy type would know my mother's missing nails and blue fingers were signs of extreme hypothermia, but there was no alternative. Staying in bed while refusing visitors and never seeing a doctor would be even weirder. People had begun to ask questions, and Mami and Bob knew it was only a matter of time before the secret police would close in on us.

I had moved back home for the time being, and on a rare night when Bob and I found ourselves alone at the table, we had a political discussion, just like old times.

"Carmencita, there's so much happening in Chile right now. The international solidarity movement has done a superb job of raising consciousness around the world. This is thanks to the work of the exiles, including your father and your uncle and aunt and cousins and all the rest of the community in Vancouver. Thanks to the election of Alfonsín here, Pinochet is completely isolated. Chile is the only country in South America living under a dictatorship now, and this makes the Yanks nervous as hell. The last thing Ronald Reagan wants is a revolution in Chile. He's pushing Pinochet to take a softer approach, call elections there. Many young people have joined the resistance but they don't want a protracted war. They are calling for an insurrection, like what happened in Nicaragua. So even though we all still have the same goals—to topple Pinochet and install a revolutionary government—and we are still working together, they have taken some matters into their own hands. They are very good. They've already performed numerous armed propaganda actions: bombed electrical towers and U.S. banks, taken over radios and TV stations to broadcast their platform, carried out a massive graffiti campaign with the high school kids. They have a series of kidnappings of major military men planned, and I wouldn't be surprised if they go for the big guy himself very soon. If insurrection is what they have in mind, they know it'll have to be quick and dirty, and the best way to get there is to go after Pinochet himself. Every month there's a million-strong rally in Santiago and all the other major cities. The poor have never been poorer or more numerous. After eleven years of living under a state of siege, people have had enough. The time is coming, Carmencita, it's coming, and precisely because of that the repression has become even more brutal."

"So what are we going to do?"

"You and Ale are going back to Canada, to be with your father. Your mother and Lalito and I won't be in Bariloche long. We'll go wherever the resistance tells us to go."

"But you've always taken us with you."

"Not this time. We've been given the order to send you back. It's become too dangerous, like after the García Meza coup in Bolivia."

"We need a plan," I said to Ale as we lay in our bunks later that night.

"I've told you. I'm gonna get Vero's family to adopt me."

185

"Well, I'm going to arrange for Alejandro to be my legal guardian. He's twenty-two, a legal adult."

"Maybe you guys should get married."

"We don't believe in marriage."

"It's not about believing in marriage, you idiot. It's about staying here. You think I believe in being adopted at fifteen? Open your eyes."

"But I'd need Mami and Papi's approval to get married. I'm only sixteen."

"So figure it out."

"How will you get them to approve Vero's parents adopting you?"

"Easy. In three years I can do what I want anyway. I'll lay out my case: I'll be happy, safe and well taken care of, and I can see Mami and Bob and Lalito anytime. They won't have to worry about me, so they can dedicate themselves to the cause without being sidetracked. Voila. Everybody's happy."

"But what about Papi? What do you think he'll have to say?"

"Papi's on the other side of the world. It's not like he knows us anymore."

But no amount of begging, pleading or tears could convince Bob and Mami to let us stay. I was not to marry Alejandro, and Ale was not to be adopted by Vero's family. On the twenty-four-hour bus trip to Buenos Aires, Ale sobbed so loudly the stewards checked to see if she was okay. I sat in a silent rage as the vast country of Argentina passed outside our window.

As the airplane to Vancouver took off, Ale grabbed my hand.

"You have only two years before you reach adulthood. I have only three. Before we know it," Ale said, "we'll be masters of our own destiny, Carmen. We'll be our own bosses, and we'll come back here to stay." She loved Argentina more than anything.

As our plane crossed the equator and left the South American winter behind, I kept hearing Alejandro's final words: "Don't worry, Skinny. I'll get to Canada come hell or high water. I'll bring you back here, and together we'll join the resistance."

PART THREE

THE
DECISIVE
YEAR

20

I T WAS A hot July afternoon when Ale and I landed in Vancouver. Papi and Aunt Tita had moved into a housing co-op, where Uncle Boris, Aunt Magdalena, my cousins Gonzalo and Macarena, and other Chileans were waiting with a barbecue. It was three years since Papi had completed his doctorate in physics. He was thinking about changing his surname to McGuire, he'd told us, since prospective employers refused to give him the time of day when they saw the Spanish name at the top of his resumé.

"To the return of my daughters!" Papi toasted with a pisco sour.

"To the return from the Return!" offered my uncle Boris.

"To the return," I repeated as I took a sip of lemonade. I studied the new grey in Papi's hair. He'd been furious when he'd found out that Ale wanted to be adopted by a rich, right-wing Argentinian family and I wanted to marry a twenty-two-year-old man. Anything to avoid coming back and living with our father, as he saw it. I could see the terrible hurt in his eyes.

Two months later, Mami, Bob and Lalito returned to Vancouver as well. The secret police had come close to capturing them, they confessed. If Bob and my mother had looked discouraged before, now they looked defeated, grief-stricken, on the verge of collapse. It wasn't long before Bob moved into a place of his own, and Mami wailed on the couch for weeks. They'd been through so much in their seven-year relationship, she sobbed. How could any couple survive so much danger and terror, such superhuman expectations? As for Lalito, he was only four and had already seen it all.

Papi was at a loss now that his two malleable girls had turned into young women with minds of their own. Ale was constantly sullen and withdrawn. I was in love. True to his promise, Alejandro arrived in Vancouver at the end of the year with plans to take me back as soon as I turned eighteen. He'd jumped through hoops to get there. First he'd gotten himself fired from the nuclear plant so he could collect fifteen hundred dollars in severance pay. Then he'd hitchhiked to Buenos Aires, where he besieged the Canadian consulate for a tourist visa. Finally a receptionist took pity on him and told him he had forty-eight hours to produce a return ticket to Canada and five thousand U.S. dollars in spending money. He'd gone to a rich Buenos Aires aunt to borrow the cash, which he planned to return as soon as he'd flashed it at the consulate. Then he'd obtained a reduced-fare ticket through a friend with connections to the Mob. When he'd presented his ticket two days later at the Aerolíneas Argentinas counter, not sure if it was real or a forgery, he'd sweated right through his winter jacket. His ticket was accepted, though, and for the first time in his life he'd seen the world from the sky.

Alejandro got an under-the-table job on the assembly line of a tofu wiener factory, and the two of us moved in with my mother and Lalito. As in the past, our household regularly put up speakers and musicians from Nicaragua, Guatemala, El Salvador and Chile who were passing through town. And as before, I had nothing in common with my Canadian classmates.

"Wanna go to McDonald's after school?"

"No, I have to go home."

"Why?"

"Ernesto Cardenal, this revolutionary Nicaraguan poet and pastor, who's now the minister of culture for the Sandinista government, is staying at our house, and my boyfriend and I are gonna drive him to his speaking engagement at the United Church tonight. You're welcome to come, he's—"

"Naw. I have to pick up some drugs at my dealer's, and then there's a pool party at Todd's. You could bring the poet if you want. Oh, right, he's a pastor too. Sorry about that."

At the tofu factory, Alejandro met four Guatemalan refugees who were survivors of the dictator Efraín Rios Montt's torture chambers. He learned about the United Fruit Company's coup against Guatemalan president Jacobo Arbenz Guzmán in 1954 (Arbenz's crime had been to nationalize the banana plantations) and the revolutionary efforts in Guatemala since then. Hearing that many of Argentina's torturers had fled the country only to offer their expertise in Guatemala and El Salvador filled him with shame and rage. He immersed himself in Vancouver's Chilean exile community, where solidarity work was the reason to live. He didn't have to return to his beloved Argentina, he decided. He would go wherever the two of us were needed for the revolution.

Bob, who'd remained in our lives as my stepfather, was in charge of our political education. We studied Chilean resistance documents and writings on other revolutions around the world: Algeria, Vietnam, the ongoing struggle in El Salvador. The Return Plan was still in full force. The hundreds of Chilean resistance members who had fought alongside the Sandinistas in Nicaragua were confident the same outcome could be achieved in Chile. As Bob had intimated back in Bariloche, there was talk of an assassination attempt against Pinochet. Many hoped his death would be followed by an armed insurrection, which would enable a provisional government to be set up. Even those resistance members who believed in protracted war rather than insurrection—the only two successful insurrections in history had been the Bolshevik Revolution in 1917 and the Sandinista triumph in 1979, we learned in our readings—were preparing for the outcome of a successful assassination.

Comrade Marcela trained Alejandro and me for life in the underground. She'd held a high position in our movement at the time of the coup and been trapped in downtown Santiago for weeks. It was there she had honed her survival skills. Her version of "hiding" had involved going out often, dressed like a businesswoman. After a while, the military men who patrolled the streets were greeting her warmly. Her check and counter-check skills (the ability to decipher when you are being followed and to lose the tail in the calmest manner possible) became so refined that she knew exactly when to get on or off a bus, duck into a store or disappear into a church. When the time was right for her to seek asylum at the Canadian Embassy in Santiago, she'd done so. Alejandro and I knew there were other resistance members preparing to go back, but we could only guess who they were. Even in Vancouver, each cell was trained separately and by different people. Alejandro and I constituted a cell of our own. During my grade twelve year, I mastered advanced algebra and acted in the school play, but I also learned the most crucial lesson about surviving in the underground: the importance of security must never, ever be underestimated.

As part of our preparations, Alejandro and I set up a small network of helpers who each promised to send us twenty U.S. dollars a month once we left, to be used at our discretion: for bribes when dealing with corrupt civil servants and border guards, for post office box rentals, for materials to make fake documents, for bus tickets and long-distance phone calls, for extra food when we had people to hide. We quit volunteering for a non-profit radio station's Latin American news show and stopped attending political events. Instead, we hung out with my classmates. While my mother interpreted for Rigoberta Menchú, a Guatemalan activist, during her stop in Vancouver, Alejandro and I went to parties crammed with teenagers in a drunken or drug-induced stupor.

Mami, who taught adult literacy in Vancouver, was getting ready for her first trip to Contra territory. The Reagan-backed counter-revolutionaries, made up mostly of death squad members from the Somoza years, were invading Nicaragua from their Honduras base, and she planned to offer her services as a popular educator in that region of the country. Uncle Boris and Aunt Magdalena had started a non-profit coffee house in East Vancouver that presented music groups, poets, plays and speakers from all around the world. My aunt managed the front of house. My uncle ran the information centre in the back, where he set up a library of revolutionary books and held political education meetings for young people. For income, he still worked as a janitor at night. While I studied for my final exams, Alejandro saved every penny he made at the tofu factory for our return south.

I WAS EIGHTEEN YEARS and seven months old, seated in a Lima café, the day I took the resistance oath. My voice low, I leaned in and spoke: "I am committed to giving my life to the cause. I will die for the cause if need be. From now on, my entire life is dedicated to the cause, which takes precedence over everything else. If I am captured by the enemy, I vow to reveal no information, even if that means being tortured to death. If I realize I am going to break under torture, however, I will hang on to any information I have for the first twenty-four hours after my capture, to allow my comrades time to hide. If I give my comrades away within the first twenty-four hours of capture, I will be executed by the organization. I will always follow the orders of my superiors. I will never speak of the organization or of my involvement in it to anybody."

Lucas and Juan, the men to whom I addressed the oath, gazed calmly at me from across the table. I'd almost cried with excitement when I first met them; I'd recognized Lucas immediately from the days when my family had housed him in La Paz. He'd pretended not to know me, but the sight of his nails, crooked from torture, still produced a sharp pain in my chest. Juan, a bespectacled full-blooded

Quechua Indian, had scars from bullet wounds on his forearms, as if he'd held his arms up to protect his face.

Just as I finished reciting the oath, a bomb went off down the street. The café's windowpanes shook furiously. My knees hit the table so hard that our papaya milkshakes almost went flying. Lucas and Juan grabbed the glasses a millisecond before they slid off the table. Not a hair on their bodies moved, not a single goosebump formed on their skin. I looked around. The necking teenage couples necked harder. The Indian-blooded waiters in their starched jackets kept whistling as they wiped tables and counters. I heard military boots behind me, running past the open door of the café. I didn't pass out, which would have been humiliating. Lucas and Juan were big fish, and I was just a tadpole. But as they took a final sip of their drinks, I knew I'd passed the test.

"Welcome to the resistance," Juan said, raising his glass.

Alejandro had taken his oath in an unfaltering voice. My admiration for his courage grew daily. I was gripped by fear: of torture, of a hideous death, of betraying my comrades. I worried that my political convictions weren't strong enough for me to keep my commitment, even to a cause I believed in so deeply. My politics and my personal life had always been enmeshed, but they'd also been at odds with each other. I kept these fears to myself, though, trying outwardly to match Alejandro's bravery. As of this day in May 1986, we were both revolutionaries in our own right.

Lead in the mouth, a queasy, cold feeling in the pit of the stomach: these were everyday feelings we'd grow accustomed to, according to Juan. He reassured us we'd get to the point where he was. A secret policeman had followed him through three countries, he told us, sitting directly behind him on every long-distance bus ride he took, until he'd confronted the culprit at a midnight station stop in the Argentinian pampas: "If you have a problem with me, tell me now. Otherwise, get out of my fucking face." And that was the end of the secret police agent. He'd disappeared into the bathroom, never to be seen again.

Juan told the anecdote as if it was the most natural thing in the world to confront a torturer in public while Operation Condor was in full swing. But I wondered whether I could endure a life in which the Terror never abated.

Alejandro and I had landed in Lima a week earlier. By now, Peru was embroiled in civil war, which meant that bombs went off regularly in middle-class neighbourhoods, and civilian casualties were commonplace. Our plane had arrived at midnight, well past curfew. In the taxi on the way into town, we'd passed thousands of soldiers patrolling the streets, their faces blackened with shoe polish. Tanks and Jeeps inched along, the only other vehicles out at night. Soldiers shone flashlights into the taxi at roadblocks, studying our passports and the driver's safe-conduct papers. At our colonial-style hotel, the watchman unlocked the gate with trembling hands. A helicopter circled above, its searchlight following our every move.

It was seven years since I'd been in Lima. Shortly after my family and I had passed through, the Shining Path had declared war on the government, hoping to take power and create what it referred to as a pure Communist society, complete with a cultural revolution. According to the Shining Path, other revolutions, including those in Cuba and Nicaragua, were revisionist, and the organization's belief in armed struggle stretched to civilian targets, including peasants and union organizers who did not embrace their ideology. Triumph for the Shining Path no longer seemed far-fetched. Its strategy of circling Lima from the countryside seemed to be working, and it boasted the support of a huge part of Peru's population, especially in the highlands.

As part of our cover, Alejandro and I had spent our first few days in Lima visiting the city's amazing museums, which displayed solid gold Inca artifacts studded with emeralds and five-thousand-year-old intact mummies from the southern desert. We'd been caught in the middle of a protest while drinking coffee on an outdoor patio. The American businessman sitting next to us, wearing an impeccable Armani suit, kept his eyes glued to the *Wall Street Journal* as hundreds of women from the schoolteachers' union passed by, waving banners and shouting for better wages. Soldiers were beating the protesters with batons. One woman, small and round like my mother, fell to the ground, hands shielding her face while four men pounded her arms, legs and ribs. She kept shouting through it all. Following the businessman's lead, we'd stayed at our table, Alejandro in his knock-off jacket, me in my tube skirt. When the tear gas hit, we pulled out our hankies, paid the bill and strolled away from the area, trying to look nonchalant.

Back at our hotel, sobs and convulsions seized me. That had been happening since the day we'd left Vancouver. As soon as we'd boarded the plane, my body had unleashed a tsunami of tears so ferocious I was sure I'd die of dehydration. There was no sign yet that the torrent of tears had come to an end. When we went out, I hid my eyes behind mirrored sunglasses. There was nothing to do but let the storm run its course.

I replayed our orders in my head.

"You will be living in Neuquén, Argentina, where you will join the flying club. You will both learn to fly small planes, and then you'll fig-ure out ways to fly into Chile undetected to drop off people and goods. Your house will be a safe house for comrades coming and going. As soon as you get to Argentina, you must get married, so that our com-rade here can get her Argentinian papers. You will present yourselves as an apolitical, petit bourgeois, hip couple and mix with that kind of crowd. Obviously, you'll both need to find jobs, and you'll live in a high-end neighbourhood. Is this all clear?"

My secret dream that we'd be urban guerrillas in Santiago was dashed. But the order gave Alejandro a spring in his step. He'd be going back to the country he loved, and he'd become a pilot, the childhood fantasy profession of many boys.

Alejandro fell into a placid siesta while I lay awake next to him, turning my head whenever my ears filled with tears. Should I have accepted the invitation to Cuba, I wondered? A few months earlier I'd travelled from Vancouver to a Rebel Youth Brigade encounter in

Edmonton. While the temperature outside dropped to forty degrees below zero, a group of us, teenagers from across Canada preparing for the Return Plan, spent twelve hours a day attending political education classes. We slept in sleeping bags in the basement of a Chilean family home, and the women of the community had banded together to cook us elaborate meals. At night there was singing and cumbia dancing. Some of the kids fell in love, but we were all using fake names and had been instructed to lie about which city we came from, so it wasn't clear how "Freddy" from Regina (wink wink) was going to keep his promise of phoning "Camila" from Calgary once he got home. On our last night in Edmonton, our teachers pulled four of us aside, two girls and two boys. At sixteen and seventeen, we were the oldest of the bunch.

"You four have excelled this weekend," one of the teachers told us. "Fidel has offered full scholarships to four Rebel Youth from Canada to study medicine in Cuba. After you've finished your education, you will go to Chile to serve the people as doctors. By that time, we hope, Pinochet will have fallen and we will have a provisional government in place. You would leave for Cuba two months from now. Everything would be paid for."

"But we haven't finished high school," one boy said.

"It doesn't matter. You have all shown outstanding academic skill and true commitment to the cause. We know you will be able to learn quickly."

"What about our parents?"

"We are talking about seven years in Cuba, studying medicine at one of the best schools in the world, sugar cane cutting in the summers and trips in between to countries that need medical help, whether they be in Latin America, Africa or Asia. This is an opportunity that should not be passed up. Your parents will undoubtedly agree."

I hadn't told my parents or anybody else about the offer, however, and I turned it down a week later. Alejandro had come all this way to get me, and I couldn't just pick up and go to Cuba. Also, I wanted to join the vanguard. Seven years seemed like forever, and I was done with missing all the action. I was almost an adult, and it was time to be at the centre of things.

Now I'd discovered I would definitely not be in the vanguard. "Rearguard" was how Lucas and Juan had described our position. I imagined myself in Cuba, surrounded by internationalists, flying to Angola to offer medical aid. I imagined myself in Nicaragua, alongside my mother in Contra territory, helping out with the literacy campaign. I imagined myself anywhere but here, in the heart of Lima's civil war, about to embark on a journey that would take me further underground than I'd ever been, to a cold Patagonian desert town as far from Santiago and the vanguard as it was from the moon. But I'd just taken the resistance oath, and I was no longer a Rebel Youth, I was a militant. From this moment on, putting my personal desires before my political commitment would be an act of treason.

A burst of machine-gun fire cracked through the afternoon. Alejandro turned in his sleep. A six-year war continued with ferocity outside these four walls. But the war within me had only just begun.

21

ANY EXPERIENCE IS good, any experience is good, any experience is good. I repeated the mantra to myself like a Hail Mary. Juan had given it to me on our last day in Lima.

"Life is so much bigger than we are, comrade. Always remember that we're here for a greater cause. The struggle begun by Simón Bolívar a century ago is ongoing, and we are here only to add our grain of sand for the liberation of our continent. Within this context, any experience is good. This knowledge got me through my years of exile, confronting a solitude I hadn't experienced even in jail. Remember, little comrade: any experience is good."

"Stay calm, everybody! I've got everything under control!"

The man shouting those words was a U.S. mercenary wearing mirrored aviators. His forearms were covered in scars, and the stench of booze oozed from his pores. Waving a semi-automatic above his head, he staggered up and down the aisle of our train car. "Don't worry, folks! It's fully loaded and ready to go."

It was noon in the highlands, and our train had been stuck for three hours in the middle of nowhere. Alejandro and I were seated in the tourist car, surrounded by European backpackers. A week earlier, this very train had been ambushed by members of the Shining Path. They'd pulled out all fourteen European and North American travellers and shot them in the head. The message was clear: whites get out of Peru. Now here we were, our train at a standstill and tensions running high. The mercenary had taken it upon himself to defend us. I took a deep breath and stood up.

"Please sit down. You're scaring people."

"You speak English?"

"Yes. Now please sit down. You're making people very nervous."

"Why didn't you tell me earlier you spoke English? I've been dying to have a decent conversation for months!"

"Well, let's talk, but please sit down and put the gun away." I gently steered him to his seat.

"Okay, lady, sure."

"And you should stop drinking. You were drunk when you got on the train this morning, and all you've done is drink since then."

"You've got quite the woman here, soldier. Hang on to this one," he said to Alejandro.

For the previous half hour, Alejandro and I had been in quiet discussions with the two big Sicilians sitting across from us. They wanted to overpower the mercenary from behind, take his gun away and cold-cock him. I'd argued that if his gun went off in the process, people might be injured or killed. Nobody in the tourist car knew whether to be more terrified of the Shining Path or of this rabid, pickled mercenary. The Peruvian waiters and porters had disappeared, locking the doors behind them. We were left to our own devices.

"Where are you from, missy?"

"Canada. How about you?"

"South Carolina."

"What are you doing here?"

"Looking for the Shining Path. I'm gonna take 'em down."

"How old are you?"

"Sixty-five and still going strong."

"What happened to your arms? The scars, I mean."

"Maggots. I'm just back from a month in the Amazon."

"Your government sent you there?"

"Naw, I'm retired. My wife put a restraining order on me, so I took my savings and came down here to flush out the Shining Path."

"All by yourself, under nobody's orders."

"That's right."

"Tell me more about yourself."

The other passengers started to relax. As long as I could keep him talking, everything might be okay. It was a rare opportunity to talk head-on to the enemy, I said to myself. Any experience is good.

"Well, let's see. I was a GI in the Second World War. And I haven't stopped serving my country since then. Done Korea, Vietnam, El Salvador and everything in between. Got paid $150,000 in cash to wipe out an African village once."

"I see. So you must love Ronald Reagan."

"Reagan? I hate Reagan! Boy has no aim. Tries to bomb Tripoli and all he murders is Gadhafi's nine-month-old baby. Ma'am, if you're going to bomb Africa, bomb the whole damn thing!"

"So, uh, where are you headed now?"

"La Paz. I was there in the early eighties. The War on Drugs."

"Oh, of course. Did you get the drug traffickers?"

"You don't think we were actually after the drug traffickers, do you, woman? You're smarter than that. We were after the dissidents. But I love La Paz. That place is the heart of South America. All those people want out of life is love."

Tears started to pour down his face. I patted him on the back. Through the window, I could see a group of Indian boys frolicking in a huge puddle next to the train. The sun shone down on them, making the boys' bodies glisten like gold.

"Just relax," I told my companion, continuing the back patting. Eventually, he passed out.

"Quick! Get his gun!" one of the Sicilians said to the other.

The tourist car passengers let out a collective sigh of relief once the mercenary was relieved of his weaponry. Alejandro and I glanced at each other, steeling ourselves for what lay ahead. If the train got fixed, if the Shining Path didn't ambush, if we weren't caught beforehand, we'd reach the Bolivian border the following morning. I hugged my purse to my chest and eyed the bags sitting in the rack above our heads.

BY NOON THE NEXT DAY, we were at the border, crammed into the Toyota minivan we'd hired in the town of Puno. Our fellow passengers were a Bolivian couple with two small children, a towering German backpacker, a young California hippie couple and a Bolivian woman about my age. The driver had announced early on that he'd need twenty dollars from each of us to stave off harassment at the border, and everybody but the Bolivians had complied.

The border was exactly as I'd remembered it: a lone shack in the middle of the highlands with two plainclothes guards wielding sub-machine guns. It was dead quiet this time around, though, not like when my family and I had crossed at the height of the Virgin of Copacabana's celebrations.

The driver handed over our passports, the twenties on top. Bored stiff and looking for some action, the guards weren't going to let us through so easily. Peering through the window, their eyes rested on the young Bolivian woman and me. One of the guards ordered the driver to slide open the passenger door.

"These two señoritas can come with me, along with their baggage."

The young woman walked into the shack as if she owned the place, but I froze for a second. Any experience is good, I reminded myself. My knees trembled, but maybe no one would notice. Taking the oath, attending daily meetings for those ten days in Lima, seemed like peanuts compared with this. As I stepped into the shack, the musty smell of a packed-dirt floor assaulted my nostrils. My eyes took a few seconds to adjust to the dark, a sharp contrast to the brilliant colours outside.

I was carrying five incriminating items, distributed across my pack, my purse and my person. Alejandro carried another five.

Alejandro and I had made the items at night, following Juan's instructions, in several different Lima hotel rooms. We'd moved every three days for security purposes. Alejandro was an electrician by trade. He'd learned a great deal at the nuclear plant in Bariloche, and he approached our assignment with zeal, even finding ways to make the items more compact. One night I'd sat handing Alejandro components while we watched Shirley MacLaine, who was making a movie in the Andes, speak at a press conference on TV, apologizing to the citizens of Peru for suggesting that Machu Picchu had been built by aliens.

One of the border guards had taken a seat behind a metal desk with an array of rubber stamps covering its surface. "Reason for travelling to Peru?" he asked the Bolivian woman as he studied her passport. Standing at his side, the other officer caressed his machine gun suggestively.

"This," the woman snapped, exposing a dozen electric shavers in her shoulder bag. Leaving one on the table, she grabbed her passport and walked out like the queen of the highlands. I'd spent countless hours trying to master the art of showing no fear, taught by older, highly experienced resistance workers. But watching this eighteen-year-old smuggler, I finally got it.

"What's this?" the second guard demanded.

He'd opened my pack and was holding up a gift box, perfectly wrapped and tied with a pink silk ribbon. He shook it. Two of the items we'd made rattled inside. I snatched the box from him.

"This is a gift for Señorita Lorena de Jesús Calderón Cabral. Her father is a direct adviser to the president of Bolivia, and you will surely understand that I do not want it ruined." I grabbed my passport from the seated guard, plunked two ten-dollar bills on the table and walked out, legs shaking so hard I wasn't sure I'd make it to the idling van.

The driver gunned the minivan out of there like one of the Dukes of Hazzard. My body was drenched in sweat, my heart banging against my chest. But I looked over at Alejandro and winked. The young smuggler chewed on a wad of gum as she studied her painted nails. She'd sell the shavers at the black market the following day and go back to Peru to do it all again.

When we got to Copacabana, our driver told us we had half an hour to pray, stretch and buy food before we left for La Paz. I followed the Bolivian woman into a temple. A thousand candles burned inside, and the murmur of prayers filled the air. The smuggler lit a candle, placed it at the Virgin's feet and got down on her knees to thank her for the safe passage.

FOR ALMOST A YEAR, Bolivia had been under the iron fist of Víctor Paz Estenssoro. Although his government was not a military dictatorship, it might as well have been, since the once-revered leader of the 1952 revolution that had nationalized Bolivia's tin mines and redistributed the land was now a full-fledged neo-liberal. Elected under false pretenses, Paz Estenssoro had turned his back on his popular supporters and, through a state of siege, had imprisoned hundreds of labour activists, leading a campaign of terror against anybody who opposed the free market economy. The extreme poverty in one of the world's poorest nations had become even more extreme, as had the extreme wealth of a few. Overrun by thousands of peasants who begged on the streets, La Paz also boasted a slew of new glass skyscrapers and a gated community of mansions that Beverly Hills billionaires would have envied. Social services and government spending had been severely cut; price controls were cancelled, wages frozen and the borders flung open to anyone wishing to engage in the free trade that had flooded Bolivia with imported goods. Malnourishment was widespread, and unemployment stood at 30 per cent.

Alejandro and I spent our first night in La Paz at a hotel just off Plaza Murillo. The following day we walked up the lane to my old friend Lorena's house and knocked on her door. It took Lorena a moment to recognize me, but when she did, we hugged for a long time, our eyes welling up. She insisted we stay with her family for the ten days we'd be in the city. We were installed in a large guest room, our special items waiting patiently in the packs under the bed.

Lorena didn't ask why I'd never written to her, and her parents opened their home to us with no questions asked. She was a soul sister, and it was as if not a day had passed. Alejandro and I had left Vancouver wearing wedding bands. The official story was that we were moving to Argentina to start a family and were taking the scenic route to get there: Machu Picchu first, and now La Paz. Lorena was studying business administration at the private Catholic university, she told me, but she would probably never use her degree, since she was already promised to the son of a major businessman, an associate of her father's. While her older brother took Alejandro for a spin, I asked her about our old friends.

"How's Félix?"

"Oh, his aunt sent him to the States on an exchange, and he seems to be having a good time there."

"What about Fátima?"

"She and her family had to go into hiding after her father was arrested for masterminding the kidnapping of a super-wealthy Belgian who was here on business. They came out of hiding a year later, and now she visits her dad in jail every week. He's missing all his teeth and nails from the torture, and he can't walk now. It's pretty bad."

I'd always known secret things happened at Fátima's house, but I'd assumed they were connected to the dictatorship, as with Lorena's family. "Oh, my God. Well, how about Ernesto?"

"Never seen or heard from again, although word on the street is that his father is a military adviser in Guatemala. So I guess that's where they are."

My heart did a double flip, but I kept a straight face.

"Do you want to see Liliana? She's still around."

"No, Alejandro's a bit jealous of my past, so it's best if we hang out just with you and your family."

"Of course. My promised one is very possessive too, and I love it. Well, my darling friend, I feel so selfish and lucky to have you all to myself. And my family's so happy to have you here. I've missed you more than words can say, and I'm grateful that life has brought us together again."

A street boy had joined the small army of slaves who now worked at Lorena's house. He approached bearing a silver tray.

"Meringue, Señora Carmen?"

The boy shined the family's shoes, went shopping for bread and helped wax the floors, Lorena told me, all in exchange for food and a stack of hay on the kitchen floor to sleep on. He looked about seven, and I was shocked to learn he was twelve.

"Malnutrition," Lorena whispered. "If it hadn't been for my father, who saw him crying all by himself at Plaza Murillo, he'd be dead by now. My mother says to leave him be, but I've taken it upon myself to teach him how to read and write."

When Alejandro returned, we retired to the guest room on the pretense of needing a nap. The afternoon he'd spent with Lorena's brother had left him agitated.

"It was incredible, Skinny. He's driving me around this gated neighbourhood in his brand-new Mercedes, and he starts telling me about all the stuff he's learning at med school, how the cadavers they work on come from the morgue and are mostly poor Indians who have died violent deaths, including by torture, or teenage Indian girls who self-aborted. Next thing you know he's comparing a doctor's training to a torturer's, saying how in the first year of med school you're urged to puke and faint whenever the urge hits you so that you can get it out of your system, and that what gets you through it all is the knowledge that you're doing this for the good of humanity. He said torturers are also urged to puke and faint when they witness their first torture sessions. Once they get to the point where they're doing it themselves, they understand that what they're doing is for the good of humanity, essentially ridding the world of another type of cancer."

I held him tight while he cried.

"It's so lonely to be around these people, Skinny, to be seen as one of them. How are we going to survive without like-minded people to talk to?"

"We'll just have to talk to each other."

On our last night in the city, Alejandro and I found the address Bob had given us before we'd left Vancouver. Getting past a pack of wild dogs took a while, with much waving of sticks, but it was worth it. When Adriana opened her door, I felt at home for the first time since our arrival in La Paz.

"Carmencita! And this must be your compañero."

Adriana was happy to hear that everyone was safe and sound in Canada and immersed in solidarity work.

"So, tell us. What would you like us to do?" She burped her four-month-old baby as her husband boiled water for coca-leaf tea.

"At this point, it's just good to know that you are here, in case we ever need a place to hide in La Paz."

"Our house is your safe house."

"And we'll give you some money to open a post office box under an assumed name, in case we need to correspond with you."

We spent the rest of the evening playing old Beatles records and listening to stories about Bolivia from our hosts, both hard-working teachers and leftists. Too quickly, it was time to leave.

"We'll send you a note once we've reached our destination safely," I told Adriana.

"Anything for our comrades, Carmencita. Anything."

22

I'D HAD THE runs for the entire ten days in La Paz. Unluckily for me, they were now accompanied by extreme bouts of vomiting. Things would have been manageable if we'd been back at Lorena's house, but instead we were on a twenty-four-hour train ride from La Paz to Villazón, on the Argentinian border. Our packs could never leave our sight, an almost impossible requirement with me running back and forth to the bathroom and a car so full that people were lying underneath our seats and in the racks above our heads. Then there were the robbers. The train was packed with them, and they carried razors between their fingers.

By the time we reached Villazón, my gut was wrung of every last drop. As usual, the trip had taken almost twice as long as scheduled, because of breakdowns and the fact that whenever we passed a cornfield, the train would slow down to five miles an hour. This allowed the train workers, and many of the passengers, to jump off, grab a few ears of corn and jump back on. People ate the raw corn on the spot.

Crossing the border on foot was a piece of cake. Smugglers, pickpockets, backpackers from around the globe, businessmen, adventurers, families and vendors crowded the crossing, and after passing the guard two twenties we were waved through. Just like that, we were in La Quiaca, Argentina's northernmost city. At the station there, we boarded a second-class bus heading south.

We were startled awake at four in the morning. "Everybody off the bus!" a male voice barked.

Alejandro and I scrambled down the steps with everyone else and waited by the side of the highway. The bus drivers checked the tires, cigarettes hanging out of their mouths, while the Argentinian federal police released two German shepherds onto the bus. All the luggage was pulled off to be opened. Most of the passengers were Bolivian families who had come to look for work in Argentina, and two men in plainclothes shouted in their faces.

"You think we want your filth in a civilized country like Argentina? Well, you'll see what's coming to you if we find anything illegal. You'll see what an interrogation really looks like."

Alejandro and I stood silent.

"We know there are people on this bus transporting something of great interest to us. You can turn yourselves in right now, or you can wait till we find your goods. And believe me, we'll find them. So, what's it gonna be? If you turn yourselves in, it won't be as bad for you. Here in Argentina, we like people who co-operate."

When the dogs came off the bus, they went straight for my open packs. One of the men shone a flashlight in my face. I knew my pupils must be dilated, and I knew that dilated pupils signalled fear. Marcela, Lucas and Juan had taught us that. A rat clawed at my spine. But then something happened. It was as if someone had split me open with a machete, pulled out my terrified heart and thrown it on the ground to die, leaving my chest an empty cage. My pupils shrank, and my breathing slowed. Out of the corner of my eye, I could see the dogs making a mess of my clothes and toiletries. The items were carefully stashed, though, and impossible to find, I hoped, without tearing everything apart.

Within fifteen minutes we were back in our seats as the bus pulled out onto the highway. No one had been thrown into the police cruisers.

All the bags had been closed and returned. Parents held their crying children close, and the sound of frightened whispers filled the bus.

"Welcome to Argentina, dear Bolivians," Alejandro muttered.

I was wondering how to get my heart back into my body. I was numb, my breath shallow. It was critical to stop the fear, but did that mean having no feelings left at all? If that was the only way to keep doing the work, it was a price I was willing to pay.

WE ARRIVED IN Villa María, Alejandro's hometown, in the early morning on a cold, cloudy winter day. His parents, María and Paco, were waiting for us at the bus station with open arms. Tears ran down María's face as she patted her son's head. As the three of them hugged, rocking together like a boat on the sea, Paco's legs vibrated with emotion. I stood to the side, my hands clasped in front of me, listening as the bus station came alive with the shouts of newspaper vendors and the hiss of espresso machines. On our way to the car, Paco offered me the crook of his arm, but María remained aloof.

Villa María's cobblestone streets were clean, and already the sidewalks were full of ladies in housecoats and curlers sweeping and washing the pavement in front of their doors. María and Paco's house was long and narrow, with a freshly waxed floor and a gleaming table where we sat to have croissants and coffee. As the day wore on, María started to warm up to me. I walked with her to evening mass, and that seemed to help. Her beloved son was back in Villa María only long enough to marry a woman she didn't know, and though she'd accepted long ago that he was an atheist, it still hurt her that her only boy would not have a church wedding.

My grandmother Carmen had a phone in her house by now, so I'd called her from La Paz and invited her to come. My grandfather had died a year earlier. Because of the blacklist, Mami and Uncle Boris had mourned him from afar.

When there was a knock on the door the next morning, I leapt up from the table and ran to open it. There she was, holding the same large cake box she'd brought to Bolivia for my fifteenth birthday. She wore a widow's frock and the grey winter coat she'd had for years. Her 1940s suitcase was at her side.

"Abuelita!"

"Why didn't anyone inform me that Villa María is two days' travel from Limache? I thought it was just over the border. And then there I am at the Mendoza bus station, telling a taxi driver to take me to Villa María, and he doesn't understand me. Finally he realizes I'm talking about Villa María, Córdoba, and that it's two provinces over. I had to sit on a bus for another day to get here!"

"I love you, Abuelita," I giggled into her hair.

"Now, let me go so I can get a good look at you."

We stood on the sidewalk together as she shook her head, hands on her hips.

"You're a woman now. A woman."

Alejandro and I were getting married for political and immigration purposes, and that was that. I'd been announcing to the world since the age of eight that I would never marry, and as far as I was concerned, I was just doing some necessary paperwork, taking care of legal matters in a town I didn't know, surrounded by strangers. My wedding dress was a fuchsia satin tube skirt with matching top. María and Paco's next-door neighbour had curled my hair, and my new sister-in-law had made me a bride's bouquet of dried flowers. Alejandro's relatives and family friends crowded around us in the civil registry as we exchanged our vows. My only blood present was my grandmother, and she cried as she signed her name next to mine. She was my witness, the person I loved the most in the world.

"Why were you crying, Abuelita?" I asked at the reception as we sat watching people dance.

"Because I hate that son of a bitch so much."

I'd never heard her swear, and I almost fell off my chair.

"Alejandro?"

"No, no. I'm referring to Pinochet. Because of him I'm here, in a foreign country, watching my exiled granddaughter getting married far from her rightful home. You left when you were six years old, Carmencita. Now you're eighteen, and I've lost it all. I've lost it all."

As my heart expanded painfully in my chest, I rose and staggered to the bathroom. Inside a stall, I bent double, flooded with homesickness—for my parents, my siblings, all that was familiar. My feelings had returned with a vengeance, and it took all I had to get them under control. Back at the table, I choked down the cake that had taken my abuelita three days to make and two to transport. I held her hand tightly in mine.

The following day we saw my grandmother off at the bus station. Her beloved dog Muchacho awaited her in Limache, as did her new vocation. Since my grandfather's death she'd started making figurines, brooches and earrings, described in detail in the weekly letters she'd sent to me in Canada. After spending fifty years kneading dough for bread, pies and pastries, she'd begun to people her solitary house with witches, babies, cats, trolls, and invented creatures that sprang from her agile hands. The dough told her what to do, she explained, and she used toothpicks for the finer work. Food colouring gave her creations a soft pastel glow or the brightness of the rainbow. Once a month, her sister Perlita, one of the three virgins, came to visit from Santiago and took my grandmother's crafts back to the boutique in the Plaza de Armas gallery, where they sold like hotcakes. I was wearing her wedding gift that day, a brooch and matching earrings so delicate people had gasped when they learned they'd been made by her hand.

After waving goodbye from the platform, Alejandro and I picked up our bags and walked to another part of the station. Twenty-four hours later we would start our brand-new life. We had two hundred dollars to our name.

23

A N EIGHTY-MILE-AN-HOUR WIND greeted us in Neuquén. Dirt, garbage and the odd tumbleweed flew through the freezing air. We locked away our bags at the bus terminal, first visiting the bathroom so we could transfer the goods we were carrying to the inside pockets of our coats and our money belts. It was noon, meaning we had two hours before businesses shut down for siesta. The city was booming, we knew. People from every corner of Argentina were arriving in droves, since this was the oil capital of the region, with work to spare. We headed for the closest rental agency, leaning our bodies into the gale.

The rental agent frowned when we told him what we could afford. "There's not much I can do for you for 150 australes," he said. "The cheapest place I've got right now is 170. I suppose you have no guarantor?"

"No, we just got here, and we don't know a soul."

"What do you do?"

"She's an English teacher, and I'm an electrical engineer," Alejandro lied. I'd completed a night course in English as a second language in Vancouver, but a teacher I was not. Alejandro was merely an electrician.

"Oh well, then, you'll both have jobs within the hour. I'll tell you what. For 170 australes I'll throw in the damage deposit and I'll co-sign. Seventy years ago there was nothing here. Now look at us! Hop in the car and we'll drive out to your new place. If you like it, you'll hand me the money, sign a few papers and we'll be all set."

The austral, the new currency introduced in 1985 by Argentina's president, was now worth more than the U.S. dollar. Alfonsín had frozen wages and cut government spending, and much of the country had fallen into private hands. The plan, referred to as "structural adjustment," had been imposed by the International Monetary Fund and the World Bank, which had agreed to refinance Argentina's $50-billion foreign debt if Alfonsín followed their conditions. Most Argentinians had urged Alfonsín to refuse the deal. The debt, accumulated by Argentina's military during the dictatorship, had been used mainly to buy arms to terrorize the population and to fatten the military leaders' Swiss bank accounts. But the military still held a great deal of power, and Alfonsín worried that refusal would mean another coup, financed and orchestrated by Washington. As we'd learn, the situation was the talk everywhere—in cafés, on buses, at work.

We drove through town in the agent's tiny Fiat till we crossed the Transnational Highway. A few fat prostitutes in neon spandex leaned against posts, waving lethargically at the passing trucks. Now we were on dirt roads, and the tumbleweeds were plentiful. There were few finished houses here, just half-built structures and huge circular tents. Children in ripped sweaters ran through the streets as packs of dogs followed. Women in multicoloured skirts with gold teeth leaned in the open doorways of rooms just large enough to accommodate the bedding on the floor.

"Gypsies," the agent informed us. "Originally from Romania. Just ignore them, and they won't bother you. They deal in cars, and they can be trusted to sell you a good one. For everything else, stay as far away as possible. They'll steal your money and your children, and tell you lies."

We turned onto one of the dirt roads, and the agent stopped in front of a completed house. He went to the front door and came back with a woman in her fifties, who led us around the side of the house. We passed five metal doors along a dirty passageway. She opened the sixth one.

"This is it."

The door banged against its flimsy frame as clouds of dirt flew in. It was a tiny apartment with a ceramic floor. The kitchen consisted only of a sink. The bathroom had a lidless toilet, a sink and a pipe protruding from high on the wall that served as a shower. The bedroom was barely big enough for a double bed. There were no closets or cupboards. The lone window looked out onto a dumping ground, where small children and dogs played in mounds of garbage.

"It'll go by the end of the day," she said.

"Okay. We'll take it."

"You kids married?"

"Yes. We got married yesterday."

"Okay, I'll throw in a small stove and fridge. Consider it my wedding present."

The rental agent dropped us off at the bus terminal so we could pick up our packs. It took us forever to walk back to our new place. Exhausted after our journey, we collapsed on the bedroom floor and fell into a deep sleep. When I awoke two hours later and stepped out into the "yard," I saw a newborn puppy lying dead a few feet from our window.

BY FIVE THAT AFTERNOON Alejandro and I were having coffee and croissants on Argentina Avenue, Neuquén's main street. The downtown was bustling after siesta, in spite of the wind. We studied a map of the city.

"Okay, Skinny. You go your way, and I go mine. We'll meet back at the house at ten o'clock. Let's hope we'll both have jobs by then."

As I walked along Argentina Avenue, I noticed that all the jeans in the store windows were the same price as our rent: 170 australes. ("Pay in 17 monthly installments of 10 australes!") Even underwear cost 12 australes. ("Pay in 4 monthly installments of 3 australes!")

Within two blocks of the main artery, I spotted a bronze plaque on the door of a small white building that read: "English Institute of British Culture."

A young woman wearing a blue smock clanged away at an ancient typewriter behind the reception desk, using only her index fingers. She was chewing on a great wad of bubble gum, and she completely ignored me as she sought out the next letter on her keyboard. I cleared my throat.

"Hello. I'm here to inquire about a possible job."

The woman sang along with the tiny transistor radio by her side, tossing her head a little. Her frizzy brown hair stood out a good foot from her face. An entire can of hairspray must have been emptied to reach the desired effect.

"Is there someone I could speak to about—"

She let out a sigh and rolled her eyes. "Miss Mary!" she yelled.

A tiny, very old woman dressed in a plaid skirt suit emerged. She inhaled deeply on the cigarette as she looked me up and down.

"Come with me," she ordered in a crisp British accent.

I followed her into an office, where a woman in her late thirties sat behind an antique oak desk. She had jet-black hair and blue eyes. A large diamond flashed on her perfectly manicured hand, the nails painted a fire-engine red.

"I'm Miss Silvina. Do sit down." She extended her hand. Her English pronunciation was perfect, despite her heavy Argentinian accent. "Please tell me about yourself."

"Tea?" asked Miss Mary.

I nodded.

"I am Carmen. Miss Carmen from Canada. I just arrived today—"

"Ah. A native speaker," murmured Miss Silvina with appreciation.

Within an hour, I'd been hired as head of the institute's language laboratory, at a wage of 150 australes a month. I spent the rest of the evening installed at my post at the front of the lab, correcting the pronunciation of rows of students in headphones who listened to cassettes of English conversation and repeated phrases into small microphones.

Getting home was a feat. There was no electricity in the Gypsy neighbourhood, which meant you navigated the dirt roads by the light of the moon, if you were lucky, or by the faint light emanating from tents and open doors. The roads were packed with people. I'd played stupid when my new boss at the institute asked where I lived, pointing vaguely toward the river.

"Be sure never to go to the other side of the Transnational," Miss Silvina had warned. "Gypsies live there. The men are rapists, and the women are whores. They're all robbers with sharp knives." I clutched my purse to my belly as I battled the wind. Dogs ran barking at my feet. As male voices swirled around me, I couldn't decide if I was more afraid of being intercepted by secret police or of being kidnapped by one of the bands of men who loitered on the corners.

Alejandro was waiting for me in our new apartment. He'd landed a job at the hydro plant as an electrical draftsman. His shift started at 6:00 AM and finished at 2:00 PM, just when my workday began. His salary was 200 australes a month. That would leave us with 180 australes for living expenses after rent.

"There are lots of post office boxes available for rent in town, Skinny. There are also some money transfer agencies around—I guess everyone's sending their families a little something. We'll ask our bosses for advances, rent a post office box and mail a note to Lucas and Juan in Lima as soon as possible. And to our helpers."

We never spoke out loud about the goods we were carrying, for security reasons. I looked to where Alejandro was pointing now. He had dislodged a few tiles in the bedroom and dug out a small hole underneath. I stashed the goods I had in my coat and purse alongside his.

"Let's go eat."

As we walked back out through the Gypsy camps, the people nodded.

When we got home at midnight, we saw a light on in our apartment. Suddenly I couldn't breathe. No one here knew us. No one would care if we went missing.

"Oh, there you are," our landlady said as she opened the apartment door from the inside. "I just thought I'd drop off a few things for you."

She'd laid a thin mattress on the floor in the bedroom, covered with starched sheets and a couple of blankets. A pot, a frying pan and two sets of cutlery, plates, cups, and bowls rested on a small card table flanked by two folding chairs in the living area. We thanked her for her generosity.

A part of me wanted to forget it, to leave all of this behind. I'd dreamed of fighting alongside my brothers and sisters in Chile, not being stuck in this cold outpost. Alejandro was fearless, but what about me? Would I be able to survive even the loneliness?

IT HAD BEEN four years since the collapse of Pinochet's "economic miracle" in Chile, and huge sectors of the middle class there were defaulting on mortgages and credit payments. Unemployment stood at almost 50 per cent. The monthly mass protests that had begun in 1983 hit their pinnacle in early July 1986, with a national general strike. The opposition, united in a new coalition called the Civic Assembly that included unions, political parties and grassroots organizations, had managed to rally a cross-section of Chilean society, and hundreds of thousands of people were taking to the streets in open defiance of the laws that made protests illegal. People erected barricades in the working-class neighbourhoods and shantytowns, and there was street fighting between the military and civilians who wielded slingshots and Molotov cocktails. Dozens of resistance bombings, designed to show that the dictatorship was not indomitable, had left half the country in the dark. The blackouts allowed people to bang pots and pans outside their homes without fear of being seen and created difficulties for the thousands of soldiers patrolling the country and raiding homes at night. The dictatorship responded with hundreds of arrests, ten murders and a state of siege, imposing strict censorship on the press and filing criminal charges against protesters and journalists. The Civic Assembly's attempts to start a dialogue with Pinochet about an eventual transition to democracy were also met with one of the government's most gruesome public displays of repression since the days of the coup. Two eighteen-year-olds on their way to a rally in the middle of the day were intercepted by the military, beaten, doused with gasoline and set on fire. Carmen Gloria Quintana survived; Rodrigo Rojas died four days later. Rojas, the son of exiles living in the United States who had returned to photograph the historic general strike, became a symbol for the thousands of returnees. Quintana represented all the impoverished, courageous Chileans who were willing to act in spite of their fear. Pinochet had once again defined the nature of the struggle: if 1986 was going to be the decisive year, as the resistance had dubbed it, then we'd better be prepared for full-on war. In Neuquén, where fifteen thousand undocumented Chileans lived in shantytowns and worked as peons, construction workers and maids, news of the general strike and the public burnings travelled swiftly through the streets.

On a sunny Saturday morning, Alejandro and I made our first visit to the supermarket. Advances on our wages had allowed us to buy basic food items on a daily basis, mostly bread and cold cuts, but now we'd gotten our first paycheques, and we'd be able to stock up for some real meals. Manoeuvring our cart down the crowded aisles, we behaved like children at an amusement park, jumping with joy at the prospect of buying tomato sauce, gnocchi, provolone cheese, steak, potatoes, spices, oil and a box of tea. We'd noticed a telephone company right next to the supermarket, so we planned to call my mother and Lalito as soon as we were done shopping. Then we'd go home and cook lunch, sleep siesta and spend the evening strolling around downtown with the rest of Neuquén. Maybe we'd bump into some of my workmates and have coffee with them. Penélope, the institute's rude receptionist, was turning out to be my first friend in Neuquén. She was a twenty-eight-year-old single mother, funny as hell in a deadpan kind of way. Tomorrow Alejandro and I would take the bus out to the flying club—our second trip there since our arrival—to find out more about lessons. We'd finance them with the money our helpers in Canada had started to send us. Our facade was this: Alejandro had always dreamed of flying, a common enough hobby for Patagonia's elite, and I was just along for the ride.

"We've gotta get these alfajores!" I salivated in the cookie aisle.

Alejandro, behind me with the cart, was studying a jar of maqui jam. At the end of the aisle, a middle-aged man in a brown polyester pinstripe suit with an empty cart feigned interest in a box of Criollita crackers. He looked up, and our eyes met for an instant. The hairs on the back of my neck stood on end. A queasy feeling seized my gut, and my knees almost buckled. I turned slowly toward Alejandro. As I dropped the alfajores into the cart, I said in a quiet voice, "We're being followed. There's a Chilean secret police agent at the end of the aisle."

Alejandro knew better than to look back over his shoulder. Making a superhuman effort to keep our wits about us, we continued at the same pace up and down the aisles, putting our check and counter-check skills into practice. The man followed, maintaining a half aisle between us. Brown-skinned, obviously from a poor neighbourhood, he looked like the typical torturer who did the dirty work for the dictatorship. The fact that he was here, in Neuquén, following us in a supermarket told us that Operation Condor was intact and fully functional. We knew that 179 Chilean resistance members had disappeared in Argentina since 1973.

As we lined up at the checkout, we noticed the man joining a line farther down. He glanced at us and smiled, keeping his lips together. I grabbed a tabloid magazine and pretended to read about a popular television diva while we waited for our turn with the cashier.

"Now," Alejandro whispered.

I dropped the magazine into the cart, and we walked briskly out the automatic doors. Losing ourselves in the crowd of people on the sidewalk, we slipped into the telephone company next door. We'd noted on our way into the supermarket that the phone company had mirrored windows, impossible to see through from the outside. These were things we kept track of, now that we were in the resistance. We'd locate all entrances and exits and formulate at least two getaway plans, whether we were in a restaurant, at work or on the street. We were learning to categorize people at a glance: informer, agent, possible helper, militant.

From inside the telephone company, we saw the man run outside and look in all directions. His right hand reached for something under his jacket. Was he carrying a pistol or a semi-automatic? Three men who also looked Chilean were waiting in a grey Peugeot 504 nearby, dressed in suits and dark glasses. No doubt they too were armed to the teeth. The man in the brown suit jumped into the passenger seat, and the four tore off at high speed. The car had two antennas, one in the front and one in the back: the mark of a secret police car.

Alejandro and I stood behind the glass for what seemed an eternity, in silence. My spirit left my body and hovered just above it as I caught snatches of long-distance conversations coming from the phone booths.

"Mother, please. They have supermarkets in Neuquén. In fact, there's one right next door. Where do you think I am, the Wild West?"

"I love you, I can't wait to see you . . ."

"Not at all like I expected—"

"Cold, windy, the biggest piece of shit—"

"I think it's safe to go now," Alejandro said.

"What?"

"I think it's safe to go now."

"Go where?"

"I don't know."

It was futile to wait for my spirit to join my body again. I realized as I stood in that Patagonian phone company that maybe it never would. This was the biggest sacrifice I'd have to make. The body cannot take chronic terror; it must defend itself by refusing to harbour the spirit that wants to soar through it and experience life to the fullest. And so it was that, as we stepped outside into the glaring light, got on the first bus we saw and zigzagged our day away, my spirit was left back in the phone company along with the mirrored windows and the echo of voices connecting to far-off homes.

When Alejandro and I arrived home late that night, grocery-less, we collapsed onto the bed and fell into a desperate sleep, clutching each other like terrified children. The wind picked up, sending the metal door rattling, the dead bolt banging back and forth in its lock. At any moment a kick could replace the howl of the wind. Four pairs of shoes could run into the house and bear our bodies away, leaving the door helplessly banging and dusty footprints on the just-waxed floor.

24

THE JAM-PACKED YELLOW bus wove at top speed along the Alam-
eda in downtown Santiago. The faces on the bus were like my own,
and the voices too. I inhaled the smell of diesel as my ears registered
the cacophony of a late-winter city night. The bus honked constantly
at the thousands of pedestrians who darted through the traffic, a clas-
sic Colombian cumbia blaring from its speakers.

Our handing off of the goods had been a success. A letter we'd
received in our post office box in Neuquén, addressed to Señor Soto,
had gone on and on about the weather and the vineyards in Mendoza.
When we'd ironed the back, brown letters had appeared, outlin-
ing in detail how we were to make the delivery. Alejandro and I were
instructed to enter Chile in jeans and jean jackets as a young couple
hitchhiking through the country, a common activity for middle-class
South American youth. The operation had to be completed over a
weekend, a challenge since Santiago was twenty-four hours away from
Neuquén by bus.

We'd arrived at Terminal North, one of three long-distance bus
terminals in Santiago, on the Saturday night. The place was always
teeming with secret police and informers, and we knew that everyone

from the kiosk owners to the bathroom attendants was bribed to report any suspicious activity. We'd grabbed our backpacks and strolled casually to the corner. A car with the right licence plate numbers and two people inside stopped at the light. The back door swung open and we jumped in, trusting that comrades awaited us, not the secret police. Otherwise, torture would begin immediately; the first twenty-four hours were always the worst, since information was freshest then. But within minutes the exchange was over. We handed over the goods, which we'd transferred from inside the lining into the usual compartments of our packs, and were dropped off ten blocks from the terminal.

When we'd alerted our superiors in Lima about the secret policeman in the supermarket, they'd advised us to keep our check and counter-check skills honed and practise them twenty-four hours a day. If we saw a secret policeman again, we should let them know immediately. Otherwise, we were to continue as before. You couldn't crumble and throw in the towel over something like being followed. Since that time, our apartment in Neuquén had also become a safe house for resistance members passing through.

Operation Condor sowed fear in insidious ways. One was to spread rumours that the resistance was infiltrated: that behind every contact you had, every letter you received, every instruction you were given lay an infiltrator, an informer, an agent, a torturer. Because of this, it was difficult to recruit new members. The belief that the resistance was run entirely by Pinochet's dictatorship, in order to trap people, was ingrained so deeply that people laughed each time new graffiti appeared in strategic places around Santiago. Commuters passed wall after wall of red-painted slogans proclaiming that 1986 was the decisive year, but most believed the graffiti had been put there by the military to give police an excuse to raid more homes, to arrest more people, to reinstate curfew. I'd had my own doubts after seeing the secret policeman at the supermarket. How could they have got on to us so quickly in Neuquén? At what point had we shown up on their radar: Lima? La Paz? Villa María? All the way back in Vancouver? And who were Lucas and Juan, really? What if Lucas had become an informer, or had always been one? Why were they sending us to the heart of Santiago to drop off the goods? Doubts ran through my mind in an endless loop. I assumed Alejandro had his doubts, too, though neither of us expressed them to the other. We understood that the paranoia bred by the dictatorship was another way they tried to break us.

After a quick walk around La Moneda Palace, which still bore signs of bombing on the day of the coup—"I have to see it, Skinny, I just do," Alejandro had pleaded—we boarded a midnight bus to Osorno. From there, we'd take a bus to Neuquén, crossing back over the snowy Andes, arriving late Sunday night, just in time for work on Monday. It was hard to watch the country I was dedicating my life to pass by outside the window.

BY MAY 1987, Alejandro and I had moved into an apartment on the top floor of a high-rise on the most coveted corner of downtown Neuquén, where we continued to lodge resistance members on a regular basis. Although I liked our more comfortable central quarters, I'd felt a pang the day we left the wrong side of the tracks. Sometimes when I'd walked the dark roads at night, I'd heard men murmur, "There she is," in Spanish, not Romanian, so I'd understood they were looking out for me. That neighbourhood had been a safe place for us. The police steered clear of those roads, afraid of a people who leapt to defend themselves if one of their own was hurt. Chilean labourers had no such luck with the police or other authorities, as I saw when I made my weekly pilgrimage to the government building in pursuit of my Argentinian national identity card. While I stood in line for hours with the requested paperwork, some U.S. dollars for bribe money tucked in my hand, I watched the Chileans who were trying to get a work permit—which would end their undocumented status—be publicly humiliated again and again.

We were renting our new place from our closest friend at the flying club for the same sum we'd been paying in the Gypsy neighbourhood.

His father had given him the place for dalliances, he said, but now that he was engaged, he wouldn't be needing it. Once we had a presentable apartment in an appropriate location, I started giving private English classes in the mornings and on weekends, charging a pretty penny.

I'd become friends with many of the teachers at the English Institute of British Culture, and one in particular seemed perfect for recruitment as a helper. Alejandro and I shared many meals with Ximena and her husband, Agustín, who taught electronics at the technical high school. They were both leftists from Córdoba; her father was a military man who had refused to participate in Jorge Videla's 1976 coup and so had been kept in jail for the entirety of the dictatorship, tortured almost to death. Now someone in Neuquén would know if we'd fallen and could notify the right people as soon as possible. "To the great avenues opening again," Agustín said, tears in his eyes, as we raised a toast.

Alejandro was well on his way to becoming a licensed private pilot, learning on Tomahawks and Cessnas. We'd already done a preliminary flight into the Chilean Andes, planning to play dumb if we were intercepted. We couldn't afford flight training for me yet, so I did two more border runs by land—dropping off goods each time—wearing fashionable clothes paid for in monthly instalments. That was my everyday look now. My hair was permed and streaked with blond highlights, my makeup heavy, my shoulder pads huge. Documents arrived regularly in our post office box, and we'd spend hours poring over them: in-depth analyses of the situation in Chile, instructions about our next move and information on world politics to contextualize it all.

The Terror came in waves, sometimes forcing me to hang on to walls as I walked down the street. Once it hit me as I waited in a bank lineup. The world started to spin, but before I could faint and draw unwanted attention, I'd sat down cross-legged on the marble floor and dropped my head into my hands. When people inquired, I explained I suffered from terrible migraines. I'd made my way home slowly, covered in cold sweat.

The much-anticipated assassination attempt against Pinochet had happened the previous September. His convoy had been ambushed on a quiet country road in the Maipo Valley, an hour out of Santiago, where Pinochet kept a weekend home. The eighteen-strong guerrilla force managed to kill five of the general's men, but the rocket launcher meant for the dictator had jammed. A grenade tossed under his car had also failed to go off. The window of Pinochet's bulletproof limousine was riddled with submachine-gun fire, but to no avail. Within minutes the attack was over. The resistance fighters escaped in their fake secret police cars, M-16s pointed out the open windows. Their disguises were so convincing, all the military roadblocks opened up for them as they sped through.

Two hundred people had contributed their skills to the assassination attempt. It had been modelled on similar actions, most notably the assassination of Nicaraguan strongman Anastasio Somoza in Asunción, Paraguay, in 1980, and was so carefully planned it had seemed foolproof. Its failure wasn't the first major blow for the resistance during the decisive year. In mid-1986, a ship carrying $30 million worth of arms for the resistance had been seized by the Chilean military after people broke under torture and released key information.

The assassination attempt had unleashed a wave of repression that extended to the Chilean shantytowns in Neuquén. Many were arrested in nighttime raids and sent back into the hands of Pinochet. The Cold War was still the excuse for suppressing workers' movements in the rest of Latin America, but change was in the air. Mikhail Gorbachev's anti-Stalinist approach as the Soviet Union's Communist Party general secretary pointed to the end of the Cold War soon. Right-wing dictatorships were falling in every country from the Philippines to Paraguay. It looked as if Nelson Mandela's release from jail was imminent, making a future African National Congress government in South Africa a real possibility. The first intifada was raging in Palestine; the Sandinistas had prevailed in Nicaragua, despite the Reagan-backed Contra war; and the FMLN was likely to seize power in El Salvador. As for Argentina, we'd just survived the first coup attempt against Alfonsín.

Alejandro and I had awoken on Easter Sunday 1987 to the news that a coup was well under way. While we burned all our documents and flushed the ashes down the toilet, millions took to the streets around the country. In Neuquén, forty thousand people, a third of the city's population, congregated outside the government building to protest the coup, clasping hands and singing the national anthem. It was a strange sight to behold: the rich mixing with the poor, illegal Chilean construction workers singing the Argentinian anthem alongside wealthy women in Vidal Sassoon haircuts. We watched from our high-rise, longing to be on the street below. Our radio was tuned to the live broadcast from the Plaza de Mayo in Buenos Aires, where a million people had gathered and the sound of warplanes flying overhead could be heard. Dozens of secret police agents lay on the tops of the buildings around us, invisible from below, taking pictures of the faces in the crowd with their high-tech zoom lenses.

The military apparatus and the secret police were still intact in Argentina, and Alfonsín's transgression was to allow trials for crimes against humanity, which had been ongoing for two years. February had been the deadline for survivors to charge their torturers, causing a mad scramble of filings in which another 450 current military officers had been named. The Easter coup was quashed, but the cost of that victory was still to be revealed.

"HURRY! GO MILK the cow!" my grandmother ordered.

She stood in the doorway of her yellow wooden house, hands on her hips, mischief in her eyes. I waded through two feet of water that covered the sidewalk, resigned to the fact that I'd just ruined a pair of shoes it would take me a year to pay off. The delivery boy from the general store had ridden his bike through the flooded streets, carrying my suitcase in his basket. It was early winter, and a third of Chile was under water because of torrential storms. Every year it was the same story: floods, mass evacuations, people in the shantytowns left to stand shivering on the side of the road with their babies in their arms. The bus that had brought me to Limache from Santiago had passed countless families on the shoulders of the highway, an expanse of water behind them, bundles at their feet. They stood on the side of the road because there was nowhere else for them to go. They weren't waiting for a bus, because they couldn't have afforded the fare. They simply stood and waited for something—anything—as their lips turned purple from the cold and their babies trembled in their wet woollen clothes.

My grandmother handed a bunch of coins to the grocery boy and winked. I wrapped my arms around her, kissing her cheeks and the top of her head.

"Abuelita! What are you talking about? You have a cow now?"

"Shhh! Don't yell! You might spook it. The cow is not mine. It belongs to someone from up the road. All the orchards are flooded, and the fences came down, and the cow's confused. It's been standing in the middle of my orchard for a day now, mooing away. I tried to milk it, but the water reaches up to my hips. The bucket's in the back. You go do it."

"Abuelita, I've never milked a cow, and it's not like I'm going to start now."

"Not so loud. We're taking its milk, so it shouldn't be advertised."

I waded around to the back of the house. Sure enough, there was a lone cow mooing softly in the middle of the water. My grandmother appeared at the back door, gesturing for me to get going.

"Abuelita, that cow will knock me over with a good swift kick, and then lean on me till I drown. Forget it. Besides, I've been travelling for forty-eight hours to get here. My travel money ran out way back in the south, and I haven't eaten for twenty-four hours. I need a hot cup of tea with condensed milk."

"All right, come in. The witches will keep us company," my grandmother said.

Her dining room table had become her work area, with my grandfather gone. Sure enough, we drank our tea among witches. There were dozens of them. Witches on brooms, witches on chairs, witches on bicycles, witches wearing black hats and red lace stockings.

"Why witches, Abuelita?"

"Because witches are illegal. That's a good enough reason for me."

Each time I'd come to Chile to make a delivery, after that first time with Alejandro, I'd stayed on for a few days with my grandmother. This was my fourth venture inside. Once I was over the border, I'd press myself against the window of the bus and devour that long, skinny country with my eyes. But standing in line as a life-sized portrait of Pinochet stared down at me, waiting in the loaded silence punctuated by the stomping of military boots, a bark here, an order there, sent me into a free fall of fear. I'd heard that the life expectancy of a person who starts doing border crossings was only two years. That knowledge could eat me alive, I realized, causing me to break and do something stupid, or it could spur me to refine my skills. So even though I was twenty pounds underweight, completely frigid (Alejandro had given up reaching for me at night) and suffering from dizzy spells, I'd worked hard to master the skill of killing my heart whenever I crossed the border. First I conjured Juan's voice, ordering me to remember why I was doing this, reminding me that all experience was good, precious, unforgettable. Then I'd invoke the machete-wielding man in Coroico slicing the bull's throat and yanking out its heart. Sometimes I also conjured up my three great-aunts, who'd made their fortune smuggling goods across this very line. By the time I reached the wicket to present my passport, my pupils were shrunken and my heart left behind, a squashed tomato on the floor. I'd answer the border guard's questions with a steady hand and a steadier gaze. Then I'd be let through, with whatever goods I'd wrapped and sewn into the lining of my new suitcase. As I rode through the Andes, I'd will my heart to enter my body again, and with it would come the release of the breath I'd been holding for the last two hours. If my great-aunts had known they were an inspiration for their militant niece, they'd have had to increase their dosage of the tranquilizers they loved to pop.

My grandmother was looking at me sternly. "I want to tell you that whatever it is you're doing, it's not going to work."

"I don't know what you're talking about, Abuelita." I took a sip of my tea and tried to get warm, a project that usually took all winter.

"We both know what I'm talking about, and I'm telling you it's not going to work. Why? Because we live in a country of cowards."

"Abuelita—"

"Don't interrupt me. In what world is it okay for people to watch two youngsters being beaten, doused with gasoline and set on fire? First the soldiers beat them, and people watch. Then the soldiers take their half-conscious bodies to a side road and beat them some more, while people pull their curtains and cower in their houses. Then the soldiers set them on fire, and people dive onto their bathroom floors. It makes me sick to be a part of this."

"Abuelita, people are terrified."

"I don't care. If every one of those households had gone outside and defended those children with whatever they had, any weapon, even if it was just a chair, and if every household did that every time something like this happened, then I'd say to you: go ahead, granddaughter, continue doing what you're doing, because we stand a chance. But here, here in this cursed country, there's no chance of anything. You tell me people are scared? Well, let me tell you something: there's nothing more dangerous than the poison of fear. I've seen fear turn people into informers, monsters, turning in their own friends and neighbours. You're dealing with a country sick with fear, Nieta, and I wish I could say that what you're doing is going to work, but it isn't, it isn't."

"I don't know what you're talking about."

She pulled out her hanky and wiped her eyes. I stared straight ahead. She grabbed one of her half-made witches, took up a toothpick and started to do some fine work on the face.

"Having said that, God knows if I was young I'd be doing what you're doing. Being old and tired, all I can do is go outside during the blackouts and bang my pots and pans. Did you know I'm the only one on this street who does it? Because of Pinochet's fortress on the corner, and the secret police agents who live next door. When a fat old woman is the only one who's not afraid to make some noise, when the youth of this country have been broken down to that point, then there's nothing to be done. After the blackout I'll be trimming the flowers out front and the neighbours will pass, saying, 'I heard your pots and pans last night, Señora Carmen.' I look them right in the eye and say, 'Yes, and where were your pots and pans, you coward? Aren't you ashamed of yourself?' Then I get back to my camellias. They just drop their heads and walk a little faster."

The assassination attempt on Pinochet might have failed, but now, six months into 1987, the lid seemed to be coming off the country. The fact that it was possible to get that close to the strongman himself gave people courage and hope. I'd been a witness to this on the buses I'd taken to get to Limache. Shockingly, many of the passengers had spoken loudly against the dictatorship. I'd kept my arms crossed and my mouth shut. The last thing I wanted was for our bus to be intercepted.

"But, Abuelita, people are starting to speak up."

"They can speak all they want, Nieta, but it's a long way from speaking to doing. To think that unspeakable son of a bitch is claiming our patron saint as his saviour."

My grandmother took her new witch on a little spin through the air. "What do you mean?"

"Haven't you heard what he's saying about the Virgin Carmen, the patron saint of Chile? The one you and your mother and I are all named after? The one who protects our borders? According to Pinocchio, the Virgin Carmen protected him from being killed. He's shown the bulletproof glass on TV countless times. He claims that the gunfire created the shape of the Virgin on his window, that she came to him in the form of bullets that were never meant to penetrate his flesh. He loves to go on about his devout Catholicism, but even the Pope agreed to come to Chile only on the condition that Pinocchio get rid of the exile blacklist. I check that list in the newspaper. It's down to five hundred now, and both your mother and your uncle are still on it. Their names are published for all to see, so everyone can know that they're considered terrorists, that they're not allowed into their own country. But you'll see, you'll see. As soon as their names are off, any day now, my children will come back, and I'll throw a party for them right here in this house, and I'll show the neighbours that my children are good. My children are good."

I stayed with her for a week. She fed me, massaged my back with cologne, prepared hot water bottles, washed and ironed my clothes and let me lie in bed all day reading my parents' old books. I devoured Hemingway's *A Moveable Feast* and Galeano's *Days and Nights of Love and War*. My grandmother's house was a capsule, a place where my mind roamed and I laughed in my sleep. I fantasized about the day I'd live there again, when Chile was free.

The day I left, my grandmother waved to me from her front door. I stood up straight, locked my jaw and headed down the street to catch a bus back to Santiago. When I looked back, she mouthed the words "Be careful."

Her yellow house framed her round body. The camellia bush shone in the winter sun, and my grandmother's face collapsed.

Go back there, I thought. Go back there and live with her forever. Just turn around. Go back to the house where the Terror doesn't exist. But that wasn't what I'd signed on for. And my grandmother had said if she were my age, she'd be doing what I was. I certainly couldn't let her down.

25

SCANNED THE CROWD as I stepped off the bus, but nobody looked familiar.

"Cousin?"

"Yes?"

"It's me, Chelito."

He placed his hand on my forearm. I blinked. This bespectacled geek was the boy I'd worshipped? I tried to find the god behind the winter coat as we climbed into a taxi.

"I'm wearing this tuque in your honour."

I giggled at the pompom on top of his head.

"A classmate of mine is a returnee from Montreal, and he gave it to me."

It was seven years since the summer I'd discovered love. Now I was a married nineteen-year-old English teacher living an underground life. The Cousin was a twenty-three-year-old playboy, going to law school at the University of Concepción, which I knew was a hotbed of resistance activities.

We drove along the wet streets of Puerto Montt. The place was famous for its fish market, which offered an array of delicacies fresh from the sea. I took in the wooden houses, the children in their navy-blue school uniforms, the dark, Mapuche-blooded Chileans striding along the glistening sidewalks in muddy boots. Uncle Carlos and Aunt Vicky had moved to this southern port town, a twelve-hour bus ride from Santiago, and I'd decided to visit them before leaving the country.

"Here she is! A woman now!"

Aunt Vicky opened the door to a large pink house overlooking the ocean. She had aged, and all remnants of the nouveau riche lady from Concepción were gone. Her face was free of makeup, and an apron was tied around her waist.

"I just finished waxing the floors, so you'll have to excuse the smell. But breakfast is on the table."

Homemade bread and a steaming cup of tea in English china awaited. Last time I'd seen this family, they'd defended Chile's "economic miracle." But they'd lost everything in the 1982 crash, and now they were in debt up to their ears. It was the typical story of Chile's new middle class. There were no more maids, no more fancy parties, exclusive clubs or private schools. They lived in a rundown rented house with only the wood stove in the kitchen to keep them warm. My uncle, my grandmother had told me, was now an underpaid accountant in a company that exported seafood to Japan. A purported aphrodisiac from these shores called "el loco" (when under the influence, you were said to be suffering from "loco fever") sold like hotcakes in Tokyo. My cousin Elena was attending secretarial school, and her brother Mario, an alternative musician in Santiago, did six-month stints on commercial fishing boats. The youngest, Gastón, was completing his final year of high school.

"Take off your coat and hat, Son, before you come to the table," my aunt ordered.

My cousin removed his tuque and bookish glasses. Smoothing his hair, he sat down across from me and winked. My body, frozen for so long, came to life with a jolt. My squashed-up heart ballooned.

When I'd made the arrangements to spend four days with my uncle and aunt, I'd had no idea the Cousin would be there on his winter break. We ran errands for my aunt and talked every night until the break of dawn. The fire ignited in me at the breakfast table raged and raged as my spirit nestled back into the centre of my body. Cocooned in my aunt and uncle's house, it seemed sometimes as if I'd never left Chile. Maybe all that existed, all that had ever existed, was the here and now: my relatives and me in the pink wooden house, going to the market every day for fresh fish and bread, conversing with one another in the shorthand families have.

But my underground life was never far from my mind. One day I asked the Cousin to drive me to the Puerto Montt flying club, located at the town's small airport. Alejandro hoped eventually to fly us both to Puerto Montt to visit Chelito's family, I told him. The man in charge came out to greet us with a warm handshake.

"My husband is only now getting his licence and will need a lot of help crossing the mountains," I explained. "Is there radar all along the way?"

"Oh, yes, Señora, tell your husband not to worry. The Chilean mountain range is one of the most radar-heavy in the world. There's no way we'll let him get lost. The radar will lead him by the nose all the way to our door."

"Thank you so much."

"Give our regards to Tomás and Andrés at the Neuquén flying club. And we look forward to meeting your husband, Señora."

"I'm sure he'll look forward to meeting you."

As we pulled up in front of the pink house, the Cousin spoke quietly. "Be careful, my little Marxist."

"I'm not a Marxist—"

"That's all I'm going to say."

A bitter laugh escaped the Cousin's lips whenever one of Pinochet's promotional spots came on TV. Outfitted in a nylon track suit, he'd wave to the camera as a deep paternal voice intoned: "The saviour of the fatherland jogs every day." Or maybe he'd be wearing his general's uniform while cradling a baby in his arms: "The saviour of the fatherland visits the Children's Hospital." Or perhaps he'd be in his cape, marching away from the camera, only to turn around at the end and salute. The night of our visit to the airport, the Cousin went further.

"Fucking old man. I was so happy when we heard there had been an attempt on his life. We hid in our houses, quiet as mice, waiting for confirmation that the monster was dead, waiting to erupt from our doors like volcanoes in celebration. I ran it in my head over and over again: which neighbour I'd hug first, which vendor I'd take in my arms, which beggar I'd kiss on the cheeks. I cannot tell you what it felt like to fall back into the abyss when we found out he'd survived. But something did change on that day. Something changed in the Chilean psyche, and that change has been growing ever since."

The Cousin cleared his throat, then glanced out the window. We were alone in the living room, each of us seated in an armchair. I kept my gaze on him, holding him fast with my eyes.

He continued, shifting his eyes to meet mine. "Last year, I went to a protest at the university in Concepción. I hadn't planned on going, but this protest was big. The head of the secret police was coming in from Santiago to give a talk on national security. The student body declared war, and before I knew it, I was shuffling to get away in my leather loafers, like an idiot, gagging from the tear gas."

He laughed and looked out the window again. I stayed stock still, not wanting to change a single molecule in the air.

"There were hundreds of other students. They were all wearing running shoes and bandanas over their faces. Their hands were full of Molotov cocktails and slingshots. They knew how to run, to dive, to hit the bull's eye even while walking backwards. A group would disperse in front of my eyes, then reappear moments later, just a little down the way. The girls were especially impressive. Tough as nails, scaling walls like ninjas, throwing burning bottles at the military. I couldn't believe these were some of the same girls I bedded on Saturday nights. As I watched, I wondered if they'd been the ones bedding me."

A smile flickered across his face.

"Anyway, I got jammed against a wall. A few of the paramilitaries moved toward me, with their guns pulled. I thought it was my last moment on earth. Their faces were shielded by Plexiglas, but I saw one of the men's eyes. They were ferocious. Wild. I wondered what drug he was on. He aimed his gun at my face, then lowered it to my crotch. There was an explosion, then darkness."

When the Cousin came to, he said, he was lying in a heap of students at the back of a military bus. Whenever new students were thrown onto the pile, the paramilitaries would kick at their ribs, heads and backs. He'd been afraid the steel-toed boots would kick his brains out.

"I lost consciousness again, and when I regained it, I was receiving the beating of my life in an underground jail. I could hear blood-curdling screams all around me, and I was making sounds I didn't recognize as my own. Once they'd finished beating me, a doctor pulled out the bullet that was lodged in my thigh. I found out later this was standard practice: Israel provides Pinochet with arms, on the condition that the evidence be removed. All but ten of us were released twenty-four hours later, and there was nothing we could do to help those left behind." He clutched the arms of his chair, his knuckles white. "I understand now why the resistance talks about being the army for the people. Anyway, they dropped me off in a shantytown ditch at dawn. Some kids spotted me and called to their mothers, 'Here's another one!' It breaks my heart to imagine the horrors they've seen in their short lives. The women cleaned me up, and a trucker drove me home. I live with my maternal grandmother in Concepción, as you know, and when the trucker laid me at the bottom of her stairs, she shouted, 'This is what you get for being a Communist, you filthy ingrate.' You know her—she held a tea party the day of the coup. She walked away, wouldn't even help me get up. My thighs were twice their size, my face so swollen it was hard to see my features. Mami came to Concepción to nurse me back to health, and after a month in bed, I was able to return to school."

We had a little laugh together. Neither of us cried. I knew that if I started to cry I might never stop. Seeing the Cousin again had already unleashed something deep in me. But I had survived thus far in the resistance by keeping a clamp on my heart, on my loins, on my tears. That couldn't change now.

ON THE LAST DAY of my visit, Mario arrived with news from Santiago. Chile had been flooded with returnees since the Pope's visit. The influx was met with disdain by some, but with great solidarity by many. Huge caravans with banners reading "Welcome Back to Your Rightful Home, Exiles!" waited at the airport for the jam-packed flights arriving daily from the United Kingdom, Australia, Sweden, Germany, Italy and Spain. Music groups like Inti-Illimani, Quilapayún and Illapu had come back from Europe, and Mario's own band had played at some of their sold-out concerts.

That night in Puerto Montt, at a nightclub on the seawall, the Cousin took me in his arms.

"I love you, Cousin," he whispered. "Please stay. Leave your husband and stay with me." My heart broke clean in two.

The Cousin drove me to the bus station the next morning, but he didn't go home after I boarded. Instead, he chased the bus in his father's car, honking as he drove alongside. When the bus slowed at a fork in the road, the Cousin slammed on the brakes, jumped out of the car and started waving his arms. "Stay!" he shouted.

The bus driver had figured out by now that this was not the secret police ordering him to pull over, but a lover driven mad with passion, a common enough sight in Chile. When he glanced at me in his rearview mirror, I averted my eyes. The driver stepped on the gas again, and we were gone.

In my suitcase were maps of underground trails from a package I'd been handed on a downtown Santiago street. Thinking of that pulled me back to reality. Once I got back to Neuquén, I'd have to break the news to Alejandro: the radar in the Andes meant we'd have to fly low through the mountains on our first delivery by air. If we were intercepted, we'd have to smash our plane against the rock face. Either that, or be shot down by the enemy. Both were better than torture, though I wouldn't live past twenty in either scenario.

My heart fluttered in its cage like a hummingbird. It would be difficult to plunge a knife into its core, but I hadn't figured out another way to cut through the fear. As we drew closer to the border, I put the Cousin somewhere far away. Even if I were to die in a plane crash, though, fuselage and limbs scattering so far from anywhere that our remains would never be found, at least I knew this much was true: I was still a sensual being.

"You travel in and out of Chile a lot," the Argentinian border guard said as he studied the stamps in my passport.

"Yes, I do."

"Why?" His eyes were steady on mine.

"Because I have family there."

"Fine. We're watching you."

"Thank you."

He stamped my passport and let me through. My tightened muscles hurt. My face, so open only hours before, was now a hardened mask.

When the bus stopped in Bariloche for an hour, I hid inside the tiny terminal. My life in Neuquén, only six hours away, could never intersect with what I'd been in Bariloche: a Bolivian girl with a Canadian father. I leaned against a wall and let my body tremble. Before I boarded the bus, a young woman approached me.

"Do you know if there are buses to Trelew?"

"No, but there are buses to Buenos Aires."

With that, I handed her the package of maps, and we went our separate ways.

26

"FLYING IS A man's sport, and I'm taking my life into my hands by sitting in this airplane with you."

"Yes, you remind me of that every time."

Two other instructors had refused to teach me, but Rodolfo had begrudgingly agreed. Having just completed the pre-flight check, we'd boarded and were now about to taxi onto the runway. I turned the key in the ignition, watched the propeller come to life and radioed the control tower.

"Listen to this, buddy, that girl's on the radio again!"

"Get her off!"

"She's piloting the Piper Tomahawk!"

I smiled to myself as I looked down at the parcels of land on the outskirts of Neuquén, divided into perfect squares bordered by poplars. When we'd reached our desired height, Rodolfo shut off the engine. We went into a nosedive, the ground coming at us fast.

"What are you going to do now?"

"This," I said.

I pulled the steering wheel with all my might and brought the nose up.

"Good. Good reflexes."

He turned the ignition back on.

"Now let's try something else. This is called Japanese eights."

We inscribed eights in the sky, with me laughing and whooping. When it was time to land, I gauged the wind and let the wheels touch the ground at the perfect time.

"Not bad, not bad. Strong stomach, good reflexes, calm and steady. We might make a pilot out of you."

He'd been hard on me, and I'd loved it. In just a few months, Alejandro and I would be ready to make our first delivery flight into Chile.

UPON MY RETURN from Puerto Montt, I'd been offered a job as a conversational English teacher for the tourism school at the National University of Comahue. My students were mostly older than I was, heavily involved in the student union movement, and I ached to live the life they led: debating over yerba maté, hitchhiking around the country during breaks, organizing rallies and protests. To them I was a super-cool young native English speaker from Canada, petit bourgeois to the core with my high-rise studio apartment, flying club antics and fashionable clothes. When the talk turned to politics, I kept my mouth shut.

My favourite of the bunch was a woman called Luisa. She'd grown up in a working-class family in the province of Paraná, in northeastern Argentina, and had hitchhiked from there to the province of Neuquén, where she'd lived on a Mapuche reserve for a year before coming to the capital. She lived at the cathedral, where the bishop—a revered human rights activist who had barely survived the dictatorship after he'd been caught using the cathedral as a hiding place for resistance members and a haven for mothers of the disappeared—let her have a small room in exchange for janitorial work. Luisa lived on nothing, so I started inviting her to our house for meals. Anytime she showed up with a slab of meat, a loaf of bread, a hunk of cheese or a jar of jam, she'd announce: "Compliments of the supermarket. I steal only from the chains, the bigger the better. Never from small businesses."

"How do you keep from getting caught?"

"Nerves of steel, mi querida, nerves of steel."

"But they have cameras."

"Oh, I know. It's just a matter of checking where the cameras are, making no fast movements, and never losing your composure. How do you think I've defied starvation all these years?"

I'd received a tear-stained letter from the Cousin within a month of my return. Since then, there'd been many more. He cracked my heart open every time. It was dangerous enough to have to lean on buildings when a wave of terror hit me. To couple that with the weak-in-the-knees sensation of illicit love was just plain stupid. And there was my secret betrayal of Alejandro. He was a comrade, a companion, a brother, a soulmate, but I'd come to realize I loved him in those ways, not as a lover. By late November 1987, the height of spring, I knew I had to leave him, and not for the Cousin. For myself. But first, the flight into Chile had to be completed.

Juan paid us a visit in Neuquén. We met him at a bus stop, then rode with him in the back seat of a bus that wound along dirt roads through the apple orchards, picking up and dropping off the peons and maids who worked in the area. We could talk safely there, as long as we kept our voices low.

"Now I want you to show me the plane," Juan said, after we'd discussed our flight plan. "I need to see how much space there is. The first time you'll drop off goods. The ultimate goal is to drop off people, of course."

"Of course."

At the flying club, we introduced him as Alejandro's uncle, visiting from Mendoza. Juan was disappointed at how small the Tomahawk was, but he cheered up when we showed him the larger Cessna.

"So you'll start with the Tomahawk, and we'll see how that goes."

"That's right."

"Excellent work."

Pinochet had announced he would hold a plebiscite in 1988, now only a month away. The people of Chile would be asked a yes or no question: do you want Pinochet to govern for another eight years? If the

Yes side won, all would proceed as usual. If the No side won, elections would be held a year later. The plebiscite was worrisome to people in the resistance. For one thing, the entire adult population would be required by law to register for the vote, providing personal information like addresses, phone numbers, place of work, names of family members and ID card numbers. Many believed this "registration" was just a way of collecting information for the secret police.

If the No side were to succeed—which seemed likely, since seventeen opposition parties in Chile had joined forces—the Christian Democratic leader, head of the opposition coalition, would win the elections that followed. There would be widespread euphoria at first. Most human rights abuses would undoubtedly cease. But the neoliberal economic structure of Chile would remain intact, and the new government would inherit a staggering foreign debt. As in Argentina, the IMF and the World Bank would demand that the new government set up a "structural adjustment plan" to repay that debt, meaning social services would not be reinstated and government spending would be cut back even further. The constitution put in place by Pinochet in 1980 would remain the same, barring the new government from prosecuting anyone for crimes against humanity and giving Pinochet a seat in the senate, as well as allowing him to keep his position as commander-in-chief of the armed forces. The secret police and other repressive apparatus would remain intact; probably dormant, but there all the same.

To many in the resistance, the plebiscite looked like the worst thing that could happen. The increasing polarization and unrest in Chile pointed to the possibility of radical change. If power could be seized soon through a revolution, the resulting provisional government could rip up the constitution, imprison members of the military, kick out the IMF, the World Bank and the multinational corporations, and work on re-establishing a democratically run socialist state.

The resistance, its members exhausted after fifteen years of persecution, was beginning to split. Some believed it was time to throw in the towel and join the coalition. Others believed the resistance still had a chance. For the latter group, time was of the essence.

"We need to organize this first drop-off of goods as soon as possible," Juan informed us. "Go to the post office box every day, and the instructions will be there."

In mid-December, Alejandro and I signed out the Tomahawk from the flying club for a day trip, loading it with goods we'd wrapped in towels and blankets and stashed inside two gym bags. A couple of young Argentinian men had dropped them off the night before at a busy greasy spoon.

Flying as low as we possibly could, we navigated through the mountain range. Alejandro had scouted the route twice earlier, accompanied by a rich daredevil skydiver who frequented the club. He made not a peep during Alejandro's "accidental" forays across the border.

"There they are!" Alejandro said now, pointing from the pilot's seat.

Two people below waved from an open field.

Thanks to Alejandro's skill, we landed safely. We unloaded the bundles and handed them to a man and a woman. They were clearly Mapuche. Within a minute it was done, with no words spoken. Everybody's hands shook.

My heart was in my mouth as we flew back. Not only because at any moment our lives could end, but because we'd achieved what we set out to do: deliver goods for a revolution whose goal was that the poor could eat, would have access to medical care and education and shelter. The other lives I constantly imagined gave way to this one. I was coasting in a plane through the Andes with a man who loved me unconditionally, a compañero who was squeezing my hand now as tears rolled down his face.

THAT CHRISTMAS EVE, my grandmother was reunited with her three children for the first time since the days of Allende. Mami and Uncle Boris had flown to Chile, filled with emotion, when the no-return list was finally erased, thanks to the Pope's continued pressure.

At dinner, I sat between Alejandro and the Cousin, symbols of the two halves of my heart. Joining us around the dining room table, to which the kitchen table had been added, were Ale, who'd reinvented herself as the head aerobics instructor at Vancouver's trendiest gym; Lalito; my cousin Elena, hiding an out-of-wedlock pregnancy from my grandmother; my uncle Carlos and aunt Vicky; my aunt Magdalena; my little cousin Sarita; my mother's new partner, Bill; and the Cousin's eight-year-old daughter, Princesa, whom he'd had with the maid I'd met in Concepción on my first visit to his home.

My grandmother beamed during the whole week-long visit. We went through the boxes she'd stored in the back, every object we uncovered inspiring an anecdote. The adults told story after story of Chile during the dark years. My grandmother was still shaken up by the broadcast on national television a few weeks earlier of a young resistance member making a confession.

"They accused that young woman of being an accomplice in the abduction of a high-ranking military man and interrogated her for the whole country to see," my grandmother said. "Her scalp was oozing pus, her eyes were swollen shut, her head was held up by a hand at the base of her skull, and they shone a light in her face while making her say into the camera that she was a terrorist, that she had helped with the abduction and she regretted it. They put her on during *María Belongs to Nobody*, the siesta soap opera, when they knew everyone would be watching. And she was rich, with a German last name, from a well-to-do family, well connected, a brilliant student from Las Condes."

There was silence at the table as my grandmother wiped her eyes. After a moment, Uncle Carlos remarked on the perfect comedic timing of the resistance: when Miss Chile had won the Miss Universe contest that winter, there'd been a blackout just as Pinochet had come on TV to use the win as a huge media vehicle for himself. Everyone laughed as we remembered that.

We dreamed about what the future might hold for our family. We made outings to Viña del Mar and Valparaíso, both packed with returning exile families. All around us, parents translated for children conversing in English, Swedish, German and French. The fifteen of us posed for pictures on the seawall and bought fresh seafood at the port, as Uncle Boris cracked one joke after another. Both he and my mother found a moment to nod knowingly at Alejandro and me. When everyone left again for Canada, my heart broke for the millionth time.

Soon after we got back to Neuquén, I told Alejandro I wanted to end our marriage. Our conversation stretched over twelve hours, during which no food or drink was consumed. Finally, lost in the maze of words that tried to make sense of what had gone wrong, he went numb. I doubled over in pain.

I left Alejandro, but I remained true to the resistance, staying in Neuquén and continuing to follow orders. I rented a downtown apartment with a roommate named Fabiana, a fellow English teacher. She was right-wing, the daughter of a decorated military man. She was a hard worker and a party girl, and we'd go dancing together. Through her I met a professional basketball player who was the antithesis of Alejandro: a macho playboy from the Argentinian middle class, with centrist politics and an anti-feminist stance. With Estéban, it was all about wining and dining, dancing and sex. He had no idea about my resistance side. I got a separate post office box, but Alejandro and I remained in constant touch. My life and heart were now completely compartmentalized.

"IS FABIANA HOME?"

"No. She won't be back till much later."

"Here they are. This is all I could get."

Luisa emptied the contents of her backpack onto the dining room table in my apartment: a dozen Argentinian ID cards. I was still waiting for my own card, checking at the government office regularly.

"I put my pickpocket skills to use during Sunday mass. Hope this helps."

It was July 1988. The plebiscite was only three months away, and the repression in Chile was relentless. The No campaign was so huge, so popular that rallies were now happening on a daily basis. The month before, the resistance had called for an underground congress, the first in sixteen years, in Santiago to discuss strategies. Alejandro went to Santiago on our behalf, but he never made it to the congress.

He'd waited on the designated corner once he got to Santiago, he told me later at a downtown Neuquén café. It was a Friday night, and Santiago was crazy with people and traffic. When a white Datsun stopped, Alejandro jumped in. There were five people in the car, and the driver told everybody to shut their eyes. Soon they were in a garage, then being ushered into a house through the back door. The walls in the house were covered with newspaper, and all the furniture had been removed. I thought of Rulo and Soledad's political education session in La Paz. "I tried not to look directly into the faces of the others," Alejandro said, "but I did notice that every other person there looked poor. Really poor. It made me proud, honoured to be in a movement with them. And relieved to see with my own eyes that we're not just a bunch of middle-class assholes telling others what to do. A moment passed, and then another door opened and a man flanked by two bodyguards came in. He seemed familiar. Then it hit me. It was him, Skinny, the leader who's always lived inside Chile, who's never left, whose pictures are plastered everywhere with the words 'Most Wanted' stamped across his face. He looked haggard, completely done for, but there was a light in his eye, and I felt admiration. I couldn't believe I was lucky enough to be in his presence."

But then there'd been three knocks on the wall, Alejandro continued. Soft, but very clear. In one second, the two bodyguards and the five men who'd been there when Alejandro's group arrived pulled out submachine guns and prepared for combat. The back door of the house opened, and wordlessly Alejandro and his companions were shown out.

"I prepared to run, but the white Datsun was ready to take us. It sped through the streets, throwing us against the car doors at every corner. At one point it screeched to a stop, and the driver yelled, 'You, the last one to get in, you're the first one to get off! Open the door and roll out, comrade, roll, stand as quickly as you can, and walk calmly

away. Make contact with your superior when you are safe and sound.'
I did as I was told. When I stood up, I realized I was by the River
Mapocho, downtown again. I walked to the long-distance bus station and came home." Alejandro took a sip of his coffee. "We should
find out soon if the congress happened. We know no one was caught,
because there's been nothing in the news about it. Catching a bunch
of resistance members heading to a congress would be Pinochet's last
trophy before he steps down, right?"

In the midst of the elation that gripped Chile, the secret police had
continued their dirty work, in the poor neighbourhoods especially,
almost undetected by the population at large. Soon after Alejandro
got back I'd received a note in my post office box asking me to assem-
ble thirty Argentinian ID cards. There were people who needed to get
out of Chile immediately, and the fastest way was to simply change
the pictures on real ID cards. And so it was that Luisa, my new helper,
came in handy.

I'd recruited her while we were having a late-night coffee at one of
our regular hangouts on a side street off Argentina Avenue.

"You know what's happening in Chile, right?"

"Yes."

"Obviously you know about Pinochet and all that."

"Of course."

"You must also assume that there's a resistance to the dictatorship."

"You always hear things, but nothing in particular."

"Well, there is a resistance. An underground, armed resistance."

"Good. I'm glad to hear it."

There was a long pause. I kept my eyes fixed on hers, then pointed
calmly toward my chest with my thumb. After a moment, her mouth
dropped open. As I put my index finger to my lips, Luisa smiled broadly.

"I need your help," I said.

"Okay."

"But you can't ask any questions."

"Okay."

By the third week of July, Luisa had managed to steal as many ID cards as we needed. The message in my post office box had included a phone number, for the first time ever. When I dialled the number from a nearby telephone company, a woman answered immediately.

"This is Clara from the company calling," I said. "Is Señor Torres there, please?"

A man came on the line. "Clarita, dear. How's the company doing?"

"It's fine. All the sales have been made."

"Good. Let's meet in two days at 10:00 PM at the office. Do you like dulce de leche pastries?"

"Yes."

"Wear your white pants, and we'll go dancing after." He hung up. I figured the office was the bus terminal, though I couldn't be sure. The reference to dulce de leche pastries was clearly the password.

When I went to the bus terminal two evenings later, it was Rulo who approached me and asked about the pastries. Within minutes we were zigzagging on foot along the streets that branched off Argentina Avenue. I'd never seen anyone do what he did with such skill. One moment we were walking; the next we were ducking into a building entrance; then we were walking again, in a different direction, all without stopping our conversation. I passed him a small mesh bag that contained a man's sweater. The ID cards were in a plastic bag tucked inside.

"We'll walk for a few more blocks and then split off," he said.

"Fine."

I waited for Rulo to say something else, but he didn't. At a corner near the top of the main avenue, he turned to me. "This is where we part. Take care of yourself, little comrade."

He disappeared into the night, and I never saw him again.

In late July, both Alejandro and I got notification in our post office boxes that the congress had gone ahead despite the initial security problems. It had been shortened to only twenty-four hours, and nothing concrete had been decided, other than that the resistance would stand by. Many citizens vocal about voting for the No side had taken to the streets, looking to the resistance as the vanguard, and we needed to be there for them, ready to go, in case the opportunity arose to seize power. Alejandro and I assumed the resistance leadership had gone away to strategize about exactly what being ready meant. Presumably it would involve bringing forward whatever arms were stashed and embarking on a public propaganda campaign, letting it be known through graffiti, leaflets and the resistance newsletter, which circulated secretly in poor neighbourhoods, schools and universities, that there was still a way for the No campaign to have a revolutionary outcome. In the meantime, we waited in Neuquén for instructions.

THE NO SIDE won in the October referendum in Chile by 56 per cent. I read the headline on a newspaper as I walked by a kiosk. My stomach flipped, but I kept my face still and continued on my way to work. Nobody on the street in Neuquén seemed to care, though I assumed that the Chilean shantytown was in a state of excitement. A great wave of loneliness hit me. Alejandro had gone again to Santiago at the request of the resistance, though we weren't sure why. So the joy and confusion and apprehension were mine to experience alone.

I'd learn later that Alejandro and Rulo had walked the streets of downtown Santiago on the day of the plebiscite. Alejandro figured Rulo would give him some kind of order if the situation called for it. The votes were still being counted as night fell. The military and the police patrolled the streets, with water cannons, tanks, Jeeps and military buses stationed everywhere. Rulo and Alejandro were standing in front of La Moneda Palace when thousands of people erupted from stores, restaurants and office buildings. Horns started honking, and people poured from cars and buses, yelling and screaming: "The No won! The monster has fallen!" Music started to fill the streets.

He and Rulo had continued to walk in silence, Alejandro told me, weeping and laughing. "To walk those streets, to watch that joy after fifteen years of terror... I cried so hard, watching the people taking over those streets and embracing one another, children running, old men pounding each other on the back. Oh, Skinny, that country lives inside my heart now, it lives inside my heart."

But it was only hours before the crackdown began. The paramilitary was ordered to clean up the streets, and Rulo and Alejandro ran down a side street with thousands of others, chased by baton-wielding cops, the tear gas unbearable, the cannon spraying acid water with such force that people were thrown against walls. Sirens and explosions replaced the music. The Santiago sky swarmed with helicopters. But at the luxurious Hotel Carrera, the lobby had been turned into an international press centre, packed with media from all over the world. In a country that had been closed to the outside world for so long, it was a shocking sight.

ON A WINDY weekday morning in November, I made one of my routine visits to the Neuquén government office to ask about my Argentinian ID card. I stood in the line at one of the half-dozen wooden wickets and waited my turn. Nervous Chileans surrounded me, as usual, their worn-out clothes washed and ironed. As always, I played the part of the bourgeois bitch, sighing audibly and looking irritably at my watch. But this time, something was different. When I got to the wicket and presented my documents, the old man who was helping came back with a file. Behind him, I caught the eye of a young, blue-eyed man sitting at a typewriter. My radar went off.

"I'm sorry, Señora, but your ID card isn't ready," the old man said.

"This is an outrage. I've been married for two and a half years to an Argentinian national, and you still can't get it together to give me an ID card."

"Well, Señora, the reason might be this."

He opened the folder and pushed it across the counter. The documents inside were all about me.

The old man held up a photocopy of my Bolivian passport, with its picture of me at fifteen. With his other hand he pulled out a photocopy of a second passport, this one stating that I'd been born in Santiago.

The floor shifted beneath me. A cold sweat broke out on my body, sending rat's claws up my spine. This was it. I'd finally been caught. But why now? Why after the plebiscite, when we were no longer a threat? I was hyper-aware of the blue-eyed man now. I took a deep breath and swallowed, and my underground skills kicked in.

"I have no idea what this is. I am not Bolivian, I never have been, and you people are obviously incompetent."

"But Señora, this is your picture on the Bolivian passport. It's your name, and it's your signature."

I raised the volume on my voice. "Do you take me for an idiot? Obviously there's someone out there who looks like me and has the same name. It's a common enough name, you fool. Do you mean to tell me that this has stopped you from giving me my ID card all this time? This country is so incompetent it's a miracle you all don't die of cholera."

I turned and headed for the door, my heels clicking loudly on the marble floor. Nobody stopped me.

There were many ways of being followed, but if someone had been following me all this time, I certainly hadn't known it. The secret police sometimes trailed people for years, waiting to see where they'd lead them. It was impossible to know why they let some people move freely and picked up others, and you'd drive yourself crazy trying to figure it out. Alejandro and I would never know if we'd really given the secret police the slip after the supermarket incident, or if they'd meant it only as a scare tactic. I zigzagged my way home on the buses. When I got there, I burned everything in sight.

That night, as I walked down the hill after my last class at the university, I heard footsteps directly behind me. I continued walking. No rash movements, no fleeing like the guilty, I reminded myself. My spirit hovered above me, my body braced for the worst. The footsteps continued until the man behind me got so close I could feel his breath on the back of my neck. When I reached the corner, I glanced over my shoulder, and a pair of blue eyes met mine.

From then on, the blue-eyed man followed me openly, in what we called the Japanese way. He sat at the table next to me in cafés, in the seat behind me on the bus. He waited on the street across from my apartment. And he bored his eyes into me. The method was designed to break you, to make you turn yourself in or run screaming into the night.

Using her student union connections, Luisa found out who the man was. "He's in the neo-Nazi youth and works at the registry to keep tabs on Chileans wishing to get Argentinian papers. He's on the secret police's payroll."

The harassment went on for weeks. Whether I was at the kiosk buying my morning newspaper or letting off steam dancing with my students, Fabiana or Estéban, those blue eyes were there. Sometimes days would pass without me being followed. I didn't know whether the secret police were about to pick me up in the middle of the night or they were giving me an opening to grab my stuff and flee. The sudden disappearance of those blue eyes was as terrifying as their presence. Just when I'd start to believe that the stalking was over, I'd turn a corner and the blue-eyed man would be there again. Finally, I sent a note to my superiors in Lima.

SHE WAS REFERRED to as La Chacotera (Chilean slang for "the fun girl") in the response I received two weeks later. I was instructed to meet her on the bench of a certain plaza at 7:30 on a weekday morning. I prayed it wasn't a set-up. And if it wasn't, I prayed the blue-eyed man wouldn't follow me there. It was impossible to know when his "workday" began. Sometimes he'd be out there from first thing in the morning until deep into the night, leaving me to wonder when he slept.

You were usually required to go to a meeting place for ten days straight until contact was made. Your contact might not show up on the first day because she was being followed or because she'd been picked up. It was only during critical times, like just after the assassination attempt on Pinochet, that the rule didn't apply. Then you went only once. If your contact didn't show up, you went into hiding.

I spotted her as soon as I arrived at the plaza. She was strolling around nonchalantly, puffing on a cigarette. The blue-eyed man, whom I'd caught a glimpse of the night before, was nowhere in sight. Either his "shift" didn't start until later today, or this was a trap. I watched myself walk toward her. My spirit perched on the highest branches of a towering eucalyptus, its scent refreshing in the early morning air. Glaringly Chilean with her big brown eyes and fleshy mouth, the woman was dressed a little too alternatively for someone in the underground. Too much funky lapis lazuli jewellery, making her look like a hippie. I wondered whether to proceed. Not wanting to cave in to the paranoia, I sat on a bench, as per my instructions, and took a deep breath. The eucalyptus filled my nostrils. She approached and took a seat next to me.

"Summer's on its way," she said.

"Yes," I responded. "The sun will rip the earth in two."

From there, she got straight to the point. "What's going on?" She faced straight ahead, looking at the empty bench across from us. The less she saw of me, the better. I explained my situation with the blue-eyed man.

"The Japanese way is in full force in downtown Santiago," she said. "One of our oldest members broke down the other day and turned himself in, complete with a briefcase full of resistance documents. He'd lived underground for sixteen years and just couldn't take any more. We can't have that happen again, comrade. This is the first I've heard of the Japanese way being used on this side of the border. You are to go on a long trip as far from Chile and its bordering countries as possible. You are to lose all contact. Come back in two months, and make contact again then."

I stayed behind for five minutes after she left, pretending to study an English text. In the mornings I taught English to children at a new private institute. As I walked in the door that day, swarmed by the eight-year-old students I adored, I noticed a car with four men in it pull up across the street. They could have been there for me, or they could have been looking for leaders of the student union from the national high school down the street.

I immersed myself in the world of "This is a table" and "That is a chair," hoping that the classroom door wouldn't be kicked open, that I wouldn't be dragged by the hair to the waiting car, my innocent students forced to witness something that supposedly didn't happen in this country anymore.

27

IT WAS LATE February 1989, and a real scorcher in downtown Santiago. I'd hitchhiked to Buenos Aires with Luisa a week after getting La Chacotera's orders, and flown from there to Vancouver, where I'd holed up for two months. Although I hadn't told anyone, including Bob or my mother, about the danger I was in, my stomach relaxed for the first time in years. I ate heartily and started to look healthy again. But Vancouver was rainy and cold, and I counted the days until I could leave it behind. Now here I was at the corner of Huérfanos and Ahumada, salivating over the lambada-inspired skirts in the window of the Falabella shop while I waited for the Cousin. A hand clasped my shoulder, and I spun around to meet those green eyes.

Within minutes we were aboard the subway, making out like desperate teenagers. I had one night before I went back to Neuquén to await orders. We rode the subway until closing, and then walked the streets of Las Condes, one of the richest neighbourhoods in the city. According to the Cousin, most of Santiago's poor neighbourhoods were inaccessible because of the burning tires and rows of nails that littered the streets to keep the military at bay. Elections had been called for December, but Pinochet's brutal reign would continue until then.

From Santiago, I flew to Mendoza, where I was scheduled to change planes. After flashing my passport, I retrieved my bags and was looking for a decent place to await my flight to Neuquén when a severe-looking woman in a light blue smock approached.

"You're coming with me," she ordered.

I followed her, the Terror colonizing my body in an instant.

The woman opened the door to a pitch-black room. I waited for her to turn on the light, but she pointed me in with her chin, enjoying the fear she caused. As the door closed behind me, I braced for the inevitable first blow.

A female voice came at me from behind. "Take your clothes off. All of them."

The adrenalin caused me to shake uncontrollably. Sweat poured out of me, feeling like pinpricks on my goosebumps. I fumbled at my buttons with fingers suddenly thick.

"Hurry up, and tell me when you're done."

She was still behind me, closer now. I tried to sense whether there were other people in the room. Secret police cars, airports, bus terminals and designated neighbourhood houses were often equipped as little torture chambers to save the hours it might take to transport a new prisoner to a concentration camp. All I could hear was my teeth chattering.

"I'm done," I said.

The woman flicked on a flashlight and aimed it at my crotch. She was in front of me now.

"Put your hands behind your head and squat."

I did as I was told. I could feel my sweat forming a puddle on the floor as I struggled to control my bowels.

My captor shone the light in my eyes, then knelt and plunged her gloved fingers into my vagina. My spirit fled through the top of my head and landed on the ceiling.

"Cough," she ordered. I did so.

"Turn around."

x

262

From my place on the ceiling I could hear myself whimper like a small child, a high, plaintive sound. It could be part of a sonata, maybe. The Terror Sonata, I'd call it. There'd be whimpers, screams, pleading, begging, crying, moaning—

The woman shoved her finger into my anus, interrupting my composition. "Put your clothes on. We'll be conducting a full search of your belongings as well."

After I'd dressed in the darkness, the woman led me by the arm through the airport. The shock of the light and the sight of fellow humans going about their business were almost too much to bear.

Three men in plain clothes waited in the next room under fluorescent lights. They searched methodically through my bags and purse, opening every package and reading every piece of paper. I stood breathing shallowly as they brought in two German shepherds. One of them jumped up on me, growling. I steeled myself for whatever was coming next. For the first time on a border crossing, I wasn't carrying any goods or secret documents. But would they plant something in my luggage, or pull out a file on all the resistance correspondence I'd sent and received in the last three years?

"You're free to go," one of the men said finally, after he'd flipped through my passport again.

I waited for a moment to see if it was a trick. Then I gathered up my things, stuffing them into my suitcases with shaking hands. When I was ready, the female guard opened the door and let me out, closing the door behind me. I found a bathroom, where I threw up green bile. In the big mirror over the sink, I saw a well-dressed young woman with red eyes and a trembling jaw.

Earlier that month, armed members of a new Argentinian movement called Todos por la Patria (All for the Homeland) had attacked an army base in Buenos Aires. The battle at La Tablada had lasted for hours, and most of the attackers had been killed. The attack had been meant to quash yet another coup attempt against Alfonsín. The militants were left-wing but misguided, with no grassroots support for their actions.

Since the Easter 1987 coup attempt, Alfonsín had passed the Due Obedience Law, which allowed torturers who had been following orders to go free, and a law called the Final Point, which put an immediate deadline on the trials. In spite of this legislation, the generals were far from pacified. In Neuquén, a fifteen-year-old student union leader had been picked up by secret police, raped and let go again. Inflation was out of control, and Alfonsín's popularity had plummeted. Since La Tablada, the clampdown at Argentina's borders had been intense.

Estéban, my basketball player boyfriend, had been traded to a Córdoba team. The city felt different without him and Luisa, who had continued hitchhiking to Brazil. Alejandro had put up resistance members in his apartment all through the summer, he told me, but other than the notes he got in his post office box with the details of people's arrivals, there'd been no word from the resistance. I picked up my privileged Neuquén existence: swimming in the river during the day, meeting friends for coffee in the evening, dancing all night. The blue-eyed man was nowhere to be seen. When the school year started again, I resumed my full-time position and checked my post office box religiously. There was nothing, even as the elections in Chile drew near. Then, one morning, a note: "Meet me at El Tío's steak house near the bus terminal at 11:00 PM on Sunday night."

I let out a sigh of relief. Silence—no contact, no tasks, no instructions—had been the scariest thing of all.

Trinidad walked into the steak house right on time, carrying her battered Samsonite, fresh lipstick on her ripe mouth. She sat down heavily and ordered a glass of wine, tucking into a plate of mashed potatoes with gravy. When she'd finished eating, she reached across the table to take my hands in hers.

"It's over, Carmencita. The resistance has dissolved. We are each to go our own way now. We tried hard, but it's time to state the obvious: we lost. Maybe in ten, twenty, a hundred or a thousand years, the society we dream of will come to be. But we've lost this round."

We gripped each other with all our might. I'd met her when I was eleven. Now I was twenty-one. She'd been the first to take me across the border into Chile. Since then I'd fed her mashed-up rice and offered her a floor to lay her tortured bones on whenever she'd shown up at my door, sometimes breathing hard and sweating, unannounced.

"What are you going to do?" I asked.

She shrugged.

"Do you have family?"

"Yes, I do."

She reached for her wallet and let a dozen baby pictures unfurl. She pointed at one: "This is Lalito when he was a newborn. I've kept him here all this time. How old is he? Nine now? These are the babies of the families who have hidden me. I look at them to remind myself why we're doing this. My babies have given me more strength than you can imagine, and they've kept me company during the lonely times. Baby pictures are of no use to the secret police, either, since they all look the same. So these babies are my family. Do I have a man? Of course not. Do you know of many men willing to wait for seventeen years while their woman goes off to be in the underground?"

We smoked her entire pack of Parliaments as we sat there holding hands across the table.

"If I ever see you on a Santiago street, can I stop and say hello?" I asked her.

"No." She glanced at her watch.

"So, that's it? What am I going to do now?"

"Oh, I'm sure you'll think of something. You've got your whole life ahead of you. As for me, I'll get to see my mother for the first time in sixteen years."

I remembered a distant time and place, the swing set in my old backyard. My best friend Arabella and I had swung on it for the last time when we were both eleven. Swinging and swinging and swinging, then jumping down from the greatest height and walking together to the waiting car, the VW Bug that would take my mother, Ale and me to the airport.

"Everything will change now," Arabella had said as we passed our favourite huckleberry bush.

"Yes, it will."

"Goodbye, baby sparrow."

"Goodbye, baby sparrow."

The farewell was our ritual ever since the day we'd found a fallen baby bird and tried in vain to nurse it back to health.

Trinidad picked up her suitcase, winked and walked away, her lopsided gait so familiar. Glued to my seat, I took in the overflowing ashtray, the empty bottle of wine, the white napkin stained with her lipstick. The tango legend Carlos Gardel, framed in a picture above the table, looked to the side with his perfect white smile, wearing a fedora and black tie. Beneath his photo, the lyrics to "Volver" (To Return) were handwritten in silver ink.

To return with my withered brow, my hair whitened by the snow of time. To feel that life is a breath, that twenty years is nothing . . .

I was falling from a great height, and the ground was coming up fast.

I am afraid of the nights peopled by memories, chaining my dreams . . . And although my old illusions have been destroyed by oblivion, I hide a humble hope in my heart . . .

The floor opened up beneath me, and I was falling, chair and all, sucked into a black hole.

"Are you all right, Señorita?" an old gentleman asked.

"What?" He was stooped over me, a steaming cup of coffee left behind at his table nearby.

"Yes, I'm fine. Thank you for your concern."

I collected my things and stood, the old man my only witness. The night was cool and windy when I stepped outside.

EPILOGUE

FEBRUARY 2010

BUENOS AIRES GRABBED me fiercely by the heart, as the South always does. I walked with my friend Peti—La Petiza, meaning "the short one"—through the city for hours at a time. Sometimes we passed the excavation sites of former concentration camps, and I was surprised to see recent graffiti celebrating the Chilean resistance sprayed on the walls along major avenues.

"The Chilean resistance has mythological status here," Peti explained. "Our youth revere it. They see it as a revolutionary movement of people who fought to the death for their beliefs, without compromise." As I inhaled the steamy air of a carnival night, I wondered for the millionth time what the hell I was doing living in Vancouver.

Peti, ten years my junior, was the daughter of parents who'd been disappeared in the 1970s for their guerrilla activity against the Argentinian dictatorship. She belonged to the so-called lost generation, coming of age at a time when ferocious neo-liberalism was eating up her country. It seemed then that our fight had truly been in vain. When I'd boarded a northbound plane in Buenos Aires on a sunny afternoon in March 1990, my heart heavy with defeat, I wasn't leaving behind only a country deep in crisis. The resistance had been spectacularly defeated in Chile. The Soviet bloc had fallen, and the Sandinistas had recently lost the elections in Nicaragua, after defending themselves against the Contras for a decade. The FMLN in El Salvador had failed in its final offensive, and just months earlier, the United States had invaded Panama. Twenty-seven thousand U.S. troops had landed in that tiny Central American country on December 20. Panama's three thousand soldiers were no match for them; El Chorrillo, a working-class suburb of Panama City, was burned to the ground by the invaders, earning it the name "Little Hiroshima." Six thousand civilians died, and the chemical weapons used by the U.S. military caused people's bodies to melt on the spot. The ostensible reason for the invasion was to "liberate" Panama from General Manuel Noriega, who was on the CIA's payroll but had become too nationalistic for the U.S. government's liking. The real purpose of the attack was to ensure that the United States retained control of the Panama Canal, due to be handed over to Panamanians ten days later.

It was the second flagrant invasion of the South during that decade. In 1983, 7,600 U.S. troops had stormed Grenada, a small Caribbean island with a population of a hundred thousand, most of them descendants of slaves. Maurice Bishop, a left-wing black-power leader, had successfully led a revolution there against Eric Gairy, a close associate of Pinochet's. Bishop set up free health care and was starting to implement agrarian reform and a literacy campaign, quite a feat in a poor nation that had gained its independence from Britain a mere five years earlier. As prime minister, Bishop aligned himself with Cuba and Nicaragua, asking for Cuba's aid in building a new international airport. Shortly after he was murdered by the head of Grenada's military, the United States stepped in to "rescue" the island from what they saw as an imminent Cuban takeover. Almost three hundred Grenadians and eighty-one Cubans (most of the latter doctors and construction workers) were killed.

I'd left it all behind, landing in Vancouver on a typically grey day. I'd gone back in pursuit of another dream: I'd decided to audition for theatre school. Once I was accepted, I threw myself into my studies. It was an interesting challenge, training my body and soul to risk vulnerability in front of strangers. During the first week of school, our voice teacher placed her palms on the ribs in my back. "When was the last time you breathed?" she asked, shaking her head. "We have our work cut out for us." The fear was intense, and it felt familiar. I managed to get through the program, hanging on by the skin of my teeth, never sharing my resistance stories with classmates or teachers. I had sworn an oath, after all. I kept a close eye on Latin America, though, and I drew strength from the acts of resistance going on there. I became an actor and a playwright, often performing my own work, which was political in a highly personal way. I led community workshops using the techniques developed in Brazil by Augusto Boal in his Theatre of the Oppressed. I ran a theatre troupe for the Latino community in Vancouver. And life would later surprise me with a son.

Latin America, like the rest of the world, was overrun by neoliberalism in the early 1990s. Argentina and Bolivia were sold off to multinationals. But on January 1, 1994, the day the North American Free Trade Agreement went into effect, the city of San Cristóbal de las Casas in Chiapas, Mexico, was occupied by an armed indigenous movement called the Emiliano Zapata National Liberation Front. The Zapatistas announced they had no interest in taking over the state: why bother? Deregulated capitalism had made sure governments no longer had any power. Instead, the Zapatistas had seized control of their rightful lands in Chiapas, calling these areas "liberated zones." Subcomandante Marcos, their spokesman, denounced the New World Order, warning that the consequences for the majority of the earth's population, the poor, would be the most dire the world had ever seen. The actions of the Zapatistas and the manifesto they'd created caused ripples around the globe. Just when it had seemed that the empire of the North would triumph, they proposed a completely different way of doing things.

By the end of the 1990s, Latin America was in the midst of a second liberation, the Bolivarian revolution. Two hundred years earlier,

Simón Bolívar had led the continent to freedom from Spanish colonial rule. This time around, people rose up against an economic model violently imposed by the United States in tandem with corrupt local elites. Today, more than ten years into the new millennium, Venezuela, Argentina, Bolivia, Paraguay, Uruguay, Brazil, Ecuador, El Salvador and Nicaragua are all practising, to varying degrees, what has been called the new socialism. Its basic tenet, based on Bolívar's vision, is the integration of Latin America through solidarity and cooperation.

Chile, for its part, has continued to embrace the neo-liberal model, at huge social cost: the disparity there between rich and poor is one of the most extreme in the world. Pinochet was arrested in England in 1998 by Interpol and charged with human rights violations against European nationals in Chile during the dictatorship. Efforts to extradite him to Spain failed. His dictatorship had come to an end, but Pinochet maintained his post as commander-in-chief of Chile's armed forces for years afterward and held a seat in the Senate until his death in 2006 at the age of ninety-one. He was never tried for crimes against humanity in his country, because the constitution he had installed in 1980 forbade it. Mainstream Chileans still consider it in poor taste to mention Pinochet's bloody dictatorship in public.

Strolling with Peti through the streets of Buenos Aires, I encountered a city full of joy and pain, of life. In the popular revolt of 2001, its citizens toppled Coca-Cola billboards and set fires in doorways of banks. The Plaza de Mayo was taken over by thousands of protesters chanting "Que se vayan todos!" (They must all go!) Argentina's people demanded no less than a new economic model, and they threw president after president out of office until they got it.

Toward the end of my visit, Peti and I met Alejandro for lunch at a local eatery. It was thirteen years since I'd been south and seen him. He'd stayed in Neuquén and become a commercial airline pilot, flying in and out of Chile on a regular basis. He'd married a woman he met at the skydiving club, an architect who spoke English fluently and designed her own clothes and furniture. The two of them had a teenage son.

We hadn't talked about our time in the resistance during our first reunion. Maybe the experience had still seemed too raw. But now I had some questions for him. The three of us settled into our seats in the restaurant, typically Argentinian with its mirror-lined walls, waiters in starched white jackets and solid wood bar.

Alejandro leaned across the table. "It's so strange to be sitting here with you, Skinny, and to be talking about all of this in a public place. Do you realize you're the only person who knows the other me? How do you tell a fourteen-year-old boy who's lived a life of privilege that the Chilean resistance paid for his father's pilot training? How does a balding, middle-class guy like me, who goes to Houston every year to upgrade his pilot's licence, tell his wife that until five years ago there were goods stashed in the walls of our house?" He stopped to take a sip of his wine. "Both of them know I'm on the left, of course. In the late nineties, when the shit was hitting the fan in Argentina, our airline was privatized and downsized. I ended up organizing the unemployed pilots in Neuquén. Some of the airline's planes had been abandoned, so we formed a co-op and started a Patagonian air ambulance. It was a dark kind of joke to see these middle-class guys coming together because they'd lost everything. These were guys used to going to Disneyworld every year and flashing gold credit cards. So my family knows something of my politics, but they have no idea I was ever part of a revolutionary movement."

The dark-skinned waiter refilled our bread basket after taking our order.

"Do you think you'll ever tell them?" I asked.

Alejandro took a moment to reply. "I'm afraid to articulate my experience with those close to me, with people who might think I went too far. Because whenever I wonder about that, I always conclude that I didn't go far enough." His eyes were dark with pain, in a way I recognized from our years together. "I wonder if it would be easier to have the conversation if I'd been a Sandinista, riding into Managua in the back of a truck the day they won. We lost so badly in Chile. Maybe we threw in the towel too soon."

I looked outside at the lazy summer afternoon, at the trees offering shade to the passersby on the cobblestoned street.

"There was nothing more we could have done," I said. "But when it was all over, there was nobody to talk to about it. Everyone dispersed, took cover. We mourned our losses alone, weeping in corners."

Alejandro nodded. "There's nothing lonelier than watching the world being taken over by the enemy you fought so hard against. But I'm proud of our continent, proud to feel that my little grain of sand contributed to the changes taking place."

"How did you deal with the fear in those days?" I asked him.

"I didn't feel afraid."

"I don't believe you."

"Really—I didn't feel it. But it comes out now, I suppose. In my depression."

"It's all I felt," I admitted. "Fear. Terror. Paranoia."

"You never talked about it."

"I worried that if I did it could break me, us, the little world of facades we'd built to keep going. I knew what they were capable of if they caught us. But what was required was absolute commitment, body and soul. I wonder if that's one of the reasons we lost, the reason so many struggles are lost—the inhuman demands placed on those who are fighting for the dream. We lived in a state of terror, and it was unrevolutionary to feel it, let alone speak of it. I tried to be a hero, but I was just the opposite: a teenager fucking up all over the place who wanted to give everything to the struggle." I turned to Peti. "Your generation seems to understand that you don't have to let your beliefs consume you. You have your loves and your lives and your activism, and you don't let anybody dictate to you what you can do."

"Remember, Skinny, when Michael Jackson came to town?"

I smiled at the recollection. "The Thriller concert at BC Place stadium in Vancouver, 1984."

"I had just arrived from Argentina, and I wanted to go so badly."

"Me too. And yet neither of us said anything to the other. It would have been unacceptable to admit we liked something so blatantly commercial."

Peti spoke up, her voice filled with emotion. "It's incredible to listen to you two. It's how I imagine my parents would be talking if they were still alive."

The sun dropped in the west. It was time to say goodbye. Alejandro and I embraced by the side of the road, cried together for a minute. Then he climbed into a taxi and was gone. The next morning I'd fly back to Canada, but first Peti and I were heading off to see Boca Juniors play a soccer match in La Bombonera, their home stadium. It would be a religious experience, chanting with thousands of neighbourhood boys and then running with them through the streets.

In November 2010, Evo Morales, president of South America's poorest country, announced that 82 per cent of his country's resources were now in Bolivian hands. Bolivia's gross domestic product had doubled over the previous five years, along with the average yearly income per person. A literacy campaign had reached all corners of the country, and there was now universal access to health care. Amazingly, even the army had declared itself anti-imperialist, anti-capitalist, socialist, in the service of community and Mother Earth.

The previous month, the world had held its breath as the thirty-three miners trapped in Chile's Atacama Desert were rescued after spending sixty-nine days underground. Simultaneously, thirty-two members of the Mapuche nation were in the midst of an eighty-two-day hunger strike they'd staged in jail; they were facing terrorism charges for vandalizing trucks owned by the logging companies that were destroying their ancestral lands in southern Chile. They would eventually get what they wanted: to be tried in a civil court, not a military one. The thirty-three miners, dubbed heroes by the Chilean state, had almost starved to death because of dangerous working conditions—the privately owned mine had failed to meet international safety standards and should not have been operating at the time of the accident. Luis Urzúa, the last miner to be brought to the surface, a man whose father and stepfather had been union activists who were murdered during Pinochet's dictatorship, uttered these words to Chilean president Sebastián Piñera the minute he saw him: "May this never happen again."

The struggle continues. Hasta la victoria siempre. Until the final victory, always.

ACKNOWLEDGEMENTS

I WOULD LIKE TO thank Peter Campbell, Marcus Youssef, Camille Gingras and Don Hannah for reading the first drafts of what became *Something Fierce*. Thanks to Michael Helm for editing an early version of chapter 1 and publishing it in *Brick* magazine, and to Scott Steedman, who signed the book up for publication. Those participating in the 2006 Banff Playwrights' Colony, which I was attending as an actor, gathered once a week for four consecutive weeks to hear me read from the book's early chapters. I am deeply grateful for the support of those playwrights, dramaturges, directors, translators, producers and actors, whose numbers grew every week, as word of my informal readings spread. That was encouragement enough to keep writing. I would also like to thank the Playwrights' Theatre Centre in Vancouver for hosting a public reading of the first two chapters of the book.

Thank you to Zool Suleman, Adriana Paz, Mariza García, Eva Urrutia, Jorge Rodríguez, Fernando Frangella, Sarah Neville and Barbara Czarnecki. And to all my friends, near and far, for being generous enough to be my chosen family.

Thank you to Gioconda Belli and Gillian Slovo, who agreed to meet for coffee and share their experience of writing memoirs with similar themes. Their books, *The Country under My Skin* and *Every Secret Thing: My Family, My Country*, inspired me, and I was humbled by their generosity.

I am deeply grateful to the British Columbia Arts Council and the Canada Council for the Arts for their individual writing grants.

There are not enough words to thank my editor, Barbara Pulling. Her keen eye, gentle prodding and utterly open mind gave this book its shape. She demanded nothing but the best from me, asking tough questions, insisting that I go deeper, be more specific and more truthful. Without her I'd still be lost in a maze.

I would like to thank my mother for teaching me that we were put on this earth to give. I would like to thank her, a fellow writer, for her unconditional support of this book and her blind trust in me. She has allowed me to write my version of the story, and in so doing to reveal her secrets. She has taught me everything I know about passion, courage, strength, conviction and integrity. She is a woman who could have spent her life in comfort but chose to give up her privilege for a greater cause. I had the good fortune of being raised by a revolutionary, and for that I am eternally grateful.

I would like to thank Bob Everton, my late stepfather, for urging me to write this book in the months before he died. A true internationalist, he fought for causes locally and globally until his last day on earth. To quote Bertolt Brecht, "There are men who fight for a day and they are good. There are men who fight for a year and they are better. There are men who fight many years and they are better still. But there are those who fight their whole lives: these are the indispensable ones." Bob's exemplary life leads me in my decisions every day.

I am grateful to my sister, Ale, a very private person, for accepting my writing of this book, even if her version of the story is completely different. Thank you to my brother, Lalito, who when asked if he wanted his name changed, responded, "It's an honour to be in your book." I would like to thank my father for his trust and faith in me, for supporting and championing my choice to follow my calling as an artist, and for agreeing not to read this book. The information in it would be too much for his weary heart to bear. I would like to thank my cousins, aunts and uncles, who lent their quiet support to this book.

Thank you to my grandmother Carmen, who passed away in 1993, and whose spirit has been with me through the writing of this book. It is only recently that I learned she was a helper of the resistance, providing her services as a messenger. Thank you to my uncle Boris, who passed away in 1995 and whose spirit is also always with me.

Thank you to the man I call Alejandro, great love of my youth, compañero, friend and brother. I could not have written this book without your blessing and permission.

Thank you to one of the founding members of the resistance, who, on his deathbed, made me promise to tell this story, because it has not been told enough, because it is a story that must not die with the people who lived it.

And my grateful thanks to all those who came before, those who are fighting now and those who will continue to fight for a better future for all. I am awed, inspired and humbled by your dedication to the struggle, whether you are in the Gaza Strip, in India, in Mexico or in Bolivia, continuing to support Evo. I stand in solidarity with you.

PAUL DZENKIW

CARMEN AGUIRRE is a Vancouver-based writer and theatre artist who has worked extensively in North and South America. She has written or co-written eighteen plays, including *The Refugee Hotel*, which was nominated for a 2010 Dora Mavor Moore Award for best new play. Her most recent one-woman show is *Blue Box*. Aguirre has sixty film, TV and stage acting credits, including lead roles in the Showcase series *Endgame* and *Quinceañera*, winner of the Grand Jury Prize and the Audience Award at the 2006 Sundance Film Festival. *Something Fierce* is her first book.